LA SANTA MUERTE IN MEXICO

EDITED BY WIL G. PANSTERS

La Santa Muerte in Mexico

History, Devotion, & Society

University of New Mexico Press *Albuquerque*

© 2019 by the University of New Mexico Press
All rights reserved. Published 2019
Printed in the United States of America

ISBN 978-0-8263-6081-6 (cloth)
ISBN 978-0-8263-6082-3 (electronic)

Library of Congress Cataloging-in-Publication data is on file with the Library of Congress.

Cover photograph | Young woman with Santa Muerte statuette, Tepito neighborhood, Mexico City, March 2013. Photograph by Anne Huffschmid.

Spine photograph | Young man with Santa Muerte statuette, Tepito neighborhood, Mexico City, November 2010. Photograph by Anne Huffschmid.

Designed by Mindy Basinger Hill

Composed in Fanwood, Fairfield, and Avenir LT Standard

In loving memory of my sister Dorry

CONTENTS

List of Illustrations   *ix*

Preface   *xi*

1 | La Santa Muerte: History, Devotion, and
   Societal Context | *Wil G. Pansters*   *1*

2 | Saints and Demons: Putting La Santa Muerte
   in Historical Perspective | *Benjamin T. Smith*   *58*

3 | Dances of Death in Latin America: Holy, Adopted,
   and Patrimonialized Dead | *Juan Antonio Flores Martos*   *84*

4 | La Santa Muerte as Urban Staging: Notes on the Images
   and Visibility of a Transgressive Performance | *Anne Huffschmid*   *111*

5 | Moving In and Moving Out: On Exchange and Family
   in the Cult of La Santa Muerte | *Regnar Kristensen*   *136*

6 | Devotion That Goes Skin Deep: Tattoos of La Santa Muerte |
   Judith Katia Perdigón Castañeda and Bernardo Robles Aguirre   *158*

7 | Afterword: Interpreting La Santa Muerte | *Claudio Lomnitz*   *183*

Bibliography   *193*

About the Authors   *214*

Index   *219*

ILLUSTRATIONS

Figure 1.1 | Kneeling Santa Muerte devotee, Mexico City, 2015   28

Figure 1.2 | Santa Muerte devotee, Mexico City, 2015   28

Figure 1.3 | Blessing of Santa Muerte images, Mexico City, 2015   29

Figure 4.1 | Woman with Santa Muerte statuette, Mexico City, 2013   123

Figure 4.2 | Man with Santa Muerte statuette, Mexico City, 2010   123

Figure 4.3 | Enriqueta Romero, Mexico City, 2013   124

Figure 4.4 | "Coordinator of La Santa Muerte," Mexico City, 2013   124

Figure 4.5 | Tattoo of church in flames, Mexico City, 2010   124

Figure 4.6 | Santa Muerte statuettes, Mexico City, 2010   125

Figure 4.7 | Tattoo of Santa Muerte with scythe, Mexico City, 2010   126

Figure 4.8 | Enriqueta Romero during rosary, Mexico City, 2010   126

Figure 4.9 | Woman with Santa Muerte statuette, Mexico City, 2010   126

Figure 4.10 | Boy with Santa Muerte image, Mexico City, 2010   127

Figure 4.11 | Girl with Santa Muerte statuette, Mexico City, 2010   127

Figure 6.1 | "Santa Muerte of the Wind" tattoo, Mexico City, 2010   176

Figure 6.2 | Santa Muerte as empress tattoo, Mexico City, 2010   176

Figure 6.3 | Winged Santa Muerte tattoo, Mexico City, 2010   176

Figure 6.4 | Warrior Santa Muerte tattoo, Mexico City, 2010   177

PREFACE

Mexico has a rich history of iconic images that are widely recognized by national and international audiences, elite nation builders, and popular groups alike. These icons are believed to represent core features of Mexican history, culture, and society. Some of them originate in the domain of religion while others are rooted in social and political struggles. While some enjoy an undisputed and lasting force and presence, like the Virgen de Guadalupe, others may fall into oblivion. Emiliano Zapata, a key icon of the Mexican Revolution, for example, is no longer the subject of state-orchestrated hero cults but preserves an iconic significance in the popular imagination. Some icons are firmly and broadly enshrined in official and social discourses: think of Miguel Hidalgo as the icon of Mexican independence, or Benito Juárez for nineteenth-century liberalism. Across Mexico, thousands of streets, squares, hospitals, and schools are named after them. Still other icons originate from, and remain much more confined to, the domain of popular culture. The *lucha libre* wrestler Canek is perhaps a good example, as are many popular Catholic saints such as San Judas Tadeo and Juan Soldado. But, irrespective of their origins and societal presence, they are always subject to shifting processes of meaning-making. What they symbolize is not some unmediated and ahistorical meaning or essence but the result of negotiations among different social actors conditioned by shifting social, political, and cultural discourses and practices. Despite all efforts to fix or stabilize its meanings, national iconography is always dynamic.

In recent decades, Mexico and Mexicans have experienced profound changes in almost every societal domain: the economic system, the political landscape, and cultural flows and practices, including changes in religious allegiances, in social and demographic terms, in the country's place in the world, in the rule of law, and in violence and insecurity. This book is the result of a project first formulated in 2013 to examine the social production of new (or reinvigorated) icons, cultural practices, mythologies, and popular heroes at the beginning of the twenty-first century, against a background of shifting social and cultural realities and a weariness with iconographies associated with twentieth-century national development, perhaps most importantly that of "the Revolution" itself. The objective was to organize the 2014 Día de Mexicanistas at the University of Groningen around this broad theme. This was also thought to be a particularly appropriate topic for the occasion of the retirement of my colleague Hub. Hermans, who specializes in literature and other forms of cultural production in Spain and Mexico and who, twenty years earlier, had been a founder of the Groningen Centro de Estudios Mexicanos. As a token of appreciation for his leading role in promoting Latin American and especially Mexican studies at the University of Groningen, this book is dedicated to him.

Soon after the initial project was formulated, we decided to narrow its focus to one of the, if not the most, significant iconic images and saints in contemporary Mexico, La Santa Muerte. This focusing was also intended to enhance the coherence and productivity of the planned scholarly encounter. It was clear that, since 2000, the cult of La Santa Muerte had grown vastly in influence and popularity throughout Mexico and beyond its borders. To understand the historical roots, devotional practices, and broader social conditions of the cult's expansion and change, the Centro de Estudios Mexicanos brought together a unique group of scholars from different disciplines (anthropology, history, religion, cultural sociology) to work on different aspects of the cult. As it turned out, the conference, held in November 2014, was the first-ever international scholarly gathering dedicated entirely to La Santa Muerte.

Bringing together colleagues from Mexico, the United States, and several European countries, all of whom are studying that visually stunning icon of Mexico's posttransitional and neoliberal violent democracy, constituted a challenge in many ways. With the exception of coauthors Judith Katia Perdigón and Bernardo Robles, and Claudio Lomnitz, all contributors to this volume participated in the Groningen meeting. I am grateful for Perdigón's and Robles's willingness to come on board at a later stage. Although Lomnitz, unfortunately, was unable to attend our deliberations in Groningen due to his teaching obligations in New York, he contributed a thought-provoking afterword to this volume. Laura Roush, who due to pressing personal circumstances was unable to contribute to this volume, played a valued role at the meeting itself and remained very helpful afterward. The input and engagement of Benjamin Smith (Great Britain), Juan Antonio Flores Martos (Spain), Anne Huffschmid (Germany), and Regnar Kristensen (Denmark) during the conference and the extended rewriting and publication process were an inspiration for me and a crucial reason for my ability to bring this project to a conclusion.

Other scholars (José Carlos Aguiar, Andrew Chesnut) delivered papers and participated in the debates in Groningen but eventually withdrew from the publication project. Thinking back, they contributed to turning the meeting into a fascinating example of "science in action" marked by academic *protagonismo* and touchiness. In hindsight, one sees that this was likely related to the strict focus on the relatively new phenomenon of La Santa Muerte; it turns out that, given the scarcity of novel research topics, competition and rivalry are as common among scholars as among the contending saints on sale in the crowded, esoteric market stalls of Mexico!

The organization of the conference enjoyed the support of numerous people. First of all, the dean of the Faculty of Arts, Gerry Wakker, provided additional funding to make the special occasion of Hermans's retirement at the conference possible. I greatly appreciate her gesture, as well as the funding from the Groningen Research Institute for the Study of Culture. I would like to thank Eduardo Ibarrola Nicolín, then Mexico's ambassador to the Netherlands, and Sandra López, the embassy's cultural attaché at the time, for their lasting support to the Centro de Estudios Mexicanos in general and the Santa Muerte conference in particular. I am also indebted to my colleague Bob de Jonge for his wise advice during the preparation phase and his organizational and logistical help. Several colleagues from the Universities of Groningen and Utrecht commented on papers and chaired sessions: Anne Martínez, Martijn Oosterbaan, and Kees Koonings. Their input was much appreciated. A special word of thanks goes to Nuala Finnegan, who runs the Centre for Mexican Studies at University College Cork in Ireland, for her perceptive comments and pleasant companionship. The conference would not have gone as smoothly as it did without the help of my student assistant Stan Aalderink. An outstanding student, Stan also turned out to have valuable hands-on problem-solving qualities. Finally, I would like to express my appreciation for the professionalism and helpfulness of Paul Kersey, who translated some chapters and copyedited others.

During the period of writing, feedback, rewriting, editing, peer review, and additional rewriting, I was fortunate to receive ongoing support and input from two key people. Clark Whitehorn, executive editor of the University of New Mexico Press, provided guidance and encouragement from the moment I first approached him at the Latin American Studies Association's busy book fair to discuss this project. His uncommon blend of editorial professionalism, amenable personality, and human perceptiveness was key to the process of transforming the idea for this volume into a reality. Ben Smith, meanwhile, provided feedback on different versions of my introductory chapter and was always open to discussing the vicissitudes of this project. His intelligence, wittiness, and broad knowledge of Mexican history, society, and culture have left an imprint on this volume far beyond his own chapter. I will never forget our regular conversations in the Cape of Good Hope Pub in Warwick about La Santa Muerte, Mexican drug trafficking, archives, books, football, snooker, Brexit, and, most importantly, our wives and daughters.

Much of my reading and writing for this project was done during stints at my mother's house. Although in her eighties, her care for, and interest in, my personal well-being and work have remained boundless. I cherish the memories of those unusual days of warmth, conversation, hard work, and good food.

WIL G. PANSTERS
Utrecht/Groningen, February 2018

LA SANTA MUERTE IN MEXICO

1 | La Santa Muerte
History, Devotion, and Societal Context

We got into a taxi at our hotel in downtown Mexico City for the long drive along the Calzada de Tlalpan to the southern part of the city. Sitting next to the driver, I immediately noticed two small images of La Santa Muerte on the dashboard. When I also observed that the driver was wearing a discreet chain and bracelet with Santa Muerte symbols, I decided to ask him about it. For the next forty minutes he—let's call him Ricardo—spoke openly and extensively about his relationship with La Santa Muerte, turning the journey into one of those exceptional moments of fieldwork that occur from time to time in the Mexican megacity. Five years earlier, Ricardo had confronted a very serious "family problem," which he did not elaborate on and which, out of respect for his privacy, I decided not to ask about. Trying to resolve his problem, he had appealed directly to God on numerous occasions, but to no avail. It was then that a friend, a Santa Muerte devotee, invited him to visit her shrine in the Tepito neighborhood and beseech her for help. Ricardo agreed, though cautiously at first. He promised La Santa Muerte and his friend that if she would resolve his problem, he would tattoo her image on his chest near his heart. And so it happened; Ricardo quickly unbuttoned his shirt and proudly showed me his tattoo. Since that day, he has been a Santa Muerte devotee, worshipping her in a manner that reflects his discreet devotional outer expressions: he attends rosaries regularly but not every month; keeps a small multicolored figurine of La Santa Muerte at home; and gives her an apple every few weeks with some smaller items, because "no le pido mucho" (I don't ask much from her).[1]

Being a taxi driver in the Mexican capital comes with insecurity and risks. Since La Santa Muerte has a reputation for providing protection, I inquired whether Ricardo also petitions the saint in this respect. He answered my question in the affirmative but was quick to add that just a week earlier he'd been the victim of an armed robbery in broad daylight in the southern part of the city when a fare suddenly threatened him with a gun and forced him to hand over the car's radio, a mobile phone, a GPS system, and fifty pesos in cash. Ricardo stressed that he was not beaten or otherwise physically harmed, suggesting that La Santa Muerte at least protected him from that. As so many common citizens suffer violent assaults in contemporary Mexico, often for limited financial gain, his view does not come as a surprise. In a soft voice, he spoke about his desire to lead a life of honesty, respect, and openness in family relations, work, and religious beliefs. He believes in caring for his family through honest hard work and invests in having an open, trusting relationship with his children and wife, who has converted to Protestantism. Proof of this is that the couple does not quarrel about their divergent religious convictions; after all, they both believe in the supreme force of God ("Dios es primero"). Tolerance toward the Santa Muerte cult and its devotees is, however, not a matter of course in Mexico. In fact, Ricardo says, for many people, La Santa Muerte has a bad reputation, since she is associated with crime and criminals. He knows that some people from the criminal (under)world are indeed attracted to the cult and participate in rosaries, but there are many others, men and women, young and old, among the devotees who survive, make a living, and build social relations based on truthfulness and sincerity.[2] Many Santa Muerte devotees also continue to worship Mexico's most important Catholic icon, the Virgin of Guadalupe. It appears that folk Catholicism, as opposed to the beliefs of the church hierarchy, is able to accommodate the cult in daily practice. Others are less open-minded.

Ricardo talks about the assertive intolerance of one of his brothers-in-law, who is a Christian pastor, which has led to unpleasant exchanges during family get-togethers. On one occasion, when Ricardo arrived to celebrate Father's Day, his brother-in-law said that the "devil" had come to join them! On others, people have told him that worshipping La Santa Muerte would send him straight to hell. But he is not particularly impressed by the threat of the hereafter: "Which hell?" he asks rhetorically, and then adds: "¡El infierno está aquí!"—"Hell is right here!" When I ask what he means by that, he tells me, first of all, about the pain he suffered when his father and then his mother passed away while he was just a child. The grief blackened his existence and overwhelmed him with loneliness and hurt so that it felt like hell. While hell manifested itself in Ricardo's individual suffering, it also took a more general shape in the form of social and economic marginalization coupled with insecurity, violence, and fear. Among Mexico City taxi drivers, such feelings are by no means uncommon.

Ricardo is one of the tens—perhaps hundreds of thousands—of people in Mexico and elsewhere who have become devotees of La Santa Muerte since the beginning of the twenty-first century, a period in which the cult has gained a "spectacular" visual presence through a wide range of social and cultural expressions and forms. In TV documentaries and journalistic accounts about Mexico's security crisis and drug-related violence, La Santa Muerte appears as the patron saint of drug traffickers, criminals, and police officers. The Internet contains huge amounts of highly diverse information: in the summer of 2016, a Google search for "Santa Muerte" produced more than five million hits! The great variety of Santa Muerte objects sold in popular markets across Mexico makes her presence tangible everywhere. While at the end of the 1990s the range of Santa Muerte figurines on sale was still limited, since then the change has been remarkable (Kristensen, 2016a, p. 408). During a Sunday morning stroll in the República Market in the city of San Luis Potosí in August 2015, I counted no fewer than twenty market stalls with Santa Muerte articles on sale. Some belonged to herbalists, who offer candles and amulets; others are popular pharmacies that sell all kinds of alternative medicines but also Santa Muerte figurines, lotions, incense, and prayer booklets. Some are small, but others are enormous with literally hundreds of artifacts related to distinct folk beliefs on display. When I inquired about the demand for these products, the young owner of a large and carefully ordered shop was quick to tell me that he and his family were not Santa Muerte devotees but instead worshipped Saint Jude Thaddeus, the saint of lost causes. Even so, they were businesspeople, and since Santa Muerte articles enjoyed a larger demand than others, they stacked their shop with sculptures both large and small, bracelets, pendants, and trinkets. At the entrance to another shop stood a glass shrine with a huge black statue of La Santa Muerte. Here, and across Mexico, these popular markets, where low-income families buy vegetables, fruit, meat, and chicken, get haircuts, eat breakfast or lunch, and acquire all kinds of products for their physical, psychological, and spiritual well-being, La Santa Muerte has obtained a prominent position in *herbolarias* and shops selling items related to Santería and folk Catholicism.

Clearly, there is a growing market for Santa Muerte merchandise, but what does that tell us about the beliefs and practices of the clients who buy these items? How many such clients are there to begin with? Since when has she been around, and where? How does Santa Muerte devotion relate to Catholicism? What does being a devotee mean in terms of beliefs, rituals, and symbolism? What are the key features of Santa Muerte devotional practices? How is the Santa Muerte cult connected to broader religious, cultural, and social processes, institutions, discourses, and actors? What does La Santa Muerte "do" or "perform" to so successfully attract followers in contemporary Mexico's religious market? What are the underlying historical, social, and cultural roots and causes of the cult as we know it today? And, finally, which concepts and analytical frameworks should we employ to understand this phenomenon?

These and other questions are addressed in this book. In order to properly introduce and contextualize the contributions to this volume, all of which focus on specific dimensions of the Santa Muerte cult with the help of apposite conceptual perspectives, this chapter strives to achieve four aims. The first is to provide the reader with a general introduction to the main features of the Santa Muerte phenomenon. Second, it achieves this through a critical reading of the available scholarly literature, thereby offering a comprehensive state of this emerging field of study. Third, it identifies and examines the principal debates and points of contention in this field. Finally, it points out how the chapters in this volume contribute to these debates and to deepening our understanding of the Santa Muerte cult. In summary, the overall, ambitious aim of this chapter is to develop a broad historical, ethnographical, and conceptual framework within which the rest of this book can be read.

LA SANTA MUERTE: STUDYING A POPULAR RELIGION "IN THE MAKING"

Research on La Santa Muerte has a brief but prolific history. With the exception of occasional references by previous generations of anthropologists, the cult only became an object of study when it grew in spectacular fashion in the early twenty-first century. As such, it provides a fascinating laboratory for the study of a popular religion "in the making." In 2007, the Spanish anthropologist Juan Antonio Flores Martos wrote that scholars had barely begun to research La Santa Muerte. Existing journalistic accounts, such as those of Edgar Escobedo Quijano (2005) and Laura Castellanos (2004), and writings by other observers—Juan Ambrosio (2003), for example—were, in his view, fraught with a "superficial, sensationalistic vision for [popular] dissemination that has explored—and exploited—this cult" (2007, p. 281).[3] Although his assessment was perhaps broadly valid, it was not entirely accurate. At the time of his writing, three scholarly texts had already been published, and they remain compulsory points of reference. In a short 2005 article, the late Mexican anthropologist Elsa Malvido laid out the iconographic and religious precedents of the emerging Santa Muerte cult, and in the same year the US-based anthropologist Claudio Lomnitz published his major study on the history of death in Mexico, which briefly addressed the Santa Muerte cult. Interestingly, in 1998, John Thompson, a freelance American scholar of Mexican folk religion, published an excellent academic paper that examined his encounter with La Santa Muerte in northern Mexico in the 1990s and traced its broad European origins.

Thus, when Flores Martos first published on La Santa Muerte in Veracruz, a pattern in the study of the cult was already emerging. Information and scholarly knowledge about La Santa Muerte came from three main sources. First, journalistic interest in the cult has remained very strong, both in Mexico and abroad (Gil Olmos, 2010; Lorusso, 2013). This includes not only reports in newspapers, magazines, and books but also documentaries, films, and a vast store of information on the Internet in the form of blogs and websites. Two factors have been important for this continued attention. The appalling events surrounding drug trafficking and crime, as well as aggressive government policies particularly after 2006, have resulted in brutal violence, disappearances, and omnipresent death throughout Mexico. In addition, visual representations of La Santa Muerte in the modern media have spurred interest, even fascination, especially since they are often, albeit one-dimensionally, connected to the world of crime and violence.[4]

Second, Malvido's seminal article inaugurated the first wave of studies from Mexican anthropology, for which much of the field research was done around 2005. Publications by Katia Perdigón, who published the first book on the "polemic subject" of La Santa Muerte (2008a, p. 15), and Perla Fragoso (2007b, 2011) reaffirmed the establishment of La Santa Muerte as a valid object of scholarly research.[5] Since then, contributions have grown and diversified. While the first spate of publications dealt almost exclusively with the cult in Mexico City, over time research appeared on its manifestations in other parts of Mexico (Bravo Lara, 2013; Higuera-Bonfil, 2015). The theme was also taken up increasingly by scholars from disciplines other than anthropology (Gaytán Alcalá, 2008; Villamil Uriarte & Cisneros, 2011) and by graduate students (e.g., De la Fuente, 2013; Yllescas, 2016). Taken together, this growing corpus of scholarly work has significantly improved our understanding of the dynamics and complexity of Santa Muerte devotion.

Third, the early work of Thompson and Lomnitz constituted the starting point of a strong and increasingly diverse involvement of US and European scholarship (mostly published in English) on La Santa Muerte, which, unfortunately, is sometimes overlooked by Mexican researchers. The first to delve into the phenomenon were anthropologists. Although his first encounters and interviews date back to 2002, the Danish anthropologist Regnar Kristensen engaged in prolonged fieldwork on the cult from 2005 to 2009. His are probably still the most theoretically sophisticated and ethnographically comprehensive accounts (2011, 2015, 2016a). The Mexico-based US anthropologist Laura Roush (2012, 2014) was also among the first to do extensive fieldwork, as was the aforementioned Flores Martos on popular religion in the port of Veracruz. Similar to Mexican academia, one observes a diversifying and broadening trend in non-Mexican scholarship. Andrew Chesnut, a student of religion, published the first (critically received) English-language book on La Santa Muerte (2012b).[6] In addition, the Polish anthropologist Piotr Michalik (2011, 2012), the Italian philosopher of religion Stefano Bigliardi (2016), the German cultural sociologist Anne Huffschmid (this volume), and the French anthropologist of religion Kali Argyriadis (2014) have all made interesting contributions. A recent development involves studies that focus not so much on the Santa Muerte cult itself but that look comparatively at its devotional practices and meanings (Martín, 2014; Oleszkiewicz-Peralba, 2015).

The global expansion of the study of La Santa Muerte during this brief period has meant that our understanding has begun to mature and move in different historical, ethnographic, and conceptual directions, even though the three sources of knowledge identified above do not always feed on each other effectively.[7] While this body of scholarship has begun to chart the social and conceptual terrain of the cult, it also contains contrasting approaches and debates; hence, much empirical and interpretative work still lies ahead.[8] This book aspires to make a substantial contribution. My review of existing scholarship revolves around three main questions or thematic fields, which order the remaining part of this chapter and form a framework for the subsequent ones: What are the most significant historical and symbolic roots of La Santa Muerte (devotion)? How can the contents and symbolic meanings of the cult's current devotional practices be described and understood? What socioeconomic, political, and cultural forces intertwine to form the wider context of the spectacular emergence of Santa Muerte devotion and its major features? In other words, this chapter will look backward at the history of La Santa Muerte, inward at key devotional forms and practices, and outward at its societal context as I combine historical and ethnographical substance with conceptual analyses.

1. LOOKING BACKWARD:
HISTORY AND CULTURAL REPERTOIRES

The author of the first scholarly book on La Santa Muerte, Katia Perdigón, initially came to know about her in the 1970s through an aunt who prayed and talked to an image of La Santa Muerte on a medallion. Later, as a trained anthropologist, Perdigón studied the phenomenon as it underwent a transformation from "underground and personalized veneration" to public visibility and devotion. But with the reinvention of the cult after 2000, "nothing was the same" (2008a, p. 14, my translation).[9] In the early 1960s, doña Enriqueta ("Queta") Romero also became acquainted with La Santa Muerte through an aunt. Forty years later, she played a decisive role, unintentionally at first, in turning her image into a massively and publicly revered saint when, in September 2001, she placed a life-size statue of La Santa Muerte in front of her house. The skeleton figure in Calle Alfarería, in the heart of the notorious Tepito neighborhood in downtown Mexico City, attracted attention and elicited manifestations of devotion as people placed candles and small offerings there.[10] Today, it is the most revered Santa Muerte shrine in Mexico (see Kristensen, 2016a, pp. 402–3). Understanding the remarkable transformation from that hidden, almost clandestine Santa Muerte devotion to the public congregations of thousands of devotees constitutes a challenge for contemporary scholarship and a major aim of this volume: what were the main forces and factors behind the extraordinary qualitative and quantitative evolution of the cult?

Encountering La Santa Muerte: Infidelity, Prisons, and Numbers

The recent history of the devotional practices of the Santa Muerte cult in Mexico City can be recounted, in part, through the personal experiences and memories of Perdigón and doña Queta going back to the 1970s and early 1960s, respectively. Flores Martos situates the beginning of the expansion of the Santísima Muerte cult in the port of Veracruz in 1993 (2007, pp. 274–75), the same year in which the cult began to emerge in Tuxtla Gutiérrez (Chiapas), while its origins in Chetumal (Quintana Roo) go back to at least 1986

(Higuera-Bonfil, 2015, p. 98; Bolaños Gordillo, 2015). In a groundbreaking article, John Thompson mentions that in 1992 he first bought a folded piece of paper with an image and a prayer to La Santa Muerte in the northern border town of Nogales (Sonora), and describes how just a few years later Santa Muerte objects became available in the United States (1998, p. 407).

However, there are oral accounts of Santa Muerte devotion that date back to the 1940s, but nothing earlier than that. Devotees told Kristensen about a skeletal figure found beneath the floor of a house in Tepatepec (Hidalgo) in 1965. Although the figure had little in common with the current La Santa Muerte and was actually venerated as San Bernardo, more recently devotees from Mexico City began to consider the Tepatepec figure the oldest San Muerte statue (Kristensen, 2016a, pp. 407–8). Written sources also exist, and more will surely be found in the near future as anthropologists and others continue to document the social history of the cult.

While Isabel Kelly (1965, p. 108), who did fieldwork in the Laguna area of northern Mexico in the 1950s, only mentions "santa muerte" prayer cards in passing, Oscar Lewis's celebrated *The Children of Sánchez*, based on fieldwork in the second half of the 1950s in Tepito, stands out as the key early ethnographic account of the cult. Lewis narrates the story of Marta and her husband, Crispín, who is not only physically abusive but also a womanizer, a man "without morals." When her sister tells her about Crispín's recent philanderings, she recommends praying to La Santa Muerte for nine consecutive nights to make the husband stop cheating and bring him back, "beaten and tied, to fulfil his promises." Interestingly, Marta told Lewis that others prayed to the souls of Juan Minero, San Antonio, and San Benito in attempts to return unfaithful husbands or lovers (Lewis, 1963, pp. 289–91). The earlier, monumental *A Treasury of Mexican Folkways* (1947) by the anthropologist Frances Toor also mentions Juan Minero and La Santa Muerte but, above all, refers to the use of magnetic stones in relation to love magic. It is the more "sophisticated folk, especially those living in and near cities," who consult sorcerers to carry out magical rituals to win back lovers or husbands. Toor understood the urban roots of this demand, since "in the cities, where life is complicated and there is more infidelity than in the villages, one finds many love charms," which can be acquired easily in markets. Regrettably, she does not specify exactly where or when she obtained the following short prayer to La Santa Muerte: "Beloved death of my heart, do not leave me unprotected and do not leave 'John Doe' tranquil for one moment—molest him, mortify him, make him restless so that he will always think of me" (Toor, 1947, pp. 141, 143–44).

This specific request to La Santa Muerte is still common today. Red-colored Santa Muerte candles that represent love and passion sell more than any others (Chesnut, 2014, p. 11), and a box with nine small red rudimentary Santa Muerte candles I acquired in the San Luis Potosí market contains prayers for such a *novenario*. On the second day, the devotee would address La Santa Muerte as follows: "I want you to do me the favor to bring [name of a specific person] to my feet, humiliated and remorseful, so he will never again leave me, as long as I need him." All these small but significant traces and testimonies from the 1940s, 1950s, 1960s, and 1970s highlight the role of women in Santa Muerte devotion in the secluded space of the home in Mexico City and other urban areas.

There is, however, clear evidence as well of a history of Santa Muerte veneration beyond the home, namely in the Mexican prison system, another space shielded from the public gaze. Kristensen (2015, pp. 6–10) recently concluded that this practice gained momentum in Mexico City prisons in the 1990s, when populations rose sharply (see Azaola & Bergman, 2008).[11] After 2000, when the number of street altars dedicated to La Santa Muerte exploded, a strong correlation was found between their geographic distribution and neighborhoods with high prison populations. But the relationship between prisons and the Santa Muerte cult is by no means limited to Mexico City. Some years ago, a criminological study claimed that La Santísima Muerte could be found throughout the national prison system. The cult was widely known and practiced by male and female prisoners alike, who maintained altars in their cells, painted her image on walls, made figurines from different materials, and had her tattooed on their bodies (Payá, 2006, p. 243). Francisco Goldman (2014, p. 207) recalls how, in the 1990s, a friend photographed the Islas Marías federal prison (about one hundred kilometers off Mexico's western coast) and told him that he encountered La Santa Muerte.

More revealing perhaps is the testimony penned by Linda Denegri about her stay in a women's prison in the early 1970s. A middle-class woman, Denegri had murdered her abusive husband, the influential journalist Carlos Denegri, for which she was imprisoned for several years. At times empathetic but occasionally condescending, her stories about life in the infamous Cárcel de Mujeres in Mexico City shed a fascinating light on the abuse of women; the corruption and extortion; the arbitrary legal system; and drug consumption and trafficking during the administration of President Luis Echeverría (1970–1976). When Denegri stumbles upon La Santa Muerte, she is stupefied to hear her fellow inmate Pilar claim that "she is more powerful than life . . . and if you become a devotee she will accomplish more things than all the saints in whom you believe." Pilar had a small altar in her cell, which others visited to pray and leave requests, "obviously [with] some coins" (Denegri, 1978, p. 29). Venerating La Santa Muerte seems to have formed part of Pilar's larger toolkit of spiritual self-help, which contained *limpias* (cleansings) to alleviate daily prison predicaments or resolve long-standing legal problems (Denegri, 1978, pp. 81–84).[12]

In summary, there is sufficient evidence that during the second half of the twentieth century, La Santa Muerte was venerated in the secluded environments of private homes and prisons in Mexico. Although it would be very difficult to estimate the number of devotees before 2000, there is no doubt among most observers that after doña Queta "went public" and began to organize rosaries, the number of street altars and devotees increased sharply. In 2008, the Mexico City metropolitan area was estimated to have around three hundred street altars (Kristensen, 2015, p. 8), and the increase in the number of private altars has most likely kept pace with this trend. Today, despite the territorial expansion of the Santa Muerte cult, central Mexico is still considered its "heartland" (Bravo Lara, 2013, p. 13).

The new visibility of the cult, through rosaries and the sale of artifacts, certainly helps gauge the number of devotees, but it may also be misleading. In 2012, Chesnut estimated that 5 million Mexicans worshipped this image, extrapolating from the (equally approximate) sales of votive candles and other Santa Muerte paraphernalia (2012b, pp. 8–9). At the end of 2015, he labeled the growth of the cult "astronomical" and upped his estimates to between 10 and 12 million devotees in Mexico, Central America, and the United States (McNearney, 2015). If we assume that 75 percent of this mean (i.e., 11 million) were Mexicans, that would give a figure of 8.25 million Santa Muerte devotees, or one of every fifteen Mexicans (!), plus 2.75 million in Central America and the United States. No one questions the transnationalization of the cult through migration networks, underground connections, and the Internet. Indeed, altars and services have been recorded from New York to Los Angeles and along the US-Mexican border (Chesnut, 2012b; Panfalone, 2014), while the presence of La Santa Muerte in Guatemalan prisons is widespread.[13] Chesnut's estimates, however, seem unfounded and methodologically weak (Kristensen, 2015, pp. 5–6). An empirically rigorous survey of Mexico City street altars in 2008 suggested that there were perhaps thirty thousand devotees praying monthly in public (Kristensen, 2015, p. 8). If we assume for a moment that this represents only one-third of all devotees—since many may worship while confined in prison or prefer the privacy of their homes, like our taxi driver Ricardo—and that the number of devotees has almost doubled since 2008 (as Chesnut seems to suggest), then we reach an estimate of two hundred thousand in the Mexico City metropolitan area. Santa Muerte devotees can be found across Mexico, but since nearly one-fifth of the country's population lives in the greater Mexico City area, and because most observers agree that this is the cult's heartland, it seems reasonable to guesstimate the total number of devotees at one million. Another half a million from Central America and the United States would make a maximum of 1.5 million: a truly impressive number of adherents for a cult that was virtually unknown just fifteen years ago.

Religious and Iconographic Roots

In recent years, several scholars have commented on the historical roots of Santa Muerte devotion beyond the ethnographic references from the second half of the twentieth century. While the latter are relatively self-evident, research into the deeper origins of this cult is particularly challenging in methodological and interpretive terms. What are the main findings and controversies? To answer this question, I examine two approaches to the cult's origin. The first involves tracing specific popular religious practices and iconographic traditions in Mexico or New Spain that bear a resemblance to today's worship of La Santa Muerte. The second focuses more on symbolic and iconographic complexes that formed historically in Mexico and Central America around death and the dead, constituting cultural resources upon which contemporary religious practices have drawn creatively. In other words, while the former emphasizes certain (iconographic) clues and similarities, the latter concentrates on broader social and cultural contexts.

Some years ago, Lomnitz (2005a, p. 489), for example, suggested that today's Santa Muerte cult in Mexico City might have evolved from the cult of San Pascualito in southern Mexico, which has its roots in colonial times. In 1960, in Tuxtla Gutiérrez, devotees who represented San Pascualito (or San Pascual Rey) as a skeleton in a coffin decided to break away from the Catholic

Church and join the schismatic Santa Iglesia Ortodoxa Católica Mexicana, which had barely survived from the time of the Cristero War (1926–1929). Their decision resulted from a drawn-out religious conflict in the 1950s, during which the cult and its annual fair became particularly popular but also increasingly discredited by mainstream Catholicism. The church denounced devotees as superstitious, as the revolutionary state had done before, in 1914, when revolutionary troops attempted to burn San Pascual's effigy because it was considered idolatrous. Later, in the early 1930s, state-led religious persecutions forced the cult underground. Devotion to the skeletal San Pascual in the first half of the twentieth century most likely dates back to the 1870s, when a confraternity placed an image of the skeleton in a coffin in a church in Tuxtla.

This development appears to be a revitalization of a colonial cult that had antagonized church authorities centuries earlier, though the anthropologist Carlos Navarrete, who studied that cult extensively, is the first to recognize that the historiographic gap is so large that the claim of historical continuity remains speculative and requires further research (1982, p. 35). San Pascual Bailón was a sixteenth-century Franciscan monk (1540–1592) who was beatified in 1618 and then canonized in 1690. In that period, his figure was popularized by members of the Franciscan order in what is today Chiapas and Guatemala. However, around 1650, when San Pascualito (note the affectionate use of the diminutive) was credited by local indigenous people with miraculous interventions during a pestilence and represented with the image of death, Catholic officialdom reacted furiously, accusing the devotees of ignorance, religious corruption, and disorder. Navarrete quotes friar Francisco Vázquez's account of the episode:

> And so ardent is the devotion of some towns, mixed at times with ignorance . . . for the pallid image of Death . . . [that] they call San Pascual, for they have fixed in their minds . . . that San Pascual frees Indians from death, [thus] confounding cause with its effect . . . to such a degree that in some places it has been necessary to remove the effigies of death from view. (1982, p. 29)

The church issued orders that all statues be collected from the Indians, many of whom were said to possess "two or three large [ones] placed upon their altars with offerings of flowers and perfumes," and then burn them publicly. There is additional evidence from the late eighteenth century of images of death worshipped by indigenous folk. Perdigón cites an Inquisition document from 1797 that describes how Indians in San Luis de la Paz, under the influence of peyote, engaged a figurine they called Santa Muerte in a forceful way, "tying her up with a new, wet rope [and] threatening to whip her and burn her if she fail[ed] to perform a miracle" (2008a, p. 33). The church decided to destroy their "pagan" chapel. It has been suggested that this episode forms part of the tensions that arose from the transformations in which images of Christian saints displaced pre-Hispanic *idolillos*—whose force was believed to determine the prosperity of people's homes and families—while retaining some of the latter's key features (Gruzinski, 1990, pp. 216–19). From the seventeenth century onward, Serge Gruzinski argues, these saints became key cultural media "through which New Spain's Indians invented, built and ordered their own reality" (1990, p. 218), although sometimes they crossed the limits marked by orthodox Catholicism. Because of the supposed indigenous and pagan origins of popular religious imaginations of death, encounters with the Catholic hierarchy in the New World reveal a long history of condemnation and punishment.

Having said this, the association between plagues and images of death observed in the case of San Pascual Bailón has numerous precedents in medieval Europe, where the Black Death devastated societies and triggered fears about the fragility of life and the inevitability of (sudden, painful) death. Those episodes had profound cultural consequences, not least in the emergence of new discourses and icons within the Catholic Church. It was the time of images of the so-called danse macabre, in which skeletons hold the hands of living humans and dance with them, young and old, men and women, rich and poor: death as the great equalizer. Such scenes were represented in poems, dances, paintings, stained glass, and sculptures—"dances of death" that expressed "the universal pessimism that invaded the late Middle Ages" (Navarrete, 1982, p. 18).

The overwhelming presence of death in the age of the plagues yielded a deep sense of fragile terrestrial and carnal existence and of the triumphant, sovereign power of death, sometimes portrayed as a crowned queen. The church urged people to live a "good" Christian life and to be ready for salvation when death came. A good life, in turn, prepared a "good" or "holy" death, *"buena"* or *"santa muerte"* (Perdigón, 2008a, p. 24). Treatises were drafted about how to prepare well for dying; that is, *ars moriendi* (Navarrete, 1982, p. 19). Discourses, imageries, and iconographies of death and dying traveled to the New World, an environment in which they evolved further (against the background of massive postconquest mortality) and entered into (hidden) conversations with pre-Columbian symbols and icons of death—for example, with the codices, inscriptions, and sculptures of the god of death, Mictlantecuhtli, in central Mexico. The proliferation of this imagery in New Spain was evident as skulls and skeletons became objects of veneration and cults.[14] Doctrinal framing by the church was profoundly shaped by indigenous devotees, who built relationships of intimacy with them. Despite being persecuted for "idolatry," devotees addressed the skulls on a daily basis and requested favors not granted by a distant and strict God (Fragoso 2011, p. 7), as popular religion became a fertile terrain for the give-and-take process called transculturation or syncretism (Chasteen, 2006, pp. 70–72; Taylor, 1996, pp. 51–61).

Inspired by Bolívar Echeverría's work on the Latin American baroque, the essence of which is summarized as its apparent "fidelity to classic canons, which, however, are reinvented by twisting them," Fragoso argues that devotion to death and La Santa Muerte is an expression of a "baroque ethos" (2011, p. 8, my translation). Hers is clearly an attempt to situate and understand these phenomena in the context of broader cultural processes in which people "live neither in a modern context nor in a pre-modern or post-modern one." In Fragoso's view, this engenders societal and cultural ambiguities "in which form twists the authentic meanings of content" (2011, pp. 10, 15). Here, the Santa Muerte cult is understood as an emblematic symbol of the baroque ethos in that it involves a "vitalist devotion" to sanctified death, as well as, one must add, iconographic exuberance and hyperbole. This interpretation elaborates on Fragoso's earlier, more Marxian argument concerning unfinished modernity, with its distinctive state of social vulnerability and fragility, as a fertile environment for the emergence of the Santa Muerte cult (2007b, pp. 28–33). While establishing firm ethnographic and historiographic grounds to claim the cult as a quintessential Latin American baroque religious practice seems particularly challenging, this interpretation has the benefit of opening up a perspective that looks to broader social and cultural processes and resources that seem propitious to its emergence.

Mexican Skeletons and Their Guises

In this context, two additional Mexican cultural traditions of mortuary imagery are relevant, if only because they are often brought to light by Santa Muerte devotees themselves, the cult's organic intellectuals, and several scholars. Mexico's cult of the dead (as opposed to death) and the iconographic tradition of

La Catrina (a dressed female skeleton) are well known Mexican trademarks in the global cultural marketplace. During the twentieth century, both were the subject of nation- and state-making efforts by elites, although, as Lomnitz has shown, the successful state-led construction of Mexican culture's alleged intimacy with death as a national totem is rooted in a preexisting "densely-layered repertoire of death rituals and death vocabularies," related to both state formation and popular culture (2005a, p. 58). In recent decades, the symbolic practices surrounding the Day of the Dead and the imagery of La Catrina have merged under the influence of increasing commercialization.

The Day of the Dead (Día de Muertos) is the Mexican version of the established Catholic traditional festivities of All Saints' and All Souls' Days (November 1 and 2, respectively). Strictly speaking, across the Catholic world it is during All Souls' Day that believers remember and honor their dead during Mass, often followed by a visit to the cemetery. In Mexico, the traditional liturgical requirements have become overshadowed by what one prominent researcher has called "an ostentatious display of art, poetry, and creative energy," which involves the cleaning and decoration of gravesites and home altars erected for the deceased (Brandes, 2006, p. 6). There will be special sugarcoated bread and other foods on gravestone *ofrendas*, adornments of paper cutouts, exuberant orange *cempasúchitl* flowers, a mass of sugar candies, and toys in the form of skulls (often with names on them), with skeletons and caskets on sale everywhere. The sweets are meant to be consumed. In addition, around these days, newspapers and magazines publish satirical faux epitaphs about public figures. Here, their "larger than life" presence in the mass media is mocked by portraying them as skeleton figures, thereby pointing out their transience. The abundance of sweets, the colorfulness, the humor and satire all mean that "in no other predominantly Catholic country . . . [are] All Saints and All Souls days celebrated with the kind of artistic exuberance and humor" as in Mexico (Brandes, 2006, p. 61). For many inside and outside the country, this uniqueness has become a key symbolic expression of Mexicanness itself.

Similar to the case of La Santa Muerte, Stanley Brandes has pointed out the temptation of several scholars to uncritically assume direct lines of influence from pre-Columbian representations of death and the dead to current popular religious practices of the Day of the Dead. Instead, he strongly argues that the evidence shows that "the Mexican Day of the Dead is a colonial invention, a unique product of colonial demographic and economic processes" (2006, p. 40). Whereas in Europe, as I have mentioned, the massive death toll of the plagues produced the imagery of the danse macabre, postconquest death, destruction, and suffering in New Spain during the sixteenth and seventeenth centuries transformed an originally somber Catholic mortuary ritual into something very distinctive (Brandes, 2006, pp. 41, 61). Also, while the main type of foods originated in Spain, as did the ofrenda format, the Day of the Dead had acquired its distinctive (humorous and mocking) manifestations in New Spain by the mid-eighteenth century, and these have been enhanced since the second half of the nineteenth century.

Several scholars have argued that around 1900, the consolidation of the unique features of the Day of the Dead began to coalesce with a new and more politically inspired graphic tradition of illustrations in broadsides and the penny press. Those publications formed part of an emergent urban print culture of social and political commentary and satire that catered to the popular classes. They not only addressed everyday events but also exposed the corruption and hypocrisy of the country's ruling Porfirian elites. Around the Day of the Dead, the broadsides published so-called *calaveras* (skulls), which contained satirical ballads and jocular rhymes about politicians, barmaids, and businessmen, illustrated with eye-catching engravings of "vivid and lively skeletons and skulls with grinning teeth, dancing, cycling, playing the guitar, plying their trades, drinking, masquerading" (Wollen, 1989, pp. 14–15). In circumstances that rarely allowed organized political dissidence, these satirical engravings constituted a form of popular resistance (Brandes, 2006, p. 63) and, as Lomnitz has suggested, an expression of a "radical liberal tradition of political critique" (2005a, p. 417). For José Guadalupe Posada (1852–1913), undoubtedly the most renowned and productive engraver of the time, the Day of the Dead provided attractive artistic and commercial opportunities. Although his oeuvre is broad, Posada has become best known for his calaveras, in which skeletons and skulls are imbued with a "burlesque vitality" (Perdigón, 2008a, p. 44). Among those works, the image of the Catrina has become emblematic: the skull of a "society belle" with a large, elegant hat adorned with feathers and flowers, accompanied by the text "Fun-loving Calaveras. Today's maids in their Sunday best, Tomorrow will be skeletons laid to rest" (Rothenstein, 1989, p. 137).

There is ample scholarly agreement that the enduring iconographic influence of Posada's dancing skeletons and coquettish skulls on Mexican visual culture and popular art has to do with the fact that after his death he was seen as "the precursor of modern art in Mexico," by both Mexican and foreign painters and artists (Lomnitz, 2005a, p. 418). Mexican muralists like Diego Rivera and José Clemente Orozco, and French artists like Jean Charlot and André Breton, became key conduits for Posada's fame. His work was subsequently seen as a source of inspiration for Mexican modernism, surrealism, and "populist" understandings of art, which meant a rejection of abstract art and an appreciation of figurative folk art, something that well suited Mexico's (post)revolutionary ideologies and narratives of national identity (Wollen, 1989). For all these reasons, by the 1930s "Posada and his *calaveras* had become symbolic for Mexico," and the skeleton achieved its totemic status (Brandes, 2006, p. 63; Lomnitz, 2005a, p. 419). During the twentieth century, and especially in more recent decades, the iconographic presence or influence of the Catrina has moved beyond artistic recognition and state-led nation-building into the commercialized world of tourism and marketing, often leading to a stylization of the original graphic imagery. More in general, it has meant that alongside the symbolic manifestations associated with the Day of the Dead, Posada's humanized skulls and skeletons have become part of Mexico's broad cultural and iconographic reservoir, forming two distinct, albeit related, traditions of mortuary art that national and foreign observers often perceive as, and reduce to, "one undifferentiated syndrome" (Brandes, 2006, p. 66).

The Santa Muerte cult can easily be conceived as another layer of a supposed Mexican cultural preoccupation with death and the dead. While it is erroneous to conceive the Day of the Dead, Posada's skeletons, the Santa Muerte cult, and even more so pre-Columbian symbols of death as manifestations of some deep cultural motif, it is possible to observe meaningful and dynamic connections among these phenomena. These connections are not unmediated expressions of some cultural essence but, rather, the result of specific social and political forces. Over time, these forces have formed layers and shaped practices of meaning-making by different social actors through which symbols, forms, and meanings may migrate from one place to another, becoming transformed in the process. In a thought-provoking semiotic and material analysis, Kristensen (2016a), for example, examined the genealogy of La Santa Muerte's present-day powerful three-dimensional iconography in terms of the coalescence of the two-dimensional representation of La Santísima Muerte as it appeared in prayer pamphlets, and the dandy attributes that Posada and later artists bestowed upon the secular Catrina, which since the 1980s has increasingly been commercialized as a three-dimensional figure for domestic and foreign tourists. Kristensen claims that prior to the 1990s Santa Muerte prayers were not recited in front of three-dimensional figures, and no strong evidence has yet emerged to contradict this view. Ever since, however, the frivolous human-like qualities of La Catrina (her enjoyment of tequila, cigars, and beautiful clothing) have become infused with the divine powers of older religious beliefs in La Santísima Muerte. I will come back to the consequences of this transformation for devotional practices, but for the moment it is important to point out how anthropological and historical research has established that significant features of the Santa Muerte cult are embedded in broader reservoirs of symbols and meanings, of which its devotees make creative use.

This is also evident at another level, namely the persistent symbolic association between the different manifestations of "death" through time and notions of the "great equalizer," and those of the vanity and fragility of life. This was the case with colonial images like the danse macabre that resonated with the widespread, arbitrary arrival of death in times of massive demographic decline. At the end of the nineteenth century, social and political contradictions formed the background against which critics mobilized the symbolic power of death. Posada's "dressed up skeleton showed up the arbitrary and violent nature of social inequality" (Lomnitz, 2005a, pp. 418–19). Indeed, twenty-first-century devotees of La Santa Muerte will remind anyone who will listen that this saint's immense power is epitomized by her great equalizing capacity, all the more so in a society as deeply unequal as neoliberal Mexico, for death undoes the differences between rich and poor, the included and the excluded, the neoliberal tycoon and the market woman, mestizo and indigenous, and criminals and law-abiding citizens.

Beyond Historiographic Gaps and Iconographic Continuities

The study of the historical roots of La Santa Muerte allows one to draw a number of important conclusions. First, ethnographic and journalistic accounts of Santa Muerte devotion in the secluded spaces of the home or prison during the second half of the twentieth century prompted the identification and analysis of popular religious practices and iconographic traditions that bear resemblance to features of today's cult. Here, I have mentioned devotional and iconographic precursors ranging from San Pascualito in nineteenth-century Chiapas to the indigenous worship of skeleton figures in late colonial New Spain, and to a whole set of symbols and imageries in medieval European

Catholicism that traveled to the New World, where they were transformed. Second, while several scholars have identified such historical references, no definitive evidence-based (archival) connections between early and late colonial phenomena and sources, and between them and the reemergence of the San Muerte cult since the mid-twentieth century, have yet been established. While such findings are suggestive, there are serious historiographic gaps.[15] Third, contemporary Santa Muerte practices are embedded in, and nourished by, broad and deep Mexican cultural (re)sources such as those of the Catholic Day of the Dead and the late nineteenth-century secular imagery of the calaveras. This is a mediated relationship, and there appears to be agreement about the overwhelming colonial (as opposed to precolonial) roots of the popular engagement with death in Mexico. Fourth, understanding the origins of popular religious practices demands going beyond tracking symbolic or iconographic continuities or connections to cultural repertoires. It requires situating their emergence and evolution in social, demographic, political, and economic contexts. Widespread death and destruction deeply shaped the mortuary ritual of the Day of the Dead in postconquest sixteenth- and seventeenth-century New Spain (Brandes, 2006), while the collapse of the colonial order followed by an unsettling mining boom triggered the emergence of the devotion to the Santo Niño de Atocha among mineworkers and their families in northern Mexico (Pescador, 2009). Finally, processes of national state-making promoted a Mexican "intimacy" with death as a national totem (Lomnitz, 2005a).

Benjamin Smith's contribution to this volume elaborates on this approach through his suggestive, longitudinal historical analysis of the social bases of popular religious practices and Catholic revitalization movements in Mexico. Using the concept of the moral economy, Smith examines how systems of social production and domination express themselves in particular religious and moral lexicons and imageries, and how systemic changes are expressed in, and contested through, new religious leaderships and rituals, innovative devotions, and the resignification of existing Catholic symbols. His broad analysis includes local religious cults in colonial Chiapas, the insurrectionist cult of the talking cross in nineteenth-century Yucatán, and the cult of Juan Soldado in early twentieth-century Tijuana. The result is a framework for understanding the development of idiosyncratic popular religious practices and cults in response to changing—and often threatening—political economies, class and ethnic relations, political regimes, and cultural repertoires. In the last part of this chapter, I return to this framework and review the social forces and institutions that have shaped the remarkable dynamics of the Santa Muerte cult since 2000.

Popular religions draw on existing theological and iconographic repertoires, but they also appropriate, contest, and transform them, and hence actively produce new realities. To understand this requires taking a close look at the symbols, devotional practices, and social processes that make up the current cult of La Santa Muerte. To this I turn my attention in the following section.

2. LOOKING INWARD: PHENOMENOLOGY, DEVOTION, AND POLITICS

The rosaries dedicated to La Santa Muerte are an explosion of images, colors, and symbols, public events brimming with visual and perceptual exuberance.[16] It is no wonder that a perceptive observer like Fragoso (2011) associates figurative exaggeration, extravagant statuettes, and seeming symbolic excess with a baroque sense of popular religiosity. The significance of the distinctive visibility and visuality of the Santa Muerte cult is analyzed in depth by Huffschmid (this volume). People carry Santa Muerte figurines in all forms and colors, some of them spectacular for their size, others for their elaborate detail or dazzling designs. Many devotees wear clothes with Santa Muerte imprints, while almost all bear chains, rings and other jewelry, and, of course, Santa Muerte tattoos.

In this volume, Perdigón and Robles's ethnographic account of the meanings of Santa Muerte tattoos examines the connections among devotion, bodily expressions, and society at large. Situating themselves in the field of the anthropology of the body, they show how Santa Muerte tattoos transform the human figure itself into an altar, and how that process is shaped by local and global iconographic repertoires and autobiographical inscriptions. In addition, their chapter contains the first comprehensive examination of the aesthetic (designs), devotional (bodily placement, protection, pain), and social (identity, community) meanings of Santa Muerte tattoos. In so doing, their contribution takes the study of Santa Muerte devotion to the most intimate level of corporal experience.

At the rosaries, the scents of fresh flowers, smoke, and food fill the air. There is an atmosphere of "countercultural and defiant pleasures" (Roush, 2014, p. 129), but these are also gatherings where one witnesses deep devotion and religious contemplation. People stand quietly in line for hours just to get a glimpse of the majestic Santa Muerte statue in doña Queta's shrine. Devotees can be seen immersed in inner conversations with their personal Santa Muerte statues. One senses serenity, companionship, and community.[17] Based on a critical review of existing scholarship and my own ethnographic encounters, this section tackles important components of the Santa Muerte cult as it exists today. First, I discuss the cult's expressive forms and material culture, and identify the spaces and places where the saint is venerated. Then I look at gender, family, and intimacy. After that, I examine the theological and ritual core of devotional practices. Finally, I review the organizational and political processes inside the growing cult. The section closes with an analysis of the major transformations that the cult has undergone in recent decades.

Phenomenology

Although a bewildering variety of forms exists, the typical figure of La Santa Muerte is a skeleton, traditionally dressed in hooded robes, like those of medieval monks, but also in long, colorful, elegant hand-sewn dresses. Sometimes she is dressed as a bride, all in white, such as the one I encountered in the Iglesia y Santuario a la Niña Blanca, a small public shrine situated between two nightclubs along the busy Avenida Casas Grandes in the border city of Ciudad Juárez. This large, seated Santa Muerte, a clearly recognizable skeleton with uncovered arms and upper chest called Amy, was attired in a white wedding gown with bridal veil and tiara. A well-off devotee from the United States had donated Amy to the shrine, I was told.

This particular bridal representation may remind some devotees of the disputed legend of the human origin of La Santa Muerte, which is rooted in the old European tale about the bride who waited in vain for her husband-to-be at the altar, and then, out of grief, shriveled up and died in God's house. In this version, her sainthood is related to her sacrifice as a neglected woman, a cultural motif similar to that of the *mujer abnegada* so often mentioned in studies of Latin American stereotypes of femininity (Kristensen, 2016a, p. 411). Others, however, will associate her bridal garb with a special occasion, perhaps her anniversary, that calls for her most beautiful outfit. In most cases, the hood of her tunic covers a bald skull, but other statuettes are adorned with brown or black wigs. The Santa Muerte at Enriqueta Romero's shrine in Tepito in particular has extravagantly long hair.

Most commercially produced Santa Muerte statuettes are represented with hooded robes and bald skulls, although the robes come in varying sizes, colors, and designs (such as the one in the design of Guadalajara's Chivas football club!). Figurines are made in one piece but of diverse materials (wood or, more commonly, plaster), and are easily transported. The dressed-up skeletons in private or public shrines, however, are more elaborate with real, specially made dresses, wigs, and jewelry, although it seems that devotees increasingly dress up prefabricated statuettes as well. Believers' evident willingness to spend money encouraged some to establish businesses where statuettes can be dressed and coiffed (Chesnut, 2012b, p. 8). This beautification of La Santa Muerte may also include such accessories as handbags, umbrellas, crowns, hats, and gloves. But this is nothing new, for it is a long-standing and wide-spread practice in the Catholic tradition to dress female saints in churches and chapels magnificently for special occasions, as in the case of the baroque Virgen del Rosario in the Santo Domingo church in Puebla. Dresses and accessories come in different designs that represent specific Santa Muerte identities, such as Posada's coquettish Catrina, a dancer with pre-Hispanic features who invariably wears a feather headdress, or a princess, *quinceañera*, or angel (Perdigón, 2015b, pp. 50–52). In all cases, this dressing up has an identity effect, for it entails a process of individualization, personification, or recognition and, hence, opens up a space for closeness and intimacy, an aspect to which I shall return below. Dressing up also validates her beauty, as one devotee confided to Perdigón: "[S]piritually, she is beautiful, because she gives me strength, peace, balance, and calls me to do things better every day. And physically as well, for [her] beauty is natural as it was created by God" (2015b, p. 57). In fact, one of the most common names for La Santa Muerte is La Niña Bonita, the pretty girl.

However, the symbolic or ritual meanings of dressing up La Santa Muerte go beyond representing her perceived (inner) beauty, for it is often seen as part of the transaction through which devotees express their gratitude. Also, acquiring a new dress can be a way "to pay off" a favor. The choice of specific designs and colors is guided not only by devotees' aesthetic preferences but also by the nature of the favors requested from the saint; that is, they are tools used to steer the force of La Santa Muerte in the desired direction. Finally, dressing up skeletons and rudimentary prefabricated statuettes enhances La Santa Muerte's feminine identity (Perdigón, 2015b).

Dressed up or not, prefabricated Santa Muerte images and statuettes always carry various objects that symbolize her primary powers and tasks, perhaps most importantly the scythe (sometimes a sword), with which she can cut the thread of life and which underscores her resemblance to the classic representation of the Grim Reaper. She often bears a globe of the world, which represents her enormous power over all things, since, eventually, everything dies. The scales of justice in her left hand refer to the unbiased judgments she imparts, a concept that, as we have seen, has deep roots in Catholic discourse and iconography (Flores Martos, 2007, p. 287).[18]

Shrines and Rosaries

Santa Muerte devotional practices and rituals take place in two distinct spaces: the private space of the home, where devotees worship their personal Santa Muerte figures in their own homemade altars, and public altars, shrines, or sanctuaries. Although much remains to be discovered about the evolution of devotional practices in the first half of the twentieth century, it appears that worship and praying originally took place in private with the help of colored cardstocks bearing the image of La Santa Muerte on one side and a prayer on the other, which remain abundantly available today (see Flanet, 1989, pp. 160–61; Thompson, 1998, p. 421; Perdigón, 2008a, p. 77). While it is likely that the first private altars were constructed around such two-dimensional images, it is certain that in the 1980s and early 1990s these images morphed into three-dimensional sculptures (Kristensen, 2016a, pp. 404–5; 2011, pp. 83–84). Around 1995, molded plastic statues of La Santa Muerte with an average height of twenty-five centimeters lined the tables of esoteric shops in the Sonora Market, the emblematic market close to Mexico City's historic center known for the wide range of esoteric, magical, and occult products it offers. Devotees acquired them for their private altars (Thompson, 1998, p. 423). But as the cult attracted an ever-larger following and the statuettes grew in size, it eventually burst into the public domain; hence, the erection of street altars. At the same time, some "intermediate altars" began to appear in work-related spaces. They were not set up for strictly private use but were not intended for the public at large, either. Miners in Sombrerete, Zacatecas, for example, installed a wooden Santa Muerte statuette at the entrance to the mine, to whom they commended their souls before descending to work (*Altares, ofrendas, oraciones*, 2007, p. 9).[19]

Being a Santa Muerte devotee entails constructing and maintaining an altar at home as well as participating in public ceremonies. Although devotees have had altars in their homes for decades and developed particular styles and formats, since around 2000 numerous booklets and magazines have appeared that provide suggestions and often detailed "rules" concerning Santa Muerte shrines.[20] An altar is a consecrated space with objects and images that form the foundation or embodiment of devotion. A private altar must be in a space accessible exclusively to the devotee. One important rule is that the altar is the exclusive domain of La Santa Muerte, although in practice one often finds her accompanied by Jesus and the Virgin of Guadalupe (Kristensen, 2011, p. 125). There are numerous additional, and sometimes detailed, guidelines about how, where, and when to construct an altar, and how to properly clean and consecrate one; information is also provided about background colors and the meanings of different offerings, such as candles (light), water, apples, liquor, and cigars. The choice of a particular image or statue is, however, entirely dependent on the devotee's preference, since it should always be one that transmits trust, faith, and devotion (Velázquez, 2013, pp. 19–29). Devotees are expected to commit to their private Santa Muerte, who requires respect, cleanliness, prayer, the renewal of offerings every day or week, and participation in rituals for specific purposes. One interesting example is a ritual that "unlocks any economic problem" using specific objects and proceedings, such as light, by placing a candle on a large plate and praying three Our Fathers. Then, the supplicant must show deep faith as she or he beseeches La Santa Muerte for her help in economic matters. Next, a magnet, a pyrite stone, a pendant, and a small copper powder box must be placed beside the candle. When the candle has burned up, all the ingredients are collected in a cloth sachet that the person will always carry close to the body, because it will help open up opportunities. No one else can be allowed to touch the sachet, for then it will lose its magical powers (Velázquez, 2013, p. 76)!

An interesting study of the emergence of street altars or public shrines in the metropolitan area of Mexico City concludes that there is a "before and after," marked by Enriqueta Romero's decision in September 2001 to place her huge Santa Muerte outside her house (Kristensen, 2015, pp. 548–51). This triggered public veneration and a practice that soon spread across the city and beyond, when doña Queta began her monthly street rosaries, which were subsequently emulated elsewhere. Between 2001 and 2008, the number of street altars dedicated to La Santa Muerte in the greater metropolitan area mushroomed from fewer than ten to around three hundred. Similar developments occurred elsewhere in the country. The territorial expansion of the public altars in the city was uneven. Around 2008, most were concentrated in poor areas, though not necessarily the poorest. More significantly, there was a correlation between the spatial distribution of street shrines and the ratio of the prison population of neighborhoods. Kristensen establishes a social relationship between neighborhood and prison when arguing that people who approach La Santa Muerte tend to come from urban areas with high concentrations of informal and illicit activities. These are places where ordinary people face the excesses of the "penal state" (Kristensen, 2015, pp. 552–56). The spatial expansion of Santa Muerte street altars thus reveals the social forces that appear to drive the cult, a topic I examine in greater detail in the third section of this chapter.

Depending on local circumstances, a public altar may be just that: a small or large shrine on a street corner or in an extension of a house. In principle, they are always open for worship, but there are also public altars or sanctuaries in edifices expressly built or accommodated for that purpose. Undoubtedly, the most spectacular case was the inauguration of the Templo de La Santa Muerte in Tultitlán, north of Mexico City, with its twenty-two-meter-high statue! A Santa Muerte shrine in the metropolitan area of Guadalajara used to be a warehouse, but it was remodeled with donations from devotees (Bravo Lara, 2013, p. 22). The Santa Muerte "Martita" sanctuary in Ciudad Juárez actually consists of two separate buildings in a large yard behind a flower shop called La Catrina. A small, well-kept building contains the Santa Muerte "Martita," the key figure of the shrine. Near its entrance stands an imposing black Santa Muerte figure with a scythe called Magda, whose task is to protect Martita. The larger building to her right is unfinished but has stained-glass windows with Santa Muerte motifs and is the site of weekly services. While large Santa Muerte and Catrina figures line the walls, the altar itself looks like that of a normal Catholic church with a low platform and a cross with a Christ figure.

The broader significance of public shrines is that their caretakers and/or spiritual leaders began to organize religious gatherings such as Masses, rosaries, and anniversary gatherings and fiestas, although the distinction among these is not always clear. Many shrines also offer other spiritual services by appointment, such as cleansings (limpias) of people, homes, or offices; amarres (love-binding spells); healings; and even marriage counseling. In San Cristóbal de las Casas, cult leaders are perhaps first of all *curanderos* (healers), who draw on a wide range of religious and spiritualist traditions (Michalik, 2011, pp. 168–73). At one Ciudad Juárez shrine, these services cost 150 pesos (approximately eight dollars in 2016). The services offered by the leader of an altar in Chetumal on the Caribbean coast included the preparation of potions and black magic (Higuera-Bonfil, 2015, p. 101).

The best-known and most highly publicized rosary in Mexico takes place at doña Queta's shrine in Tepito. Attendance at these rosaries has grown from hundreds to thousands of devotees, who flock to Alfarería Street clutching their own statues on the first of every month. Because the Santa Muerte cult grew and then burst into the public domain with no unified or agreed-upon liturgical formats or content, these rites were constructed in noncentralized ways from below, giving rise to interesting differences across the country. At the same time, however, they are strongly shaped by Catholic rituals. Blanca Estela Bravo Lara found that in addition to some specific elements, Mass in the Templo de la Santa Muerte in Guadalajara "does not differ much from the current official Catholic one. . . . [T]he itinerary, the prayers and rituals are executed in the same order and in very similar ways" (2013, p. 25). Laura Roush (2014, p. 132), meanwhile, concludes that the rosaries in Tepito are immediately legible for Roman Catholics (see also Flores Martos, 2007, pp. 295–96; Kristensen, this volume).

Over the years, input from Enriqueta and a series of male prayer leaders has given more uniform content and structure to the rosary services, which have subsequently traveled elsewhere. Roush's excellent ethnographic account provides insight into how rosaries begin with a prayer that asks God for permission to address La Santa Muerte directly ("Dios es primero!"), followed by prayers that deal with mysteries, which in a traditional Catholic format are meant to convey the experience of the divine in earthly beings. In Santa Muerte rosaries, however, mysteries are associated with the real-world problems of the urban poor and thus bring matters of illegality, insecurity, and different modalities of vulnerability into the heart of religious practices. In other words, an established Catholic format is colonized by popular religious concerns. One salient example is the prayer that deals with addiction, a phenomenon typically associated with the margins of urban modernity and maligned by state and religious institutions:

Most Holy Death, protector, and owner of life . . .
I ask you, I implore you, I humbly beseech you
to behold and contemplate the great anxiety I feel
for the person who is slowly being consumed by vice.
And knowing that for you nothing is impossible,
today I beg you, I supplicate,
that you return him to health,
so that he will no longer depend on any kind of drug
[and] his body recovers its vigor, energy, strength,
with the decision to never consume again.[21]

After the mysteries, the rosary continues with chants, including an Agnus Dei, and a prayer concocted entirely by the leaders of the Alfarería shrine (Roush, 2014, p. 134). The final part of the gathering contains most of La Santa Muerte's sui generis rites: a key petition for protection from all possible harm (enemies, weapons, illness, or disgrace) and, most importantly, the so-called *cadena de la fuerza* (chain of force) and blessing of images, when all participants raise their personal Santa Muerte statuettes above their heads in the direction of the shrine. While the latter constitutes the visual culmination of the rosary, the former connects devotees both among themselves and to the saint. Roush (2014, p. 136) captures the significance of the rite in these words: "Each person present is encouraged to take the hand of the next, to form a chain through which energy can flow. . . . The leader invites the congregation to concentrate on what they want to say to her. . . . A long and total silence follows." In January 2015, I experienced the chain and the blessing of the images as compelling instances of devotion and community building, as well as manifestations of the cult's self-recognition and pride.[22]

Equally meticulous ethnographic accounts of other Santa Muerte rosaries and Masses are not available (yet), but recent studies indicate that the cult has developed an emerging "shared" ritualistic and liturgical framework that leaves room for local specificities and bricolage.[23] In a shrine in Guadalajara once run by a group that rivaled the Tepito cult, for example, the preacher similarly prayed for La Santa Muerte to protect prisoners and police officers, and for money, health, love, and harmony in the family (Bravo Lara, 2013, p. 26). Other observers, however, have found devotional and symbolic practices deeply shaped by local histories and specific religious and spiritual

FIGURE 1.1 Male Santa Muerte devotee
kneeling, Tepito neighborhood, Mexico City,
January 2015. Photograph by Rigo Gallardo
Schwan.

FIGURE 1.2 Male Santa Muerte
devotee with statuette, Tepito
neighborhood, Mexico City,
January 2015. Photograph by
Rigo Gallardo Schwan.

contexts. In the port of Veracruz, Flores Martos (2007) learned not only
about a localist origin myth claiming that La Santa Muerte came into existence
after revelations to a local sorcerer in the mid-nineteenth century but, more
importantly, about how the contemporary Santa Muerte cult is enmeshed in
a religious field made up of popular Catholicism and Cuban Santería.[24] A
recent study of several Santa Muerte shrines and altars in the relatively small
city of Chetumal found diverse rituals. There, liturgical practices and fiestas
grew out of the particular histories of local congregations deeply fashioned,
in turn, by the initiatives and views of their respective spiritual leaders. For
example, during the annual anniversary fiesta for one altar, a series of folk-
loric dances was inspired by pre-Hispanic Maya death cults, while at another
shrine yearly fiestas included tropical dances, lavish alcohol consumption, and

FIGURE 1.3 Blessing of Santa Muerte images, Tepito neighborhood, Mexico City, January 2015. Photograph by Rigo Gallardo Schwan.

erotic performances by (mostly gay) male devotees intended to please La Santa Muerte (Higuera-Bonfil, 2015).

Devotion, Theology, and Ritual

La Santa Muerte shares many features with other Latin American folk saints. Her devotees regard her as miraculous, but she is not recognized by the Catholic Church. There is one key difference that is relevant for understanding Santa Muerte theology. In contrast to other noncanonical saints, La Santa Muerte is not identified with a deceased person; rather, she is the personification or sanctification of death itself, and this imbues her with extraordinary powers. Devotees themselves distinguish between the generic nonhuman *muerte* (death) and human *muertos* (the dead) and acknowledge that La Santa Muerte never lived an earthly life. They see her in ambiguous terms as a spirit who nonetheless does "saint-like things" (Kristensen, 2016a, p. 411). While the latter justifies naming her a "saint," the former explains her force and privileged position in the spiritual universe, a figure or entity close to God, placed above other saints (Perdigón, 2008a, p. 60).

Despite La Santa Muerte's unique nonearthly past, in popular religious practices devotees often place and understand her powers in the context of various other folk and canonical saints. In terms of her interventions in matters of health and healing, the cult of Niño Fidencio, which originated in the 1920s in northeastern Mexico, is relevant (Graziano, 2007, pp. 191–216). Also, as a kind of "last resort" saint, she is often associated with the canonical saint of "lost causes," Jude Thaddeus. When approached for the protection of illicit businesses or otherwise dangerous enterprises or occupations (e.g., police work), she might appear in the company of former bandit and folk saint Jesús Malverde, from the northwestern state of Sinaloa. Or, when she is called upon to support migrants attempting to cross into the United States, she stands close to Juan Soldado, the poor soldier from Tijuana who was believed to be unjustly tried and executed in 1938 and later became a folk saint (Vanderwood, 2004). Needless to say, devotees approach all of these saints with a great variety of requests.

At the core of all devotional practices to folk saints lies an exchange mechanism. Frank Graziano's groundbreaking study states that "devotion is structured by a spiritual contract that establishes mutual obligations for the folk saints and the devotee" (2007, p. 60). Like our cabbie, Ricardo, from the beginning of this chapter, who promised La Santa Muerte that he would get a tattoo once his problem was resolved, petitions to the saint come with a promise (*manda*). Failing to keep such promises once the saint has successfully brokered (with God) an intervention or miracle may have dire consequences. Despite structural similarities, what distinguishes different devotions are the content and terms of exchange. Some saints are called upon for specific purposes, while others offer solutions to many problems; some are lenient, others more demanding. Underneath the image of Saint Ramon Nonato in the Mexico City Metropolitan Cathedral, one can observe a huge pile of iron chains with locks and colorful ribbons with devotees' requests and expressions of gratitude. I once acquired a card with the following prayer: "Señor San Ramón, place a lock on any gossiper who with his tongue wishes to do me harm." Devotees thus specifically request the saint to intercede against a gossipy neighbor or colleague who makes life hard at home or at work. The quintessential exchange mechanism between a devotee and San Ramón Nonato would be to petition the saint to intercede before "our Lord Jesus Christ, so that he may . . . free us from evil tongues, protect us from the slanderer." In exchange, the devotee leaves a chain with a lock.[25] At the beginning of his wonderful study of miraculous images and votive offerings in Mexico, Graziano makes this point in general terms when he writes that devotion to images and statuettes is "primarily petitionary, which is to say motivated more by management of hardships and compensatory satisfaction of worldly needs than by salvation of the soul after death" (2016, p. 17).

At the core of Santa Muerte devotional practices lie the emic notions of *amparo* and *desamparo*, best translated as protection and loss or lack of protection; and *paro*, translated as the suspension of some activity (such as in *paro cardiaco*, heart attack, or *paro laboral*, work stoppage), but in conjunction with the verbs "make" or "have" paro also means to have backup, support from a powerful somebody, or simply a helping hand. Several scholars of La Santa Muerte have justifiably dedicated considerable attention to these notions. The need for amparo corresponds to devotees' main frustrations concerning law enforcement and other public institutions (prisons, hospitals, tax offices), accustomed as they are to the vicissitudes of informal livelihoods and the vulnerability of patronage politics. Cult prayers often begin by petitioning La Santa Muerte with the plea "no me dejes desamparado" (don't leave me unprotected) against a variety of forces, actions, or agents in different domains of social life (Roush, 2012, 2014). Unsurprisingly perhaps, the notion of amparo has both legal and religious meanings. On the one hand, an amparo is a uniquely Mexican legal procedure that allows an individual to petition a court to postpone, at least temporarily, an allegedly arbitrary or illegal act of public authority; in other words, a legal device that mediates between state and citizens (Reich, 2007).[26] In popular religion, on the other hand, the notion of (des)amparo conveys "how the Santa Muerte cult is a space for thinking about who protects whom, and from what" (Roush, 2014, p. 130).

From a theological perspective, another study compared the interventions of La Santa Muerte in human affairs with understandings of "miracles" contained in sacred canonical scriptures or narrated in other devotions. Despite the fact that devotees themselves frequently speak of "miracles" in exchange for gifts or promises, that study concludes that the nature of the exchange practices between La Santa Muerte and devotees cannot comply with the definitional threshold of traditional "miracles" for a number of reasons: first, there is no foundational narrative or miracle (such as the 1917 Fátima miracle in

Portugal); second, her interventions are seen as the result of petitionary prayer, ritual, or devotion; and third, events attributed to her are concrete and useful for devotees, mundane rather than supernatural (Bigliardi, 2016). Instead of miracles, the theological core of Santa Muerte devotion is best expressed in the notion of the paro, "a favour consisting in the stoppage . . . or avoidance of an undesirable . . . situation, analogous to favours usually exchanged among human beings" (Bigliardi, 2016, pp. 317–18). The idea that paro constitutes the theological core of Santa Muerte devotion is nested in the saint's very identity. If a problem or undesirable situation comes to an end, this is attributed to La Santa's powerful intervention, but when the course of life itself is suspended, this can also be taken to be the work of La Santa Muerte. The ambiguity of the notion of paro (favor, helping hand, and death) means that whatever the result may be, "death always triumphs" (Bigliardi, 2016, p. 319). Interestingly, in 2008 a visitor convinced the spiritual leader of the Tepito shrine that La Santa Muerte "does not provide miracles, she provides paros," which might explain why so many are attracted to her.[27]

By far the most complex analysis of the emic notions of (des)amparo and paro is Kristensen's (2011; this volume), which examines Santa Muerte devotional practices with the help of classic anthropological concepts and theories of the gift, exchange, and reciprocity, and proposes a continuum with distinct categories and correlated practices of exchange and reciprocity. It is also important to address the meaningful distinction between amparo and paro and the importance granted to time. Amparo is quintessentially about protection secured by a temporal distance—that is, protection through postponing the final encounter with danger and death. The generalized, unconditional gift exchange typical of home altars constitutes the natural and "familial" habitat that nurtures amparo. However, the balanced reciprocity typical of commercial or even utilitarian exchanges between devotees and La Santa Muerte through the *mandas* found in paros (favors in exchange for promises) reveals a distinct approach to exchange with La Santa Muerte (Kristensen, 2011, p. 155; Perdigón, 2008a, p. 65). Instructional booklets generally contain long lists of prayers and rituals for very specific requests. One contained some forty to request the protection of children and businesses, the resolution of conflicts, and the solution to problems involving health, love, or money (Anónimo, 2015). Even so, paro and amparo are notions that enable people to "engage temporarily with dangerous enemies" and express the need for a helping hand in difficult, risky, adverse, or outright threatening circumstances (Kristensen,

2011, p. 16). Popular prayers to La Santa Muerte supplicate her to intercede before God to obtain protection and favors in devotees' earthly lives.

Family and Gender

The position of La Santa Muerte in the "familial" habitat merits further attention since it reveals a key feature of the cult's devotion, namely the devotees' intimate relationship with her. Once established, Perdigón (2008a, p. 78) argues, La Santa Muerte was represented as a *"humanized* God-object, as a non-sexual body that needs to be fed and kept pleased." One of her informants identified the closeness to humans graphically by saying that "we always have death with us, we carry her inside of us, in our bones. . . . She is the one who is always with us." This emphasis on La Santa Muerte's corporal familiarity with humans apparently obliterates her nonhuman origins (as occurs with other popular Catholic saints): just as humans carry the skeleton inside, so too does she long for food, drinks, cigarettes, clothing, and attention. Devotees also impute human mood swings to her: she can be caring and loving, but also demanding and vengeful. This is a matter of theological debate: there are those, including spiritual leaders, who highlight the former, and others who state that when not treated properly La Santa Muerte becomes a dangerous "high-maintenance *cabrona* [bitch]" (Roush, 2014, p. 145).

The humanization and personification of La Santa Muerte has undoubtedly been enhanced by the transformation from two-dimensional representations to three-dimensional sculptures, and her "new" material existence has become a vehicle for extending the agency and meaning of death. This is not only because the three-dimensional figure allows social interactions, such as dressing and hugging, but also because "the statues, and particularly their eyes, conjure up a hidden inner world" (Kristensen, 2016a, p. 412). Three-dimensional sculptures do a better job of welding intimate, durable familial relationships between La Santa Muerte and her devotees. Seen from this perspective, it is no surprise that devotees lovingly speak of La Santa Muerte as a female family member: sister (*hermana, hermanita*); child (*nena, niña*); mother or little mother (*madrecita*); godmother (*madrina*); or the more informal but warm *manita* (female friend but also young female sibling). In the private space of the home altar (often in a bedroom), La Santa Muerte is a partner in everyday familiar interactions such as chatting, gossiping, and sharing food and a smoke but also in daily tensions and conflicts. Moreover, like any member of the family, she demands loyalty and defends her kin, aspects that bring us right back to a decisive feature of early Santa Muerte devotion, discussed above, in which women invoked her to chastise unfaithful, disloyal men. But over time, she has evolved into a much more complex family personality: "[S]he is now an innocent and capricious child, an understanding and awkward sister, a fair and jealous wife, a loving and castigating mother, and a tough godmother, but above all else she is committed by familial loyalty and susceptible to betrayal" (Kristensen, 2011, p. 116). The process of humanization has yielded to one of intimate personification.

These are, of course, all *female* identities. With the exception of Perdigón, who, under the probable influence of Navarrete's work on Rey Pascualito, claims that La Santa Muerte appears in feminine and masculine forms, all scholars agree on her female identity; indeed, Chesnut calls her gender "one of her most unique characteristics" (2012b, p. 7). While elsewhere in Latin America two male skeleton saints exist—San La Muerte in Argentina and Rey Pascual in Guatemala—La Santa Muerte appears to proudly follow in the footsteps of La Parca, the female personification of death introduced by the Spanish in colonial New Spain and elsewhere in the New World. This is likely explained by the fact that, despite interesting similarities, a key difference between the male San La Muerte and the female Santa Muerte is that different foundational myths about the former all include references to the exemplary lives of a shaman, a king, or a Jesuit friar, whereas, as I have shown, the latter lacks immediate human origins and is the result of the humanization of a divine force.[28]

The gendered identity of La Santa Muerte becomes visible and meaningful through the decisions and investments made by devotees to highlight her femininity. As I mentioned above, dressing her elegantly or in typical feminine outfits provides ample opportunities to sate the saint's alleged vanity. Some designs of La Santa Muerte statuettes explicitly seek to bring out female bodily contours. The most telling expression of female gender is undoubtedly a pregnant Santa Muerte. Although devotees engage in embellishing their Santa Muerte figures, there is never an intention to undo her fierce countenance and presence. In fact, in 2007 when the leader of one of the most influential Santa Muerte shrines in Mexico City transformed her into a dulcified, incarnated "Angel of Death" that, according to some, looked like his own wife, devotees widely disapproved (Roush, 2014, p. 137).[29]

But what specific values and character features does the female Santa Muerte represent? Although she operates alongside the powerful figure of the Virgin of Guadalupe, and her cult undisputedly feeds on other female Catholic saints, she in no way embodies the traditional values associated with the *marianismo* complex.[30] More than a caring and protective Mary figure, and more than just a pretty girl, the "Santa Muerte is most importantly the Powerful Lady (*la Dama Poderosa*)" with impressive miracle-working skills (Chesnut, 2012b, p. 8). This, however, does not fit easily with the theory that connects La Santa Muerte to the foundational myth about the waiting bride at the altar who shrivels up and dies. After all, that bride's subsequent sainthood is informed by her sacrifice as a neglected woman. This theory is implausible not only because of the widely accepted idea of La Santa Muerte's nonhuman origins but also because she hardly complies with the stereotypical features of the self-sacrificing woman (*mujer abnegada*). To both male and female dev-otees, she is powerful, purposeful, and, if necessary, a *cabrona* (battle-ax). A recent comparative study of "fierce feminine divinities," which includes La Santa Muerte, picks up on this feature and argues that, as embodiments of liminality and marginality, such divinities are perceived as dangerous and uncomfortable, and are often rejected, but they are also perceived as attractive because they are endowed with "wisdom, magical power and the truth about the human condition" (Oleszkiewicz-Peralba, 2015, p. 5).[31]

Organization and Politics

The growth of the Santa Muerte cult since 2000 has inevitably led to increas-ing organizational complexity, questions of leadership, and, hence, the crystal-lization of political and economic interests. Although Kristensen (this volume) argues that today the numbers have decreased from the peak years around 2006, rosaries continue to be impressive in size and organization. They require logistical planning that includes so-called *coordinadores* (coordinators) *de la Santa Muerte*, who see to it that all goes down in orderly fashion. The cult is a powerful example of a living popular religion, a key feature of which is that devotees are themselves constantly active in establishing the terms of devotion through syncretic practices and the popular appropriation of symbols, rituals, and iconographies (Rostas & Droogers, 1993). This also explains the diversity and fluidity of the cult across Mexico and beyond. However, such a reading fails to do justice to the consolidation of particular devotional formats and beliefs under the influence of different leaderships that emerged in the early twenty-first century in Mexico City and that have extended across other parts of the country.

There is agreement among scholars and commentators that, since around 2000, the Santa Muerte cult has been shaped largely by a limited number of leaders and their respective centers of devotion in Mexico City. In his chapter in this volume, Kristensen estimates that a select group of fifteen to twenty people has decisively molded devotion. Three figures and their families have been key. First, the public shrine established in 2001 by Enriqueta (Queta) Romero in Tepito launched her as perhaps the cult's most prominent and influential leader. Doña Queta enjoys enormous spiritual and social authority among the devotees who visit her altar, and over the years she has become a much sought-after spokesperson by the (inter)national media; in fact, Desirée Martín goes so far as to call her a "media star" (2014, p. 189). Helped by her congenial personality and nondogmatic theological views, Queta and her oft-changing collaborators have profoundly formed and influenced the stock of prayers, rituals, and symbolic practices of Santa Muerte devotion, perhaps mostly in an unplanned manner. Above all, she remains deeply committed to the family-run street altar. Considered the "godmother of the cult" and a "devotional pioneer" (Chesnut, 2012b, pp. 15, 8), doña Queta is probably best typified as the warden of the Tepito shrine who cares for "her" Santa Muerte, but she has never claimed any special power or sought to capitalize institutionally or politically on her widely recognized leadership and visibility (Bigliardi, 2016, p. 307; Quiroga, 2011).

This stands in stark contrast to the ambitious institution-building efforts by the controversial and vociferous self-appointed archbishop of the Santa Muerte church, David Romo, who in the 1990s founded the Iglesia Católica Apostólica Tradicional México–Estados Unidos, a traditionalist pre–Second Vatican Council Catholic church. After obtaining official state recognition in 2003 under the new rules governing state-church relations, Romo began to incorporate La Santa Muerte in his religious services in what proved to be an effective strategy, for his church began to grow. In the early 2000s, Romo established the National Sanctuary of La Santa Muerte, which he aspired to turn into the central shrine of the emerging cult in Mexico. In what has been called the most serious attempt to institutionalize the cult, Romo sought to expand it by erecting other shrines and altars and training a new generation of priests in Mexico City and elsewhere. He exerted a strong influence over local spiritual leaders, their shrines, and devotees in Veracruz and Puebla and, to a lesser degree, in Guadalajara (Argyriadis, 2014; Bravo Lara, 2013, pp. 17, 22). Also, the Parroquia del Señor de la Misericordia y la Santa Muerte in the southeastern city of Chetumal became associated with Romo's church. He led the first mass at the shrine and ordained deacons during subsequent visits (Higuera-Bonfil, 2015, p. 99). The media-savvy Romo appears to have been particularly active outside Mexico City after the Ministry of the Interior revoked the recognition of his church in April 2005. A US State Department report states that this decision came in the face of protests by the Catholic Church that led to a ministerial investigation, which concluded that including Santa Muerte devotion was inconsistent with the church's original statutes and objectives.[32] Relations between Romo and the Catholic hierarchy further deteriorated when he organized protest marches and vociferously attacked the church. In 2009, he even urged followers not to vote for the party in government (Chesnut, 2012b, p. 45).

But Romo had also made enemies inside the Santa Muerte devotional movement itself, where he was widely viewed as a "megalomaniac" (for his desire to build a Santa Muerte cathedral!) and, worse yet, as someone who wished to "centralize" and dominate Santa Muerte devotion not only spiritually but also organizationally and economically. He was accused of embezzlement, womanizing, and bad-mouthing leaders of rival shrines who refused to see him as the "true leader of the cult" and upheld the principle of unmediated exchanges between devotees and their preferred Santa Muerte (Martín, 2014, 206–7). That was also the moment when Romo introduced the "embellished" Angel of Death—pointedly described by Roush (2014, p. 137) as a "department store mannequin with a scythe"—a decision roundly rejected by devotees. By that time, his church had lost much of its former influence and credibility, and in 2011 he was arrested on charges of kidnapping and money laundering. He was convicted in 2012 and imprisoned (Vicenteño, 2012).

Some form of megalomania could probably be ascribed to Jonathan Legaria Vargas as well, the leader of a Santa Muerte church in Tultitán on the northern outskirts of Mexico City, where he had a twenty-two-meter-high statue of La Santa Muerte built. Shortly after its inauguration in 2008, Vargas was brutally assassinated.[33] Since then, his mother (curiously, also named Enriqueta) has assumed leadership of the International Santa Muerte Shrine and embarked on a mission to unite diverse shrines under her direction. Apart from a remarkable personality cult around her deceased son, she has introduced significant innovations in the cult in the form of weddings and baptisms performed in the name of La Santa Muerte. The Tultitlán shrine, which cultivates precolonial (Aztec) iconography, has grown considerably in recent years. After Romo's failed attempt to expand nationally and centralize control over the cult, it appears that Enriqueta Vargas has now launched a similar project (Chesnut, 2015). Given the background and history of the cult, it remains to be seen whether the attempt will ultimately prove successful, especially because there are counterforces. One study mentions a network of local shrines (*altares unidos*) in different parts of the country that opposes any form of institutional leadership, encourages devotees to come out into the open, and organizes yearly pilgrimages to the Tepatepec shrine in Hidalgo (De la Fuente, 2013).

The recent organizational history of the Santa Muerte cult clearly highlights the decisive role of personal leaderships.[34] For the political anthropologist, this comes as no surprise, because most forms of social and political organization in Latin America are characterized by the importance of personalistic loyalties attached to leaders and families, so there is no reason to think that religious movements or organizations would be exempt from this imperative. In the same vein, we can expect that the features of the social and political culture of personalism such as factionalism, the weight of personal (instead of ideological) rivalries, clientelist exchanges, and bossism will also manifest themselves in emerging popular religious organizations (Butler, 2005). In his important contribution to this volume, Kristensen argues that the incorporation of La Santa Muerte into the family brings with it contradictory consequences. Implicitly criticizing too strong a focus on external societal conditions, Kristensen draws our attention to the explanatory potential of the processes that take place in the intimacy of familial devotional units for understanding the dynamics of the Santa Muerte cult.

The familial form of the centers of worship has split and multiplied several times to thrive elsewhere. While this is responsible, in part, for the cult's vitality, it also engenders family conflicts and the spread of rivalries. In other words, it has consequences for the political organization of the cult. Kristensen's analysis focuses mainly on the history of a limited group of people who provided religious services at different street altars in Mexico City, and who influenced the formats and practices pertaining to home altars. An important aspect here is what Kristensen calls the consolidation of a virtuous and "Catholicized" sanctification of death. By 2005, the key features of the modus operandi of the Santa Muerte cult as we know it today had been established, and this goes a long way toward explaining the emergence of a shared sense of devotional practices and theological ideas, despite the absence of any organized congregation with central authority or an elaborate doctrine. Argyriadis (2014, p. 205) has observed how divisions based in Mexico City manifested themselves in severe rivalries in Veracruz, while I also encountered the logic of splitting in Ciudad Juárez. The Santísima Muerte "Martita" shrine, allegedly the first one in that city, was founded around 2006 by a female spiritual leader who had learned her skills in Mexico City. She trained others in Juárez, and when the number of devotees grew, another shrine was established, but clearly based on the knowledge and skills acquired in the first one.[35]

La Santa Muerte's Vitality through Multiple Transformations

The dialectic of doctrine and division, the dialogue between tradition and innovation, and the productive conversation between leadership projects and popular appropriation account for much of the cult's dynamics, vitality, and expansion. The notion of transformation perhaps best articulates what we have seen so far. Since the mid-1990s, La Santa Muerte has been transformed from an object of hidden and private worship to one of publicly lived and increasingly massive folk devotion. Numerical growth, spatial expansion, and migration are easily recognizable, but there has also been a diversification of purposes, in which La Santa Muerte has evolved from, above all, an expeditor of love magic to an all-purpose saint. Appeals for protection and support by La Santa Muerte in exchange for material and spiritual commitment by devotees have branched into many real-life domains (from sentimental to economic, legal, and existential insecurities), along with the diversification and differentiation of material forms and functions that, in part, made the former possible. Colors and specific iconic representations of La Santa Muerte are now associated with certain devotional purposes. Currently, symbolic and aesthetic mutations in the Santa Muerte cult are discernible in trends of re-Indianization, Marianization, and hybridization with Cuban Santería (Flores Martos, this volume).

The conversion of black-and-white prayer cards and other two-dimensional representations of La Santa Muerte, mentioned by anthropologists from the 1940s to the 1990s, into a proliferation of three-dimensional forms and designs has, in a way, reconstituted the cult, for it brought about deeply meaningful processes of humanization and personification, which endowed La Santa Muerte with effective agency and familial intimacy. Digital media have multiplied the cult's impact and distribution, such that increased variation, visibility, and visuality are now all key features (Huffschmid, this volume). The expansion of the cult has also translated into growing organizational and political complexities. Devotional and ritual practices have evolved and diversified. Some of these have been consolidated, but others have not. The persistence of multiple leaderships and the resistance to institutionalized centralization, so characteristic of other forms of popular religiosity as well, ensure the cult's vibrant present, despite the fact that some shared liturgical and ritualistic frameworks appear to have stabilized. The next section discusses how the cult's transformational dynamic has been conditioned by broader societal contexts.

3. LOOKING OUTWARD: POLITICAL ECONOMY, VIOLENCE, CATHOLICISM, AND BEYOND

Analyses of the historical background and the material, devotional, and political processes within the current Santa Muerte cult have hinted at the importance of its wider societal context. The debate surrounding amparo (protection), for example, signaled the societal forces behind the perceived lack of protection of citizenship rights and the dangers inherent in confronting other challenges in people's lives. Ben Smith's broad historical review of Mexico's idiosyncratic popular religious practices points to changing political economies, class and ethnic relations, political regimes, and cultural repertoires. The last part of this chapter turns attention to the social forces and actors that have lain behind the dynamics of the Santa Muerte cult since 2000.

My starting point is the dispute between the view that the growth of the cult must be ascribed, above all, to the saint's efficacious miracle work, and the position that narrows the causes to a religious expression of narco-related violence and insecurity that has pushed people to become "devoted to death." The former view takes a narrowly religious or even theological interpretation regarding the what, how, and why of La Santa Muerte. After all, ascertaining La Santa Muerte's reputation as an effective miracle worker "does not offer any explanation of either the cult's success or its structure."[36] Understanding the social origins of the demand for particular "miraculous services" leads us to engage broader societal processes and elaborate pertinent conceptual frameworks. The latter perspective—particularly influential in the media some years ago—sees Santa Muerte devotion as a direct outcome of a violent society, or even reduces it to links to the world of drug trafficking.[37] Both visions are equally reductionist and generate one-dimensional explanations. If we want to comprehend, as Flores Martos suggests in this volume, the reasons behind "the totality and complexity of practices and profiles of the people" involved in the Santa Muerte cult, we need to move continuously from the "inside" to the "outside" of the cult, and back again. This approach will take the analysis beyond an unmediated cause-and-effect mechanism of (criminal) violence and Santa Muerte devotion, and beyond an autonomous spiritual force.

Jeffrey Rubin, David Smilde, and Benjamin Junge (2014) put forward the notions of lived citizenship and lived religion to address the profound and multiple imbrications among religion, citizenship, politics, security, and economy. While "lived citizenship" requires the study of discourses of citizenship in their historical context and, above all, of "the practices and subjective meanings of citizenship for real people enmeshed in the experiences of daily life," "lived religion" similarly refers to daily life practices and meanings "predicated upon the existence of superhuman powers" in any area of social life. In this understanding, religion has no natural domain separate from practical and material concerns; or, as Paul Vanderwood would have it, "circumstances and belief . . . are always inextricably mixed in human experience: they are like scrambled eggs" (Rubin et al., 2014, pp. 11, 10; Vanderwood, 2004, p. 69). In daily life, reified distinctions do not matter. Seen in this perspective, expressions of popular religion like La Santa Muerte "can make situations meaningful and facilitate agency" particularly in "contexts where basic subsistence needs go unaddressed and survival is threatened" (Rubin et al., 2014, p. 16). One ethnographic study of a Mexico City prison found that Santa Muerte devotion served as a form and source of resistance against punitive power (Yllescas, 2016, p. 196). To understand such popular religious practices thus requires situating them, and the people involved, squarely amid the social forces that shape Latin America's zones of crisis. This is consistent with the approaches proposed by Smith, Flores Martos, and others in this volume, albeit with distinct conceptual vocabularies.

This approach also ties into concepts and ideas related to the rise of new forms of enchantment, religion, witchcraft, and "occult economies" under the conditions of millennial capitalism and violent democracies. While Nils Bubandt (2006) demonstrates the critical role of the occult politics of corruption and sorcery in Indonesia's postauthoritarian democracy, Peter Geschiere's (1997) pathbreaking study examines the enduring importance of witchcraft (*djambe*) in opposing inequalities and domination, as well as in the accumulation of wealth and power, in West Africa. What Jean Comaroff and John L. Comaroff (2001) call the global proliferation of occult-related activities refers, first, to their conspicuous irruption into the public sphere. Social groups experience their predicament as the outcome of arcane and uncontrollable forces that lie behind the creation of value and wealth together with loss of community and protection. This explains "why the ethical dimensions of occult economies . . . often express themselves in religious movements that pursue instant material returns and yet condemn those who enrich themselves in non-traditional ways." As if the parallels with La Santa Muerte's pragmatic problem-solving orientation in combination with her role as the "great equalizer" do not suffice, the Comaroffs continue: "To be sure, occult economies frequently have this bipolar character: At one level, they consist in the constant quest for new, magical means for otherwise unattainable ends; at another, they vocalize a desire to sanction . . . people held to have accumulated assets by those very means. The salvific and the satanic are conditions of each other's possibility" (2001, pp. 25–26). Is it implausible in this context to allude to the lure (and needed protections) of the magical riches that illegal businesses such as drug trafficking may generate?

What, then, are the social forces and processes that shape the daily lives of ordinary Mexicans, and of Santa Muerte devotees in particular? Which institutions and discourses affect and influence the cult's adherents and workings? Which ethnographic findings and concepts have been brought forward in the corpus of literature under review? I will now address the socioeconomic conditions of exclusion and vulnerability; the production of insecurity, violence, and impunity; and the main actors, institutions, and practices in the broader religious landscape.

Social Vulnerability, Violence, and the State

Fragoso's (2007b) early call for an approach to La Santa Muerte focusing on the social and cultural conditions of devotees themselves is still useful, since it looks at the relationships between "social vulnerability" and religiosity. The former does not necessarily coincide with poverty or even marginality, but stresses the risks and uncertainties that people encounter in their daily lives because they lack effective social protections in a wide range of domains (the labor market, health, education), characteristically identified as the result of the structural heterogeneity and fragmented modernity of contemporary neoliberal Latin America. The idea of ineffective social protections is easily linked to "disjunctive" citizenship, in which civil, political, and social rights purportedly guaranteed by the state are seriously compromised by the inequalities and mechanisms of exclusion. As a consequence, citizens confront situations alternately called vulnerable, precarious, unpredictable, or risky. Increasingly large numbers of people end up in the informal economy or in the lowest-paid layers of the formal service industry. This economic and legal precariousness extends toward informal housing, where it generates a condition of insecurity that Bolivians call "living *chuto*" (Goldstein, 2012, p. 98). As Huffschmid (this volume) explains, it is no coincidence that the historical center of Mexico City's informal economy is also the place where the cult of La Santa Muerte, as "a talisman against the risks of everyday life," began to flourish in the 1990s (Hernández, 2011, p. 39).[38]

Influenced by Peter Berger's sociology of religion, Fragoso proposed to investigate how Santa Muerte devotion is helpful in establishing an alternative order (nomos) (2007b, p. 32). Through its focus on paros/amparos, this line of research has demonstrated that asking La Santa Muerte for protection in a wide range of domains is a popular agentive response to failing state and market protection regimes. Małgorzata Oleszkiewicz-Peralba condenses this train of thought when she writes that the saint "is invoked for protection and strength, in the hope of transforming disorder into order in the private lives of often vulnerable individuals, their families, and their communities" (2015, p. 116).

In an especially suggestive analysis, the Spanish sociologist Pilar Castells Ballarín has delved into the meanings of the protective calls upon La Santa Muerte against the background of the discourse on human rights. Recognizing the transfer of petitioning from the state to La Santa Muerte, she critically points to the resulting order: "[T]he contribution of this Saint is to correct the uncertainty caused by the State's retreat from its role as bearer and guarantor of human rights. Somehow, while the State is rendering the social fabric in tatters . . . La Santa Muerte knits the broken threads into a new texture of an accumulation of individualities and a loss of citizenship" (2008, p. 20). Here, as the state delegitimizes itself and produces anomie, La Santa Muerte presents herself as an alternative actor who has the ability to reorganize that condition of anomie, though at a price: opting for La Santa Muerte as a justice-making entity not only signals the shortcomings of the state "but also means renouncing the exercise of rights and duties as citizens and, therefore, a separation from the imaginary of human rights" (Castells 2008, p. 21).

In recent years, scholarly attention has increasingly concentrated on the failure of the rule of law to ensure human rights and, hence, on the enduring need of people at the margins of the state to access protection in other ways. Several points need to be established here. First, vulnerability concerns not only bread-and-butter issues of the informal economies like erratic income and unregulated labor, but also legal insecurity and impunity. Street vendors and informal businesses, for example, are at risk of being submitted to rent-seeking extortion by administrative authorities or law enforcement, especially the police. Forced to negotiate through corrupt financial transactions, people are finding the law as a source of protection to be beyond their reach. Second, the degree of vulnerability or abandonment varies: people who make a living on the margins of society, such as sex workers and petty criminals, are usually worse off than taxi drivers who work at night in insecure neighborhoods. But people incarcerated in penal institutions probably find themselves in the most unprotected circumstances, as they face corrupt lawyers and prison guards, lack basic health facilities and decent food, and depend entirely on the protection and support of outsiders (Yllescas, 2016). Impelled by economic pressures and submitted to increasingly harsh securitization regimes, people who move along the migrant trails from southern and central Mexico to the north and beyond the US border are pushed into a zone of existential vulnerability by violent actors, state and nonstate alike (Martín, 2014; De León, 2015). Third, vulnerability as a consequence of the arbitrary application of the law is deeply rooted in the personalistic loyalties that govern what I have called the informal order (Pansters, 2009). Against the uniform application of the law, Roberto DaMatta once wrote, "I will defend myself . . . not by calling upon another universal law, but a personal relation . . . [that] enables me to bend or break the law" (DaMatta, 1987, pp. 319–20). In Latin America, the law is seen by many as an instrument of political and economic subordination that serves to maintain inequalities (DaMatta, 1991, pp. 187–88).[39] Personalistic mediation or negotiation of the law lie behind the region's insidious problems of impunity and the cynical flirtations of the powerful with invulnerability.[40] The vulnerability and lack of protection that so many Latin American citizens experience is mirrored by the protection and invulnerability of the powerful.

Atop this complex and varied landscape of socioeconomically, politically, and culturally created vulnerabilities, and this is my fourth point, has come the dramatic upsurge of violence and insecurity in Mexico, first in the wake of the economic and political crises of the mid-1990s, but above all with the escalation of criminal violence and large-scale militarization (see, e.g., Pansters, 2015; Pansters et al., 2018; Castillo and Pansters, 2007). Since 2006, the vicious dynamics of drug trafficking and other forms of territorially rooted organized crime, militarized state-securitization interventions, tens of thousands of fatal victims and disappearances, and impunity have encroached on the lives of millions of Mexicans, spreading down from northern cities (most infamously Ciudad Juárez, but also Nuevo Laredo, Tijuana, Monterrey, and others), to broad extensions of central Mexico (including Michoacán, Jalisco, and the Estado de México), and from there to the southern states of Veracruz and Guerrero.

In other words, the social origins of vulnerability and precariousness, the sense of being abandoned by the state and market institutions, and hence the development of alternative sources of authority and protection (religious or otherwise) by the people in Latin America's zones of crisis both precede and go beyond the escalation of violence and insecurity directly related to the ill-reputed global war on drugs. To see Santa Muerte devotion through the prism of drug-related violence and death alone—as a derivative, as it were—would be reductionist. However, this should not exclude recognizing, as Flores Martos (this volume) and others have done, the empirical correlation between the increase in violent deaths in Mexico and the growth of the Santa Muerte cult, both of which have, as Flores Martos found during his fieldwork in Veracruz, begun to affect the middle classes as well.

Keen on taking a broad comparative look at the cultural consequences of the ravages of neoliberalism and violence across Latin America, Flores Martos puts La Santa Muerte in the context of a growing range of popular cults to miraculous dead and saints that "condense and incarnate Death as an agent with the power to intervene in the daily reality" of many Latin Americans. His contribution to this volume analyzes the emerging iconographies of death, paying particular attention to the process of what he calls "popular patrimonialization." One particularly significant finding from his study of, among others, the Chilean popular saint Botitas Negras, is that the nature and content of the exchanges between devotees and popular saints replace the services of a distant or absent state. The chilling but fascinating case of the ritual adoption of unidentified dead in violence-ridden Colombia reveals remarkable parallels with the incorporation of La Santa Muerte into the intimate and moral order of the family (Kristensen, this volume). The ethnographically informed comparative examination of diverse cults of miraculous dead in Latin America adds valuable depth to the understanding of La Santa Muerte.

Popular Catholicism and Hierarchical Contestation

A further outward-looking and comparative perspective is Huffschmid's analysis of La Santa Muerte as an emerging urban religiosity, which focuses on the visual, performative, and spatial strategies devotees engage in to confront the existential fragility and vulnerability of their lives (this volume). This approach relates to the broader study of the postsecular world, in which religion is no longer considered a holdover from the past but, rather, is viewed in connection to the politics and social development of Latin America's multiple modernities (Rubin et al., 2014, p. 9). Studying the practices of Santa Muerte devotion provides opportunities to grasp a range of urban-religious configurations that involve the appropriations and sacralizations of secular spaces and the creation of new religious hot spots.[41]

In the case of La Santa Muerte, the role of different forms of visuality in public spaces provides the cult with a particularly interesting place-making quality. Huffschmid's analysis also enables us to position La Santa Muerte in the shifting religious landscapes of Mexico and Latin America. As a mediator between everyday life and religiosity, and as a problem-solving entity, the saint shares these features with booming Pentecostal and other Protestant churches, thereby revealing Catholicism's loss of hegemonic power and popularity. Interestingly, she takes the reader back to the early 1970s when adherents of liberation theology forged links between the Catholic Church and members of youth gangs and other marginal groups in Mexico City's poor neighborhoods, as they did throughout Latin America. But, Huffschmid argues, just as the state abandoned its aspirations to build and work with collective social actors, so too has the Catholic Church forsaken the "preferential option for the poor." In the current religious landscape, how must the relations between Santa Muerte devotion and devotees and the Catholic Church be understood?

We have seen that many devotees of La Santa Muerte continue to consider themselves Catholics. We have also observed that the devotional practices associated with La Santa Muerte—such as rosaries—are steeped in Catholic traditions. Finally, the figure of a saint who intercedes with God to help devotees is deeply rooted in Latin American folk Catholicism. However, we have also noted how at least one of the original leaders of the Santa Muerte cult fell out publicly with the Catholic Church. Over the years, several spokespersons of the Catholic hierarchy have voiced their concerns, criticism, and outright rejection of the cult. And they were taking it seriously.

In 2011, for example, a Mexican missionary movement called Apóstoles de la Palabra, which engages in Catholic pastoral work "to confront the problem of proselytizing groups and the new religiosity and promote Biblical Pastoralism," distributed fifty thousand copies of the third updated edition of a booklet on La Santa Muerte and other "superstitions" in an effort to instruct and provide guidance to pastoral workers.[42] That text clearly exemplifies the contours of official Catholic thinking about the cult. Written by Jorge Luis Zarazúa Campa (2011), it begins by arguing that the privileging of human and material development above the cultivation of strictly spiritual and religious values has left people in search of a meaningful life, thus providing a fertile environment for diverse forms of popular religiosity, such as La Santa Muerte and other noncanonical saints, but also for the use of amulets and consultations with psychics and fortune tellers. In this author's view, these superstitious beliefs and practices are, however, often perceived in a religious context and connected to popular Catholic devotions. Zarazúa Campa even states that because many ordinary Catholics have received scant education or proper grounding in Catholicism, they are easily misled by dishonest individuals. This legitimizes efforts to purify popular religiosity from such influences. The publication subsequently specifies several theological arguments to explain why La Santa Muerte is not recognized by the Catholic Church. The cult is said to represent a superstition, because devotees believe that images of La Santa Muerte have "a power" that supposedly derives from rituals of consecration; it also represents a form of idolatry, because devotees worship something that is not God. Moreover, since death simply means the cessation of life, "La Santa Muerte cannot help anybody, since 'she does not exist.'" She is not a personal being and does not have a physical or spiritual existence (Zarazúa Campa, 2011, p. 46; see also Fragoso, 2007b, p. 14). Finally, there is confusion between La Santa Muerte and the Catholic idea of a *muerte santa* (blessed death), which presupposes a life lived according to Christ's teachings. Once inside the cult, some devotees are believed to make the step toward Satanism, or at least to become associated with the terrestrial underworld of crime and drug trafficking.[43]

Theological objections aside, the booklet also mentions the social aspects of the cult. It recognizes the cult's lure, since "it responds to the most pressing needs of Mexicans, especially in the current socioeconomic context, characterized by insecurity, unemployment, loss of purchasing power, and multiple problems in interpersonal relations" (Zarazúa Campa, 2011, pp. 60–61). But it also blames the growth of Santa Muerte devotion on the initiatives of religious "entrepreneurs" and market vendors, who financially benefit from selling services and all kinds of material objects needed for devotional practices and rituals. In sum, according to Apósteles de la Palabra's publication, Santa Muerte devotion is an idolatrous superstition that shrewdly capitalizes on the needs of needy and uneducated people, who mistakenly associate it with folk Catholicism.

In the eyes of the church, such mistaken and false convictions need to be combated and corrected by earnest, faithful Catholic apostolic work. One priest in Veracruz wrote that overcoming the fear to leave the "essentially satanic" Santa Muerte cult requires renouncing it decidedly and destroying all related attributes and objects, while praying the rosary (Hernández R., 2014)! After qualifying the Santa Muerte cult as the result of "ignorance, confusion, and idolatry" grown out of the milieu of magic, witchcraft, and esotericism, another priest calls upon devotees to renounce Satan and return to Almighty God (Aguilar, 2007; see also Chesnut, 2012, pp. 53–54). A consistent argument in these and other church publications is that La Santa Muerte is intimately linked to the world of kidnapping, drug trafficking, and even human sacrifice.[44]

There is, without doubt, ample evidence of Santa Muerte devotion among members of Mexico's criminal organizations (Lomnitz, 2005a, p. 492). Home altars found by police officers or soldiers raiding the hideouts or safe houses of drug traffickers or gang members have made headlines in the mainstream media, in a framing that goes back to the 1990s (Roush, 2014).[45] The administrator of one Santa Muerte shrine in Ciudad Juárez told me unreservedly that people involved in criminal activities (from traffickers to hitmen and corrupt police officers) had frequented the shrine. It is, however, also true that most Santa Muerte devotees are not part of organized crime, just as it is likely that many of those who are involved piously worship the Virgen de Guadalupe. In the discursive framing of the Santa Muerte cult as "dangerous," the mainstream media played a key role.[46] In a thought-provoking analysis, Roush (2014) has examined key episodes in this process and suggested how adverse media framing became an incentive for the spectacular public outing of the cult and the subsequent characterization of certain spiritual leaders of Santa Muerte beliefs and devotional practices as tolerant, caring, and closely linked to Catholicism.

Even so, the links constructed between the perpetrators of gruesome acts of violence and crime and La Santa Muerte likely inspired the destruction of dozens of shrines by the Mexican military in 2009 in the northeastern border region around Nuevo Laredo and Reynoso, an area hotly disputed for years by rival criminal organizations (Loya, 2009). While some have suggested that the army was intentionally "doing the Catholic Church a favor," others have argued that the shrines were threatening "because of their association with marginalized and transgressive people in general, and especially in such close proximity to the United States" (Chesnut, 2012b, p. 114; Martín, 2014, p. 191).

Opposition to the cult by members of the Catholic clergy dates back to the very beginning of its public manifestations around the turn of the twenty-first century. After the first pilgrimage to a new Santa Muerte chapel in Santa Ana Chapitiro (Michoacán) in 1998, a conflict emerged between local devotees (and their leader from Mexico City) and the village priest, but soon the auxiliary bishop of the diocese of Morelia and the archbishop of Morelia himself came out against the cult, declaring it "a grave sin of superstition" (Vargas González, 2004, p. 108). Several priests interviewed by Perdigón expressed "inconformity, anger, and even some sarcasm in referring to her as a blasphemy" (2008a, p. 75). But as the cult gained traction and spread across the country and beyond its borders, and in reaction to David Romo's vociferous proselytizing and street protests, the upper echelons of the church became actively involved. A key moment was the public condemnation of the cult in May 2013 by the president of the Vatican's Pontifical Council for Culture, Cardinal Gianfranco Ravasi, during an official visit to Mexico: "Religion celebrates life, but here you have death. . . . It's not religion just because it's dressed up like religion; it's a blasphemy against religion." He did not forget to point to the alleged popularity of the cult among members of Mexico's drug cartels (Guillermoprieto, 2013; Vatican declares, 2013).

A few months later, the Conference of Mexican Bishops issued a declaration that debunked the supposed social roots of Santa Muerte devotion and instead disqualified the cult as dangerous: "Behind it is a kingdom of evil and people can become a victim of diabolic possession" (Conferencia del Episcopado Mexicano, 2013). Finally, during his visit to Mexico in February 2016, Pope Francis told the country's bishops that he was "concerned about those many persons who, seduced by the empty power of the world, praise illusions and embrace their macabre symbols to commercialize death in exchange for money. . . . I urge you not to underestimate the moral and antisocial challenge which the drug trade represents for Mexican society . . . as well as for the Church" (Pope Francis, 2016). Clearly, the theological and ritualistic closeness to (popular) Catholicism of Santa Muerte devotees contrasts sharply with the theological condemnation by the official Catholic hierarchy, which ranges from mild charges of ignorance, disinformation, and aberration to serious denunciations of danger, evil, and Satanism.[47]

Popular Religious Articulations

One particularly notable feature of popular religiosity is its pragmatism and malleability. Adherents to specific popular religious movements incorporate and mingle elements from adjacent religious complexes as they continuously redesign their beliefs so as to give meaning to their daily anxieties in ways that orthodox Catholicism cannot. Outside the domain established by the church, people exercise, as one scholar put it, their "religious rights" in their own ways (Bravo Lara, 2013, p. 20). As such, popular religious practices have an intrinsic political dimension: by creating new meanings, people use religion(s) to empower themselves. The popular use of religion "implies a side-stepping of the power hierarchy, in a quest for new sources of power, whether these be spiritual, the desire for self-realization or for a position that gives empowerment. . . . In the process of empowerment, popular syncretism occurs" (Rostas & Droogers, 1993, p. 10).

Over the years, anthropologists have encountered numerous examples of syncretic practices in Santa Muerte devotion that demonstrate, above all, a disposition to connect with other saints and religious traditions. Fragoso, for example, mentions an altar in Mexico City with three saints: in the middle sits Jesús Malverde, the former bandit turned into a narco-saint in Sinaloa, flanked by La Santa Muerte and Saint Jude Thaddeus (the only one recognized by the church). The skull in the iconography of the Niño de las Suertes (a baby Jesus sleeping on a skull cushion) has led Santa Muerte devotees to incorporate it into their belief system, thus transforming the original Catholic interpretation (Perdigón, 2008b). In Veracruz, Argyriadis (2014) and Flores Martos (2007) noted how Cuban Santería was digested through La Santa Muerte, and how this led to the idiosyncratic iconography of the Joven Muerte Encarnada as a beautiful, white-skinned young woman. One mother, anxious to see her daughter separated from a drug and alcohol addict, was instructed to pray to La Santa Muerte, stick pins in a piece of paper (voodoo), and prepare and bury a potion in a pot, a practice associated with Cuban Santería (Flores Martos, 2007). In Chiapas, as mentioned previously, La Santa Muerte backs up the spiritual work and indigenous healing rituals of curanderos (curers) (Michalik, 2011).[48]

La Santa Muerte's capacity for hybridization has even been called "cannibalistic" in the sense that it appropriates and devours other (folk) saints and mystical and spiritual figures (Flores Martos, this volume). In this vein, Michalik described the cult's astonishing ability to absorb other religious meanings and imageries in terms of "semiotic voracity" and "syncretic over-lap" (2011, p. 165; 2012, p. 608). The cult's internationalization through migration and the Internet, and the assimilation of global cultural products and icons (such as heavy-metal music) into Mexican popular culture, are adding additional practices and iconographies to the mix (cf. Perdigón & Robles, this volume). Interestingly, it also appears to work the other way around, as La Santa Muerte is also being incorporated into, and reworked within, Western esotericism and occultism (Hedenborg-White & Gregorius, 2017).[49]

The extraordinary syncretic practices and imagery associated with La Santa Muerte are not so much the outcome of the concordance of spiritual traditions, or of a purely mercantile logic that seeks to increase the number of devotees, but rather of their roots in Mexican folk Catholicism, which is historically made up of a particularly rich tapestry of Catholic, indigenous, African, and spiritualist belief systems. Even so, La Santa Muerte's eclectic potential stands out among that of other folk saints, an aspect that can be explained by two additional factors: first, the absence of any centralizing leadership with the ability to enforce a liturgical and theological canon (as described in the previous section) has led to particularly permeable semiotic boundaries; while, second, the universally recognizable though polysemic image of the human skeleton has created opportunities to connect with diverse systems of meaning (Michalik, 2011, pp. 176–77). Symbolic layering and richness allow myriad ways of reading La Santa Muerte's identity (Bastante & Dickieson, 2013).

Looking Inward, Outward, and Ahead

Understanding La Santa Muerte's devotional practices, their vitality and transformations, requires looking inward, outward, and backward. The notion of "lived (popular) religion" is useful, as it sets out from deep connections between different layers and domains of human existence but without falling into reductionist arguments. What we find "inside" the cult is conditioned by, and intervenes in, what happens on the "outside." A key objective of this volume is, precisely, to further enrich the conversation between these two spheres. For this reason, the preceding section looked at how distinctive features of violent neoliberal democracies have generated disordering forces and processes that constitute the "raw material" for popular religious practices in Mexico's zones of crisis. These include social vulnerability and precariousness, but also insecurity and violence, coupled with the deeply entrenched personalistic logic of "mediated" access to the law and citizenship rights, conditions that create a "demand"—so to speak—for protection and alternative ordering mechanisms and authorities, both in the sense of a "need" and a "claim."[50]

Different conceptual approaches speak of the connections between the cult's inside and outside in comparative anthropologies of the social and political bases of popular religious practices (including those in this volume). Conceptual frameworks of failing citizenship or human rights regimes, the political economy of occult economies, new urban religiosity, moral economy, and popular patrimonialization can all enhance our understanding of the phenomenon at hand. Conceptually informed "outside" interpretations of La Santa Muerte complement wider comparative (Flores Martos), historical (Smith), and sociological (Huffschmid) perspectives, adding depth to our understanding of the "inside," while Perdigón and Robles's account of the intimate form of devotion through tattoos takes into account shifting national and global iconographic markets, and Kristensen explicitly concentrates on the simultaneous movement of La Santa Muerte toward street and home.

Looking at the religious or spiritualist landscape properly speaking, I noted two interlaced but counteracting trends: articulation and pushback. La Santa Muerte devotion (partly) expands by flowing into adjoining popular religious practices, but it also encounters strategies of curtailment and opposition led, especially, by official Catholicism. This theologically and politically informed Catholic pushback has been supported by adverse framing in the mass media and (coercive) government policies. It remains to be seen how this dynamic will play out in the near future in terms of the features of this devotion.

What seems undisputed, however, is that the Santa Muerte cult's deep ambiguities are responsible for its expansion since the turn of the twenty-first century. A humanized skeleton, a sanctified death invoked to improve earthly existence, simultaneously caring and menacing, protective and harmful, at home in the liminal space between life and death, and entrenched in manifold symbolic, iconographic, and religious repertoires, La Santa Muerte is made up of multiple layers of meaning, speaks to different audiences, caters to the needs of the heart, family, economy, and security, and connects to a wide range of societal contradictions, offering alternative meanings of order, hope, protection, and justice.

NOTES

1. In general, I prefer the Spanish "La Santa Muerte," but occasionally will omit the Spanish article *La* when it benefits the phrasing, as in "the Santa Muerte cult." Now and then, some authors in this volume use the superlative degree of "La Santísima Muerte," as some devotees and documents also do.

2. In contrast to negative connotations (fanaticism, deviance) and following Frank Graziano (2007, p. ix), I use the term "cult" in a neutral sense to refer to "a community loosely cohered by belief in a particular folk saint."

3. In the same year, Perla Fragoso (2007b, p. 24) observed that until then journalistic (especially Sergio González Rodríguez's 2002 *Huesos en el desierto*) and literary accounts (especially Homero Aridjis) were largely responsible for the strong association of Santa Muerte devotion with illegal activities, and hence she argued for a more sociological approach.

4. A typical example would be an article posted by reporter Christopher Woody for the *Business Insider UK* website (March 2016). Alma Guillermoprieto (2010) is more nuanced but also frames the cult in relation to drug trafficking.

5. Often overlooked is Alfredo Vargas González (2004).

6. Two particularly sharp critical reviews are by David Lehmann (2013) and José Carlos Aguiar (2014). For a milder review, see Stanley Brandes (2014).

7. When organizing the international conference that formed the basis of this volume, I realized that researchers had, until then, cooperated very little and were occasionally unaware of each other's work. Gradually, I also learned about some (unpleasant and unprofessional) rivalries, so characteristic of current academic affairs.

8. Having said that, I do not subscribe to Michalik's argument that "virtually everything in regard to Santa Muerte remains a blank space" (2011), much less to Małgorzata Oleszkiewicz-Peralba's unwarranted statement that "there is almost no scholarly literature" on La Santa Muerte (2015, p. 104).

9. In an even earlier short article, Perdigón (2002) emphasized the need to engage in the study of the actual practices and meaning-making of La Santa Muerte.

10. For a brief social history and characterization of Tepito, see Huffschmid (this volume). A few years earlier, in 1997, small street altars were erected in the Buenos Aires neighborhood of Mexico City, but these did not become objects of public worship (Kristensen, 2016a).

11. For an excellent and wide-ranging analysis of the political, social, and security consequences of "punitive democratization" in Mexico City, see Markus-Michael Müller (2016).

12. During fieldwork in the mid-1970s in Jamiltepec in the Costa Chica region of Oaxaca, the French anthropologist Veronique Flanet encountered different devotional pictures with prayers to La Santa Muerte. Although conflict, violence,

and death constituted key themes in her work, she did not write about Santa Muerte devotional practices and only mentions that prayers were used as spells, although she does include pictures (1989, images on pp. 160–61).

13. Personal communication by Evi Kostner, who does ethnographic research among imprisoned gang members in Guatemala City, November 17, 2015.

14. Stanley Brandes (2006, pp. 58–60), for example, has pointed out that the danse macabre is a prominent antecedent of contemporary Mexican Day of the Dead art.

15. The Santa Muerte cult does not have anything similar to the ways in which Juan Javier Pescador (2009) has been able to brilliantly reconstruct the historical roots of the devotion of the Santo Niño de Atocha in medieval Spain and colonial and independent Mexico.

16. What follows is based on my observations of the rosary at the major Santa Muerte shrine on Alfarería Street in Tepito, Mexico City, on January 1, 2015.

17. See also the photographic impressions by Huffschmid (this volume), Reyez Ruiz (2010), Adeath & Kristensen (2007), Fraser (2015), and Salgado Ponce (2012).

18. La Santa Muerte is often depicted with other attributes as well, such as an owl, the night bird that effortlessly finds its way in the dark and that is a symbol of wisdom.

19. Juan Ambrosio (2003, p. 8) claims that devotion to La Santa Muerte in the mines of Zacatecas, Sombrerete more precisely, goes back to colonial times.

20. One can obtain these publications in popular markets and shrines. They invariably contain information about altars, prayers, and rituals, preceded by a brief synopsis of origins and history. Many are anonymously written. Despite certain differences, the content is often rather similar. See Del Bornio (2008); Goodman (2006); Velázquez (2013); *Altares, ofrendas, oraciones* (2007); *El libro de la Santa Muerte* (2007); Anónimo (2015); *Santa Muerte: Darse a la Muerte* (2016).

21. Fragment from "Prayer to help get rid of addictions," in a photocopied prayer guide used in the Tepito rosaries, obtained from Enriqueta Romero, January 1, 2015.

22. Perdigón also provides an interesting account of the rosary (2008a, pp. 103–8). See also Kristensen (2011, 136–38). When a tragedy hit Enriqueta Romero's family in the summer of 2016, she decided to suspend the monthly rosaries. At the time of writing (late 2017), she has not revoked this decision.

23. An exception would be Sergio de la Fuente Hernández (2013), who describes an indoor rosary in the Ajusco area in the southern part of Mexico City.

24. Localist mythology is not uncommon. In Michoacán, a prominent cult leader claims that La Santa Muerte is of Purépecha descent, the primary regional indigenous group, dating the foundational myth back to the sixteenth century (see Chesnut, 2012b, pp. 28–30).

25. San Ramón Nonato is also the patron saint of pregnant women.

26. Having said that, amparos are often used by powerful political and economic interests to postpone or entirely disrupt legal cases against them.

27. This episode is chronicled by Kristensen (2011, p. 15). It is noteworthy that Stefano Bigliardi's 2016 article does not consult Kristensen's work at all.

28. For San La Muerte, see Graziano (2007, pp. 77–111). With respect to similarities: San La Muerte is called upon as a protective agent, petitioned for miracles concerning health, work, and love, and is considered a "great equalizer."

29. Chesnut (2012b, pp. 18, 46) claims that spiritual leader David Romo's decision to drastically transform the image of La Santa Muerte from a robed skeleton to a brunette angel was a reaction to the horrific assassination of three men in front of a Santa Muerte shrine by members of the Gulf cartel in early 2007. Romo tried to dissociate his church from that highly mediated event.

30. For a critical and informative analysis of the notion of marianismo, see Marysa Navarro (2002).

31. The other deities are the Slavic Baba Yaga, the Indian Kālī, and the Brazilian Pombagira. Although I believe that Oleszkiewicz-Peralba's chapter on La Santa Muerte tends to stretch the argument about her liminal character and the transient condition of her devotees too far, interesting parallels exist. After all, and despite their differences, "these untamed divinities equipped with supernatural powers are able to transcend the accepted aspects of society and to confront a devotee with the ultimate reality—that of chaos, impermanence, and death" (Oleszkiewicz-Peralba, 2015, p. 141).

32. See US Department of State, *International Religious Freedom Report 2005: Mexico*. Retrieved from https://www.justice.gov/sites/default/files/eoir/legacy/2014/03/04/mexico.pdf

33. In a recent booklet, Heber Casal Sáenz (2016, pp. 91–96) refers to Humberto Padgett's journalistic account of kidnapping in Mexico City and the surrounding region, which mentions the connections between Vargas and criminal gangs.

34. See also the interesting analysis by De la Fuente (2013) of the leadership competition in the southern part of Mexico City.

35. Interview with David Ayala, Ciudad Juárez, July 30, 2016.

36. The quotation comes from David Lehmann's critical review (2013, p. 196) of Chesnut's *Devoted to Death*. Chesnut's book and his other publications, among them some rather sensationalist blogs and Internet postings, stress the saint's "awesome" power as the decisive explanation for the cult's growth. In fact, Chesnut even believes—admittedly being "semi-superstitious"—that La Santa Muerte "beckoned me to study her, helped me keep my eye on the larger picture, that of her cult of many colours" (2012b, p. 200).

37. References to Santa Muerte devotion in the form of altars or paraphernalia found at crime scenes or on the Internet were considered proof of this association.

38. David Bromley (2016, pp. 3–4) refers to notions of social and economic dislocations that make up an environment in which La Santa Muerte found a "folk saint veneration niche."

39. The relationships between law and social power are of course much more complex than suggested here. Social struggles for justice and equality are often inspired by legal frameworks. For the paradoxical role of law in postcolonial societies, see Jean Comaroff and John L. Comaroff (2006).

40. See, for example, Pieter de Vries (2005) and Kathy Powell (2012).

41. Raúl René Villamil Uriarte and José Luis Cisneros (2011) use the notion of the "inversion of the religious world" to speak of the ex- and reappropriation of dominant or traditional religious meanings. Because they demand recognition and social justice, these new popular cosmovisions require (public) visibility.

42. This objective can be found at the organization's website: http://www. apostolesdelapalabra.org/familia-misionera/fundador/.

43. In a remarkable passage, Zarazúa Campa states that since around 2005 Catholic priests well versed in the work of exorcism have dealt with cases involving Santa Muerte devotion. Kali Argyriadis (2014, p. 204) mentions a priest trained in the Charismatic Renovation movement who held weekly "exorcist" masses for years in Veracruz. See also Vladimir Hernandez (2013), who reported that "the rising demand for exorcism is partly explained by the large numbers of Mexicans joining the cult of Saint Death."

44. The website Church Forum: Una, Santa, Católica y Apostólica Iglesia, founded in 1993 in Mexico, contains several articles about La Santa Muerte that further develop these arguments. See http://www.churchforum.org/categoria-libre/santa-muerte.htm.

45. Kevin Freese (n.d.) includes several references to publicized raids involving Santa Muerte paraphernalia between 1998 and 2005. The author, who was working for the Foreign Military Studies Office at Fort Leavenworth, Kansas, concluded that "the Santa Muerte cult is anti-establishment and appears to glorify criminal behavior."

46. Beyond the mass media, there are films, documentaries, and fictional accounts that portray La Santa Muerte as part of the dark and violent world of drug trafficking. An example of the latter is Mexican author Homero Aridjis's novel *La Santa Muerte: Sextet del amor, las mujeres, los perros y la muerte* (2003), but undoubtedly much more influential has been the much-acclaimed novel *The Cartel*, by the North American author Don Winslow (2015), in which the vicious aberrations of a major drug trafficker are associated with his Santa Muerte devotion.

47. Bromley (2016) states that Santa Muerte veneration is on the verge of being designated a "dangerous religion." Although the church, of course, does not even consider the cult a "religion," other scholars would likely agree with the thrust of

the argument. The main problem with Bromley's contribution is methodological: it is based almost exclusively on secondhand, English-language Internet sources and ignores the empirically informed work examined in this chapter.

48. In cemeteries in Mexico City, Marcel Reyes-Cortez (2012) found Santa Muerte material objects in relation to magical practices related to interactions between the living and the dead.

49. This does not mean that occultism or occult symbols would not be present in the Mexican Santa Muerte community. For example, the black walls at the entrance to a Santa Muerte shrine in Ciudad Juárez exhibit a large tetragrammaton.

50. It is not difficult to argue that another way of "resolving" the need for alternative ordering and protective mechanisms is through the formation of self-defense forces (cf. Pansters, 2015).

2 | Saints and Demons
*Putting La Santa Muerte
in Historical Perspective*

The Santa Muerte cult forms part of a long line of Mexican religious revitalization movements going back hundreds of years. Sometimes, these movements centered on charismatic leaders, like the twentieth-century northern healer, Niño Fidencio, or the eighteenth-century peyote-taking Otomí mystic, Francisco Andrés. But often, they also focused on emblematic images or icons of folk saints. Some represented dead heroes, like the revolutionary Pancho Villa; others figure on the boundaries of history and myth, like the northern bandit Jesús Malverde or the executed soldier, Juan Soldado; others still portrayed traditional Catholic saints, like Tatu Chu, the indigenous image of Christ remade and reconfigured by Oaxaca's Triquis. The focuses of these movements differed, but all were "deliberate, organized, conscious efforts by members of a society to construct a more satisfying culture," to innovate what Anthony Wallace called "a new cultural system," which better described the immediate world of socioeconomic and political tensions (1956, pp. 264–81). This chapter offers an overview of these revitalization movements and suggests that such venerations have always carried distinct matrices of meanings. Although some aspects stayed broadly similar, others changed over time and from place to place. As we shall see, the Santa Muerte cult both harks back to this long history of revitalization movements and incorporates new meanings derived from the precarious situation of many of its followers.

Before reviewing Mexico's rich history of religious revivalism, it is worth making two broad theoretical points. First, it is necessary to examine these movements, including La Santa Muerte, in relation to the institutional Catholic Church. Most historians have approached Mexican revitalization cults as millenarian movements, designed to press for apocalyptic world transformation by the intervention of supernatural forces. For example, scholars like Paul Vanderwood, Eric van Young, Serge Gruzinski, and Jacques Lafaye have viewed the independence movement as an intrinsically millenarian rebellion, foreshadowed by a string of apocalyptic lay preachers like the Morelos cacique, Antonio Pérez, and Durango's mad messiah and underpinned by what Luis Villoro terms a "millenarian belief in the total change in the social order."[1] In focusing on these movements, historians have emphasized the distance between popular and elite religion. For Van Young, the violence of the independence movement emerged from the "yawning cultural chasms" between Spanish and indigenous "views of the human and supernatural worlds" and the "running incompatibility of popular and elite mentality and culture" (2003, pp. 41–43). For Vanderwood, priests and parishioners "lived different realities," and "popular spirituality" operated "in a spirit of defiance towards authority" (1998, pp. 175, 189).

Although such a Manichean view of Catholicism works at certain times in certain places, this chapter suggests that many of Mexico's revitalization movements were much broader, more common, and more orthodox than such an approach allows. Priests and parishioners were only rarely involved in some sort of apocalyptic struggle, their relationship on the point of anomie, rebellion, or collapse. Instead, most were engaged in constant, if occasionally fractious dialogue.[2] As Talal Asad argues, ecclesiastical authorities managed the "authorizing discourses," which "defin[ed] and control[led]" religion. The church, in an effort to "subject all practice to a unified authority," could reject some practices and accept others, authenticate certain images and dismiss the rest, "regularize popular social movements into rule-following orders, or denounce them for heresy" (1993, p. 35). In distant villages, with few if any formal links to the church, ecclesiastical authorities resisted dialogue, denounced perceived heresy, and delegitimized popular revitalization movements. In response, these movements became increasingly antihegemonic, often transforming into full-fledged rebellions.

But parishioners were not entirely powerless, and over the past five centuries priests have often been forced to "clericalize popular religiosity"—to authorize more popular devotions and images, to allow for increased lay autonomy, and to hope that they could channel these enthusiasms in suitable directions (Tackett, 1986, pp. 229–33; also Butler, 2006, p. 489). Ecclesiastical authorities with close on-the-ground relations with their parishioners have embraced certain popular revitalization movements, incorporating their beliefs (and perhaps more importantly their funds) within the formal rhythms of the church. Saints, who "trembled, grew heavy, became bigger, perspired, bruised, oozed or spurted blood," were stripped of their worldly, lay intermediaries, placed on the altar at the front of the parish church, and generated new church-approved devotions and sources of cash (Taylor, 2010, p. 29). The contemporary Catholic Church has never sanctioned the Santa Muerte cult; instead, ecclesiastical authorities have repeatedly denounced the movement as satanic. To follow La Santa Muerte is clearly a transgression. As Laura Roush argues, "You're giving a finger to the church" (2014, July 11). Yet, even the relationship between this outré cult and the church should be characterized as one of ambiguity rather than outright opposition. Most of the Santa Muerte rituals are derived from the Catholic Church. And most followers combine their devotion with visits to official churches and prayers to orthodox saints.

As a second broad theoretical point, it is necessary to study Mexico's religious revitalization movements, including La Santa Muerte, "in a creative encounter with other social activities" (N. Z. Davis, 1974, p. 314). Here, I suggest hijacking E. P. Thompson's (1971) and James Scott's (1976) ideas on the moral economy, that thick network of reciprocal arrangements underlying dominant social systems. Religious symbols, icons, and saints played a key role in both describing and stabilizing these arrangements. The moral economy may, in many ways, be better described as a spiritual economy (Gosner, 1992, p. 10). Threats to the stability of this spiritual economy, whether through large-scale socioeconomic change, state or church intervention, or violence, generated not only political movements but also new religious descriptions of community relations. Some, like the millenarian movements of the late Bourbon period, were temporary and fleeting, attached to short-lived personality cults and prophets. Other, more orthodox shifts that focused on church saints often provided a symbolic language sufficiently flexible to describe community relations for decades and even centuries.

By looking at these movements over the *median durée*, such a historical perspective can offer some insight into common processes that have generated these new cultural understandings of the world. A rough chronology of these revitalization movements emerges. Although threats to the spiritual economies of individual communities have been a common thread throughout Mexican history, large-scale national changes produced not only flurries of small-scale movements but also broader, intercommunity movements that could extend over large regions. What contemporary anthropologists of religion term "zones of crisis" periodically coalesced (Rubin et al., 2014, p. 10). As a result, revitalization movements peaked in eras of sustained socioeconomic and political change like the late Bourbon period, the 1840s, and the 1890s; and eras of violent threat like the independence and revolutionary eras. The Santa Muerte cult has emerged in another "zone of crisis"—the poor, urban barrios of neoliberal Mexico. Here, the moral economy, the traditional rules of politics, justice, and community relations have fallen apart. Although the Santa Muerte cult may face new problems, like its predecessors, it is an attempt to describe, shape, and to an extent legitimize a new social and political order.

SAINTS, IMAGES, AND THE COLONIAL MORAL ECONOMY

The links between Catholic saints and communities' moral economies go back to the colonial period. In the centuries after the conquest, they often focused on cults to the cross. New Spain's stability rested on an intricate skein of reciprocal relationships, which connected Spanish political authorities, the Catholic Church, and the sociopolitical hierarchies of individual communities. Some of these relationships worked externally. While the Spanish authorities offered security, a legal framework, and legitimacy to community leaders, the latter demonstrated obedience and collected tribute. At the same time, church authorities offered spiritual guidance, education, and legal representation in exchange for obedience, compliance, and pay. Other agreements operated internally within the communities. Individual priests put on Masses, baptized children, and established schools. In return, they expected money, accommodation, and, at the formal level at least, visible demonstrations of church orthodoxy. Indigenous caciques also played a key role. In much of central Mexico, aristocratic indigenous clans traded land use, security, and legal representation for labor, food, political control, and overt demonstrations of obedience.[3]

Religious rites and organizations imbricated this tight skein of relations. Religious rites in the form of Sunday Masses, baptisms, and individual fiestas provided spaces for overt displays of clerical control and communal orthodoxy. At the same time, they also provided villagers with assurance of spiritual contact, climactic temperance, and agricultural productivity as well as more tangible rewards like drink, meat, and links of compadrazgo. *Cofradías* often headed by indigenous caciques legitimized the village social hierarchy but also distributed food surpluses, land, and medical assistance (Dehouve, 2002, pp. 178–83). These links between the church, caciques, and village commoners were symbolized and strengthened by village saints. On the one hand, mythologies surrounding the saint often consciously drew on both ecclesiastical and indigenous traditions, offering a stable image of interethnic cooperation. On the other hand, the regular carrying of the saints around village barrios and surrounding ranches on saints' days and money-collecting pilgrimages served to impose the spatial boundaries of these accords.

For example, on May 3, 1655, Mixtecs from the *república* of Santa María Tindu in northern Oaxaca informed the resident Dominican friar that every year on the feast day of the Sacred Cross they heard music emanating from a cave on the rock face above the village. In response, the Dominicans, the Spanish alcalde, and the villagers of Santo Domingo Tonalá walked the six leagues to Santa María Tindu to investigate. When they arrived, they found that the cave could not be entered easily from the valley below. Consequently, they decided that the only way to reach the entrance was to lower somebody from the rocky hilltop above. They eventually chose a local man who had earlier been condemned to death. As villagers collected the necessary ropes, the prisoner took communion and confession with the Dominican friars. Then the assembled crowd secured him to the ropes and let him down "with much work and risk" toward the mouth of the cave. After struggling over a stone outcrop above the opening, the man "miraculously" reached the cave and clambered in. A few minutes later he returned holding a wooden cross and was hoisted up to the expectant throng. The Dominicans took the cross "with much reverence and veneration" and proceeded to parade it around the neighboring villages, where it was received "with happiness and joy." Finally, the group arrived in Tonalá and placed the cross beside the altar of the monastery church, where it would remain. The friars immediately wrote to the bishopric of Puebla and asked to establish a cofradía led by the region's indigenous caciques to celebrate the incredible find.[4]

Even the pared-down story of the Holy Cross of Tonalá is rich in symbolic significance, a tale that encapsulates the negotiations between elite and nonelite groups over the reestablishment of postconquest society. On the one hand, the tale clearly betrays the pre-Hispanic roots of Catholicism in the Mixteca Baja. The cross itself was an ambivalent symbol, used widely in pre-Hispanic ritual to represent the four winds. Caves, like that of Tindu, held multiple sacred meanings for indigenous groups as openings to the underworld, resting places of the royal dead, spaces of divinatory power, and locations for fertility rituals. In the Mixteca, caves were primarily associated with the Mixtec rain god, Dzahui, their damp, dripping interiors representative of pending precipitation. It seems no coincidence that the singing emanating from the cave of Tindu happened on May 3, not only the feast day of the Holy Cross but also the date by which rains should start in the Mixteca. Worship of the Holy Cross not only resonated with a pre-Hispanic Mixtec cosmology, which associated religious devotion with agrarian productivity, but also recemented the reciprocal bonds that linked the social hierarchy. During the pre-Hispanic period, caciques were not only the political but also the religious leaders of Mixtec communities. Through ritual fasting, blooding sacrifices, and drug taking, Mixtec caciques appeased the tutelary gods, ensured community well-being, and enhanced their own individual status and authority. In the postconquest age, they revitalized the moral economy, reprising their role as the financial backers and leaders of the cofradía. In return for obedience, deference, and labor, caciques organized annual fiestas to the Sacred Cross at the beginning of the rainy season on May 3 to plead for precipitation on their followers' behalf.

On the other hand, other elements of the story demonstrate the important role of the Dominican friars in creating the religious framework of the region. The Dominicans organized the prisoner's descent, authorized the cross as an authentic Christian symbol, managed its subsequent tour around the local villages, and established a cofradía with permission of the diocese. For the friars, the discovery of the cross reinforced their sense of divine mission. During the colonial period, numerous friars argued that the Americas had been Christianized long before the conquest. The carefully constructed fiction emerged from extrapolating upon the Acta Thomae, an apocryphal text, which claimed that Saint Thomas had preached "beyond the Ganges." During the sixteenth century, the myth of Saint Thomas wandering the world preaching Christianity started to take root in Latin America. During the 1670s, the Mexican scholar Carlos Sigüenza y Góngora compiled a synthesis of the evidence for Saint Thomas's arrival in the New World. He argued that the failure of the apostles to evangelize the Indies would have been incompatible with Jesus's commandment to his followers to "teach all people." The only apostle who was known to have traveled widely and consequently could have evangelized the region was Saint Thomas. Sigüenza y Góngora backed up his claim of Thomas's transatlantic missionary work with examples of indelible traces of feet, miraculous springs, and crosses discovered throughout Latin America, from Bahia in Brazil to Huatulco in southern Oaxaca. Thus, by discovering the cross in the Tindu cave, local Dominican friars not only accommodated Christianity within Mixtec cosmology but also tapped into a strong creole belief in the New World's pristine evangelization, which "redeemed their American patria from the stigma of having lain in darkness for sixteen centuries, isolated from revelation" (Lafaye, 1984, p. 182).

By 1700, the Holy Cross had become the centerpiece of Tonalá's spiritual calendar. The cacique leaders of the cofradía would parade the cross throughout the streets on the first Friday of Lent, on May 3, and on Corpus Christi. At the same time, numerous Mixtec locals adopted the surname "de la Cruz." Over the next century, the myth of the Sacred Cross spread throughout the Mixteca Baja, coming to symbolize the moral and spiritual economy that linked the region's colonizers and colonized. During the 1740s, the Holy Cross's mayordomos, surrounded by musicians and singers, started to wander the region carrying the icon and demanding money from dispersed devotees throughout the Mixteca. By the 1780s, nearly every village in the region contained a small *hermandad* or brotherhood to the cult. At the same time, the Holy Cross formed the root of multiple similar cults, like nearby Ihualtepec's statue of Our Crucified Lord. Tonalá thus became an exemplary center of the pact among Dominicans, indigenous caciques, and Mixtec commoners (Smith, 2012, pp. 39–43).

William Taylor (2010) has discovered more than three hundred miraculous shrines and images that were constructed during the colonial period. Most, like the cross of Tonalá, originated in the seventeenth century. Agustín de Vetancourt's 1697 *Teatro Mexicano* describes New Spain as a "network of shrines housing images that worked miracles and showed life" (taken from Taylor, 2010, p. 29). They were key to the colonial pact. By establishing a syncretic narrative of both Spanish and indigenous provenance, and forming the basis of a series of religious celebrations and organizations, local saints and perhaps more importantly cults to the cross both symbolized and legitimized local colonial moral economies. They were, in effect, spiritual economies. At the same time, in regions where similar social hierarchies had generated similar agreements, key icons developed extracommunal influence, signifying pacts in multiple villages or providing the basis for multiple similar shrines.

SOCIAL AND RELIGIOUS CHANGE
IN THE BOURBON ERA

During the eighteenth century, multiple socioeconomic, political, and cultural shifts threatened these local spiritual economies. Demographic growth generated increased demand for agricultural land and growing markets for commercial products. Powerful groups, including local Spanish administrators, priests, and indigenous caciques, usurped communal lands and squeezed community resources and labor. At the same time, Bourbon monarchs imposed a series of administrative changes designed to monopolize revenues and undercut the political and cultural autonomy of all levels of colonial society. Spanish administrators and mestizo interlopers increasingly interfered in village life. Finally, church authorities, who had regularly provided a symbolic language that smoothed out class and racial tensions, sought to reform popular religion. By persecuting drinking, dancing, cofradía landholding, and even indigenous language teaching, they reduced the benefits to the rural poor and also undercut the legitimacy of the colonial regime.[5] As contemporary anthropologists might put it, rapid social and political changes generated distinct "zones of crisis."

In these zones of crisis, communities sought to maintain social stability and rewrite the old colonial moral economies by generating a series of revitalization movements. In a handful of cases, church suppression led to insurrection. For example, during the early eighteenth century, the bishop of Chiapas, Juan Bautista Álvarez de Toledo, started to charge exorbitant sums from highland Mayan cofradías. Nonpayment was punished with imprisonment. The policy was ruinous. The capital of the cofradías declined by half, creating periodic shortfalls in essential foods and "eroding the security of subsistence." At the same time, the village elites or *principales*, who ran the cofradías and had presided over the distribution of village surpluses, saw their local authority undercut (Gosner, 1992, pp. 93–97). In response, Mayan villages started to reformulate the traditional reciprocal framework by supporting a series of new cults. In 1708 in Zinacantán, villagers built a church to an image of Saint Joseph placed in an alcove in a tree. In 1711 in Santa Marta, they followed the visions of a young woman, discovered a statue of the Virgin Mary, and constructed a new chapel for the image. And the following year, in Cancuc, they again followed the Marian visions of a young woman, placed a cross where the apparition demanded, and built another church.

As Victoria Reifler Bricker argues, these were not intrinsically radical movements. Rather, they were "creative attempt[s] to establish . . . locally inspired religious cult[s] which would be acceptable to Spanish ecclesiastical authorities" (1981, p. 59). But the ecclesiastical authorities were inflexible. On all three occasions, the church suppressed the new devotions, refusing to say Mass, burning the churches, and arresting the village elites. Only at this point did the villages rebel. They did so not by dismissing the old moral economy but rather by re-creating it on their own terms. Sebastian Gómez, an Indian visionary from Chenalhó, rallied more than twenty Mayan villages by claiming that he could appoint Indians as priests and celebrating Cancuc's Virgin of the Cross. Over the next year, Spanish forces brutally put down the rebellion (Bricker, 1981, pp. 55–69). But the pattern of revitalization movements, church suppression, and rebellion extended to other areas of the republic.

During the 1730s, Spanish forces allied with Otomí nobles to expand colonial power in the Sierra Gorda. Troops and frontier militia invaded and took the lands of poor Otomís, Pames, and Jonaces. Some priests joined in the assault, arguing that the villagers never attended Mass, never baptized their children, and were "devoted to all sorts of pagan evil." In response, poor indigenous villagers, including many women, started to congregate around an Otomí mystic, Francisco Andrés, to establish alternative community authorities and invade stolen lands. According to scattered Inquisition reports, which span over thirty years, Andrés mixed these political acts with his version of religious ritual. At these celebrations, he would celebrate Mass in his indigenous language and distribute tortillas and his own bathwater instead of the Eucharist. Finally, by the late 1760s, his followers were so incensed by official demands to close down his backland church that they beat up the local priest (Tutino, 2012, pp. 412–13; Lara Cisneros, 2007). Similarly, in Morelos, villagers combated the expansion of Spanish landholdings and debt labor by following another indigenous leader, the former shepherd Antonio Pérez, who also set up his own church in 1767. Again, he held Mass in his own house and asked devotees to pray to his hand-carved statue of Christ on the cross (Gruzinski, 1989, p. 105–72).

In both these examples, indigenous groups sought new ways of explaining the world through religious ritual. Although they criticized the church hierarchy, they were not anti-Christian or even anti-Catholic. As Gruzinski argues, by the eighteenth century, "it was no longer possible to contrast the Mesoamerican legacy with Western Christianity, between Indian subcultures and

Catholicism" (1989, p. 119). As in the case of La Santa Muerte, radical revitalization movements drew on the language of the church, even if they radically reinterpreted the lexicon in order to differentiate their programs from those of the institutional church and create a more amenable spiritual economy.

Furthermore, in general, these radical ventures were the exceptions. Outside relatively underchurched frontier regions and areas of radical socioeconomic change, most revitalizations stayed firmly within the institutional church. As economic and political pressures increased, New Spain's political administration fragmented. In central Mexico, most poor villagers sought respite not through armed revolt or heterodox religious ritual but rather through establishing new pueblos and replicating a traditional if decentralized version of the colonial moral economy. Between 1750 and 1800, hundreds of small or subject pueblos petitioned for and received status as self-governing villages or cabeceras. Yet, contrary to Eric Wolf's supposition, these were not socially flat, closed corporate communities (1956; 1957; 1959, pp. 202–32). Rather, they replicated the social hierarchies of the old moral economies, inviting or even inventing indigenous caciques to take over the running of the new pueblos and legitimizing their rule through the religious rituals and symbols (Ouweneel, 1995). As a result, myths of discovering, hijacking, or even stealing new saints abounded. New villages necessitated revitalization movements in order to describe the new status quo.[6]

NINETEENTH-CENTURY REVITALIZATION MOVEMENTS

During the nineteenth century, threats to communities' moral economies developed in two distinct waves. During the 1830s and 1840s, increasingly centralist governments started to threaten both village autonomy and communal lands. And again, during the 1880s and 1890s, Porfirian entrepreneurs took advantage of liberal land laws to privatize village properties. On both occasions, many communities attempted to reestablish a stable set of agreements among the state, the church, and rural villagers through innovative devotions. Often, the church met these revitalization movements with outright repression, forcing communities to revolt. But other times, local priests were more sympathetic, incorporating relatively heterodox devotions into the local canon of saints. Most of these movements still concerned small-scale, intra-village relations and agricultural subsistence. But some—including the cult to

El Niño de Atocha—had a broader, regional influence and focused on other forms of insecurity and injustice. As such, they foreshadowed the emergence of more urban, twentieth-century cults like La Santa Muerte.

In areas of limited clerical influence, peasants turned toward heterodox interpretations of Catholic doctrine. Perhaps the most prominent revitalization movement occurred in the Yucatán Peninsula during the late 1840s. During the preceding decades, the expansion of sugar and henequen haciendas had challenged both subsistence and the authority of indigenous caciques. And by the 1830s, radical federalist discourses, which lauded village autonomy and local democracy, had penetrated Yucatán's Mayan communities. During the centralist-federalist clashes of 1835–1847, many peasants joined the federalist militia (Rugeley, 1996, 2009). Finally, in 1847, a group of former federalist soldiers, led by both mestizos and Mayan caciques, rebelled. After a series of victories, they were pushed back toward the Caribbean coast. Here, they developed a distinct devotion to the cross. In 1849, the rebels established their headquarters in a cenote (a natural pit) just south of Tulum. They worshipped a cross carved into the side of a mahogany tree. A cult leader, Juan de la Cruz, acted as ventriloquist for the cross, voicing religious, military, and political demands. Although government forces destroyed the shrine and killed De la Cruz two years later, the cult continued. By the 1860s, rebels worshipped a series of crosses dressed in indigenous huipiles and petticoats. Three leaders now pronounced on behalf of the cult.

Just as local saints undergirded village society, the devotion to the talking cross described, explained, and legitimized the rebels' new military organization. During the insurrection, military loyalties replaced old village ties. The Yucatán militia, in which many Mayans had served, provided the model for this new form of social organization. Companies were integrated into existing kinship systems. The military company became what Bricker terms a "corporate descent group"; rituals and celebrations surrounding the cross cult were now organized along these company lines (1981, pp. 103–14).

The cult of the talking cross provides the most celebrated example of how religious devotions supported radical federalist insurrections. But outside Yucatán, other groups in underchurched areas utilized similar revitalization movements to support new social structures and relations generated by rebellion. Priests rarely visited the small Triqui village of Copala, and less than 10 percent of the children were baptized. During the 1830s, neighboring creole and mestizo landlords imposed non-Triqui authorities on the village, who started to rent out the communal lands to sugar and livestock farmers. The Triquis reacted through armed revolt, murdering the imposed authorities and hacienda mayordomos and taking to the hills to join radical federalist rebellions from 1838 to 1848. During this period, they engaged centralist troops and pillaged itinerant merchants and surrounding villages for supplies. At the same time, they imbued their movement with religious significance (Smith, 2012, pp. 108–10). In their 1845 manifesto, they charged that "rapacious priests, who charge fines for nothing and exorbitant fees for baptizing our children," had provoked their revolt.[7] Yet, they refused to renounce Catholicism entirely. In the same manifesto, they claimed they were good Catholics. And, during the decade-long rebellion, they carried with them the village image of Christ on the cross, dressed in full indigenous clothing and redubbed Tatu Chu. According to soldiers sent to track down the rebels, they believed that their "uprising and crimes" were just "as they were prescribed by the divine image" of Christ.[8] Removed from the local church, stripped of its orthodox trappings, and given a voice independent of priestly intervention, the saint represented and legitimized the Triquis' struggles against the institutional church, the centralizing state, and rapacious non-Triqui landowners.

If some movements explained and supported revolt, others formed last, desperate attempts to reestablish a rapidly disintegrating moral economy. During the first half of the nineteenth century, ecclesiastical authorities in the parishes around Tepic repeatedly sought to take control of cofradía funds, threatening village surpluses and villages hierarchies. By the 1840s, they had started the wholesale plunder of the cofradía treasuries, halting religious festivities. Like the indigenous Mayans of Chiapas more than a hundred years earlier, the Cora Indians of Santa María del Oro responded, at first, with a revitalization movement. In early 1853, local authorities reported that a thirteen-year-old boy had seen a vision of Our Lady of Atocha on the "old walls" around the Acuña ranch. According to the authorities, the devotion was already established. Pilgrims arrived from the villages around, and tales of miracles abounded. The boy spoke on behalf of the apparition, chose "11 or 12" young men to pray with him in the hills, and received pilgrims with blessings and gifts of cloth from his ragged garments.

Unlike the Chiapas ecclesiastics who had condemned the Mayan cults, the local priest was soon convinced of the boy's vision. In fact, he claimed to have seen the apparition on at least six occasions. With small-scale legitimacy ensured, pilgrims now offered money to the shrine. But the higher church authorities were less enthusiastic. Bishop Pedro Espinosa y Dávalos feared the expansion of the devotion beyond Santa María del Oro, ordering the priest to dampen popular fervor and collect the donated money. Reluctantly, the priest fenced off the miraculous walls, placed the boy in custody, and declared the cult finished. As Aaron van Oosterhout argues, with the suppression of the movement, "the already tense relationship between priests and parishioners rapidly deteriorated, and sporadic violence peppered the region." Gangs, often led by former cofradía heads, began to rob and pillage local haciendas. Within a few years, these local bands would coalesce into Manuel Lozada's pro-conservative insurrection (Van Oosterhout, 2014, pp. 167–71).

Similarly, during the 1860s, church authorities in Chiapas started to make increasing demands on the local Mayan populations. These included money for baptisms, marriages, and burials, daily domestic service, animal fodder, and firewood. In late 1867, a girl from San Juan Chamula called Agustina Gómes Checheb claimed to have seen three stones drop from the sky while she was tending sheep. The local fiscal, Pedro Díaz Cuscat, went to investigate the story, placed the stones in a box, and claimed that they were sacred. Soon, a few small figurines, to which the fiscal claimed Agustina had given birth, formed part of the "paraphernalia of the cult." Villagers built a chapel and worshipped the clay statues. But after they invited priests to say Mass at the church, soldiers arrived to suppress the movement, destroying the chapel and arresting the young girl. At this point, the cult shifted focus. Díaz Cuscat declared that the worshippers should destroy all images made by ladinos and instead crucify an Indian. On Good Friday, 1868, they refused to go to the Easter celebration in the ladino community of San Cristóbal de las Casas and nailed a young Chamula boy to a cross. Later that year, they linked the movement to the traditional village fiesta of Santa Rosa, organizing "elaborate celebrations" in order to "incorporate the new cult into the traditional festival cycle and cofradía system." Agustina was now reported to have been redubbed Santa Rosa. Suppression came swiftly, and by the end of the year, soldiers had destroyed the embryonic cult (Bricker, 1981, pp. 119–25). Like the 1712 revolt and the Acuña apparition, the movement was connected to shifting relations between villagers and the institutional church. And, as with the earlier devotions, initial attempts were made to seek church legitimation, to get official approval for this rewritten spiritual economy. Only when this failed did the movement generate revolt.

If the 1830s and 1840s witnessed an increasing rhythm of religious movements, so did last the two decades of the nineteenth century. Porfirian land reforms generated another wave of radical revitalization movements. Most famously, mestizo peasants in the drought-ridden, land-starved Chihuahua village of Tomóchic rose up in the name of the folk saint and healer Teresa Urrea in late 1891. But other, small-scale movements also abounded (Vanderwood, 1998). In 1885, Antonio Díaz Manfort, an indigenous healer from Papantla, Veracruz, combined armed insurrection against church fees, land privatization, and the influx of foreigners with complaints about civil matrimony, the regulation of religious processions, and the erosion of Catholic beliefs (Kouri, 2004, pp. 175–77). And in 1882, indigenous tobacco workers raided the Tuxtepec church, stole the altar image of Our Lady of Sorrows, placed it on a boat, and sailed it down the Papaloapan River in order, according to the local cleric, "to set up their own church."[9] All three movements emerged in regions of rapid agrarian transformation, decaying village autonomy, and, crucially, a weak institutional church. All three consciously hijacked the practices, rituals, and symbols of orthodox Catholicism to redescribe internal village relations and to challenge the local religious establishment.

Yet beyond these overt displays of heterodox religiosity, many communities responded to threats to village security, agrarian self-sufficiency, or political authority by reformulating the existing lexicon of Catholic symbols in conjunction with ecclesiastical authorities. Research on such movements is limited; they are often difficult to spot. But these cooperative movements probably far outnumbered those connected to insurrection. During the 1820s, the extension of sugar haciendas around the southern Puebla town of Acatlán had started to disrupt indigenous communities of Mixtecs, Popolucas, Nahuas, and Zapotecs. Land conflicts and intervillage violence were commonplace. In response, the local priest introduced an image of Christ, dubbed Our Lord of Peace or the Black Christ of San Pablo Anciano, in order to reestablish both intra- and intercommunity relations. Although the image was introduced from the top down by a member of the church establishment, surrounding indigenous groups soon subsumed the black Christ into their own mythology. Mixtecs, for example, held that the black Christ acted as peacemaker and intermediary between the warring spirit lords of the mountains, caves, and rivers (Taylor, 2010, pp. 177–78).

Other more cooperative revitalization movements described internal shifts in village subsistence patterns. For example, in 1873, an image of Christ of Mercy appeared miraculously outside the church of Nuyoo in the Mixteca

Alta. Within a few years, mayordomos of the village started to celebrate a fiesta in the image's honor, transporting the statue to a succession of households. At the first two houses, the owners rudely dismissed the image, but in the third house the farmer answered it cordially. According to the story, the third farmer's corn immediately started to ripen. Despite the icon's miraculous appearance, it was soon moved to the church where the local priest regularly gave Mass. The icon and the associated ritual described the tensions inherent in the village's new stress on individual household economies, but also legitimized the solution—individual mayordomos. As John Monaghan argues, "it was through [the Christ of Mercy] that Nuyootecos innovated. Its ritual and associated mythology allowed Nuyootecos to create new mechanisms for financing collective activities, to develop a moral context for new kinds of relationships between households, and to redefine households as property units" (Monaghan, 1995, p. 311).

Finally, during the nineteenth century, certain cooperative revitalization movements emerged that foreshadowed the more urban, more individualist, and more geographically diffuse devotions of the twentieth century. The shrine to the statue of Our Lady of Atocha and child in Plateros, Zacatecas, dates from the seventeenth century. By the 1810s, the image of the child Jesus, dubbed El Niño de Atocha, had started to gain an independent following. Twenty years later, the image of the child was moved to a place on the main altar. By the 1850s, the image had a substantial following among both northern settlers and miners in nearby Fresnillo. The city had witnessed a temporary mining boom during the 1830s, attracting workers from throughout western Mexico. According to believers, the Niño de Atocha provided miraculous aid to this new transient population as they suffered mining disasters, violent assaults, and everyday health problems (Pescador, 2009). Like his successors Jesús Malverde, Juan Soldado, and La Santa Muerte, the image became a "new kind of protector of ordinary people in danger or in trouble with the law on Mexico's restless northern frontier" (Taylor, 2010, p. 178). Furthermore, unlike traditional village saints, his influence spread far and wide. New print media, in the form of *novenarios* and pamphlets, spread news of his miracles throughout the trade fairs and fiestas of the Bajío and beyond.

During the Revolution, political change, social reforms, and, perhaps most importantly, roaming armed groups challenged communities' security and created "zones of crisis." As Luis González y González argues, many Mexicans were less *revolucionarios* and more *revolucionados*. They experienced the decade as one of "savage crimes, robbery, kidnappings, hanging corpses, ravished women, and religious images stripped of their Milagros" (1985, p. 5). Many responded to these upheavals by turning to religion. As Matthew Butler argues, the Revolution was a period of "genuine religious ferment as well as social upheaval." Radicalization and violence "were accompanied by innovative, often improvised response in the religious sphere" (2007, p. 2; also Bantjes, 2007, p. 224). Some kept to the language of the church. But others were founded in areas of waning ecclesiastical influence, and, like La Santa Muerte, they were deliberately provocative.

Many attempted to adapt existing symbols and rituals to this new socially fluid reality. From the underchurched north to the indigenous south, these responses were often radically anti-authoritarian, conscious rebuttals of clerical control. In April 1911, a Nahua woman, Bartola Bolaños, from San Mateo Tlacoxcalco claimed that an apparition of the nearby saint, Our Lord of Wounds, had appeared to her, complaining that the villagers of Miltepec were not treating him well. According to the woman, he spoke Nahuatl, gave out the sacraments, delivered a sermon, and directed his devotees to build a chapel and organize religious celebrations in his honor. In the absence of a local priest, Bartola and the village's mayordomos took up running the new shrine. For Edward Wright-Rios, the cult to the Nahua Lord of Wounds represents the legitimization of a new social order. On the one hand, church reforms and the military recruitment of men had shifted local power toward religious women. On the other hand, the mayordomos' control of local water resources, which happened to be located on church land, also offered these lay leaders greater control (Wright-Rios, 2009).

Beyond these apparition movements, Mexicans adopted other even more heterodox solutions. In Easter Week 1919, Chontals from southern Mexico crucified an Italian dentist who claimed to be a new incarnation of Christ. In the Chontals' witness statements, they claimed that they hoped the sacrifice would bring "security and wellbeing" to their village (Smith, 2010). In regions of Mexico with limited histories of lay-clerical interaction, similar outré devotions emerged, exposing the tensions between priests and parishioners. Devils, Moseses, Marias, and mad messiahs stalked the land. In 1912 outside Guadalajara, a "mysterious celestial figure" appeared, claimed to be the Messiah, and announced that the end of the world was nigh (Butler, 2007, pp. 11–12; J. Meyer, 1973–1974, vol. 1, pp. 287–88; Rodríguez, 2003).

The plethora of religious solutions, some deliberately extreme, revealed the breakdown of traditional interclass relations and the regionally specific decline of the Catholic Church. These idiosyncratic cults and popular apparitions gained substantial publicity. But most devotional innovations were much more orthodox. In regions with long traditions of lay-clerical negotiation and successful church education programs, priests and parishioners provided security and designed divine solutions together, producing a series of agreed-upon icons and practices with limited or no disagreement. In fact, in some regions, ecclesiastical authorities were keen to legitimize these movements in order to reintegrate the faithful into the church.

In 1911 in Tzocuilac, a small barrio of the Puebla town of Cholula, ecclesiastic authorities started to investigate a painting of the Virgin of Tzocuilac, a seventeenth-century miraculous image that had allegedly appeared one day on the wall of a cacique's house. Over the centuries, the image had fallen into disuse. The cacique's house collapsed, and the picture was exposed to the elements. But around 1910, new miracles had started to occur. After praying to the image, the sick claimed to be cured, and the crippled got up and walked. At first, the church took little notice. But in 1911, Zapatistas cut off Puebla from the traditional pilgrimage route to the Basilica of Our Lady of Guadalupe. Ecclesiastical authorities turned to the painting in Tzocuilac as a possible replacement. After a two-year investigation, which involved scientists from the Catholic University of Puebla and interviews with those cured by the image, the authorities gave their blessing. Such legitimization generated considerable support for the image throughout the revolutionary period.[10]

A similar process of conscious church-led revitalization movements occurred to the south in the Mixteca Baja. Here, revolutionary offers of land distribution were ineffective. Instead, Zapatistas and other revolutionary groups robbed, plundered, and even burned villages. Clerics and lay leaders turned to the manipulation of orthodox religious icons. In Tequixtepec, cofradía members bought new images of Our Lady of Perpetual Succor, Our Lord of the Sepulcher, Saint Joseph, Saint Peter, and Our Lady of the Rosary during the first five years of the Revolution alone. When funds were short, the clergy and the villagers also experimented with changing the names of ineffective icons. In 1914, the priest of Tequixtepec changed the name of one of the pueblo's images of the crucified Christ from Our Lord of the Sanctuary to Our Lord of Clemency, hoping that apposite nomenclature would glean better results. Hard-pressed communities also sought to change their devotional practices toward these divine intermediaries, believing that by asking for succor in a different manner, they might better harness an image's power. In 1915 Juxtlahuaca, the priest and members of the predominantly indigenous barrio of Santo Domingo took an old image of Saint James from the town's main church and placed it in their own chapel. They then formed a cofradía, purchased several cattle, and pastured them on the village's lands. That year the priest reported that "they held a much bigger festival than that of the center" and, as a result, managed to avert Zapatista invasion.

Finally, communities also attempted to change the physical form of their existing images. In 1919, Virginia Perpetua, the head of Tequixtepec's Daughters of Mary association and a famed local beata, had a vision. She claimed that if the villagers lifted the reclining Lord of the Sepulcher to his feet, placed him on a cross in the central altar of the local church, and implored him forgiveness for their sins, God would end the village's suffering. The vision, similar in many ways to the Tlacoxcalco apparition described by Wright-Rios, was radical. By voicing the vision, doña Virginia threatened both clerical and gender hierarchies. Yet Tequixtepec's visionary, unlike her Tlacoxcalco peer, understood the rules of the game, pushing the limits of orthodox behavior sufficiently to ensure divine appeasement but not too much to offend diocesan norms. As a result, the local priest quickly accepted the innovation, nailing the Christ to a hastily constructed cross and institutionalizing a celebration of the new saint on the second Friday of Lent. Ecclesiastical authorization soon followed. In 1921, the bishop agreed to bless the image, organized a Mass of three priests, and named godparents for the ceremony. Devotees arrived from villages along the Huajuapan-Tehuacán Valley, and the local priest claimed that he witnessed "much piety." Summing up the local belief in the efficacy of the providential economy, the villages called the icon Our Lord of Forgiveness (Smith, 2012, pp. 217–19).

POSTREVOLUTIONARY
REVITALIZATION MOVEMENTS

During the postrevolutionary period, revitalization movements seem to have diminished. Broader processes of secularization had some effect. Demographic shifts, migration, urbanization, and the growth in infrastructure and communications served to challenge the predominance of the village saint.[11] From the late 1920s onward, politics also played a role. Church and state became increasingly "jealous institutions" demanding both political loyalty and symbolic standardization.[12] As popular anticlericalism met official anticlericalism, heterodox movements were often subsumed into general state anticlerical campaigns. Here, transfers of sacrality took place from orthodox Catholic saints onto secular revolutionary heroes (Bantjes, 1998, pp. 15–18). Emiliano Zapata and Pancho Villa both gained substantial quasi-religious followings (Behar, 2003, pp. 203–24; Brunk, 2008, p. 99). In a similar way, orthodox clerical movements were regimented and subsumed into church resistance to this anticlerical movement during the 1920s–1930s and again from the mid-1950s to mid-1960s.[13] Official, nationalist church icons like the Virgin of Guadalupe or Cristo Rey often became centers of village worship (Torres-Septién & Solís, 2004). These new symbols not only stabilized intracommunity relations but also linked villages to Catholic nationalism and political Catholicism.

Yet even during the mid-twentieth century, some revitalization movements still slipped between the institutions of the church and the state. They peaked in periods of reduced church-state tension and occurred in regions of low institutional influence. At first, they tended to emerge in remote indigenous regions, far from the diocesan headquarters. But by midcentury they had also started to develop in the fast-expanding barrios of Mexico's major cities. These new cults, like those to Juan Soldado or Jesús Malverde, answered more immediate, urban concerns often linked to the distribution of political power or the provision of justice. As such, they formed the immediate predecessors to La Santa Muerte.

One of the most widespread agrarian revitalization movements occurred in the predominantly Nahua region of La Huasteca during the 1940s. During the postrevolutionary period, nonindigenous caciques like Juvencio Nochebuena had carved out an extensive area of dominance in the region. Here, they took over communal lands, creating huge fictitious ejidos where wealthy mestizos ruled. At the same time, they also usurped Nahua identity, co-opting upwardly mobile Nahuas to defend the arrangement and to speak on behalf of their "race" (Schryer, 1990, pp. 140–41). Robbed of traditional farmlands and deprived of space within the *indigenista* framework of the state, excluded Nahuas turned to a consciously heterodox religious movement, which played with both the state's and the church's estimations of acceptable indigenous behavior.

In 1944, Nahuatl-speaking devotees started to worship the Aztec corn goddess Seven Flowers (Chicomexochitl). The movement started away from La Huasteca's agricultural heartland in a dried-up lake in the northern tip of Puebla. It then spread throughout the isolated forests of northern Veracruz and into La Huasteca. According to Frans Schryer, the followers witnessed the miraculous appearance of maize kernels and other agricultural produce on the forest floor. After being picked up by young children, the maize kernels were carried in procession to local temples (usually private homes), where locals engaged in a night of dancing and singing. These revelries involved girls dressing as the corn goddess. Such rituals were designed to revive agricultural production for the devotees (Schryer, 1990, pp. 182–83).

If some movements confronted agrarian capitalism and sought a spiritually buttressed alternative, other indigenous movements sought to provide a buffer against the material attractions of modernization. During the 1940s and 1950s, logging companies started to prey on the lands of the Tepehuán of southern Durango. As the companies brought cash incentives, alcohol, and modern consumer products, agrarian grievances fused with cultural divisions. Links between village elites and nonelites started to disintegrate as some embraced the companies' offers while others resolutely rejected them. Finally, in September 1956, a young Tepehuán woman saw an apparition of the Virgin of Guadalupe. About half a meter high and dressed in fine silk, the virgin spoke to the woman, ordering her to obey her mother and father, embrace the *mitotes* (traditional dances), and refrain from "using" or "wearing" Mexican things, especially *huaraches de hule* (sandals made from tire rubber). The apparition gained a considerable following. Tepehuán villagers built a chapel, slaughtered goats, and burned their "foreign goods." At the suggestion of the Virgin, they even halved the price of commercial goods sold among themselves. The movement, however briefly, reestablished the old status quo, the old ways of organizing the community and dealing with the outside world (Riley & Hobgood, 1959).

Until the early twentieth century, most Mexican revitalization movements were predominantly rural. Although they often bled into broader political programs, they centered on the provision of physical security, agricultural production, and community coherence. There is limited research on urban revitalization movements for a variety of reasons. On the one hand, modernization theory, with its stark dichotomies between rural and urban, the religious and the secular, stamped the works of the social scientists that scoured Mexico's cities from the 1960s onward. Many were either uninterested in religion or dismissed religious practices as the dying vestiges of rural living. On the other hand, even in the poorest, *paracaídista* barrios, the state, the Catholic Church, and Protestant and Pentecostal establishments had greater influence than they did in far-flung indigenous regions. These channeled attempts at community building through relatively acceptable official rituals, practices, and symbols. Mexico City's squatter settlements adopted the names of revolutionary heroes and situated their struggles within broader historical struggles for land, access to modern infrastructure, and education (Cornelius, 1975; Vélez-Ibañez, 1983; Ugalde, 1970). Provincial cities' poorer barrios ran local branches of Acción Católica Mexicana (Estrada M., 1963, pp. 45–47), and Guadalajara's poor sought protection, social services, and jobs through the Church of La Luz del Mundo (Dormady, 2007; De la Peña & De la Torre, 1990). However imperfect, demands for subsistence and citizenship were organized and transmitted through large institutions, not small-scale, organic religious movements. These institutions, in turn, shaped internal and external community relations.

But there were exceptions. Spiritualist churches grew enormously. By 1963, there were 175 Spiritualist temples in Mexico City alone. The religion, which blended the beliefs of nineteenth-century preacher Roque Rojas with female empowerment and the offer of spiritual solutions to health problems, was particularly popular in the poorer barrios of the country's growing conurbations (Poniatowska, 2002; Lagarriga Attias, 1975; Kearney, 2004, pp. 156–59).[14] But other cults concentrated on individual saints. In Tijuana in 1938, soldiers killed the convicted child rapist and murderer Juan Castillo Morales. To deter an angry mob that threatened to burn down the police station, they staged a public incident of *ley fuga*, shooting Castillo Morales in the back as he allegedly attempted to flee. After his death, rumors started to circulate that Juan was innocent and that he had been set up by his superiors. Blood was said to seep from his shallow grave; locals heard his ghost demanding vengeance. And over the decades, followers established a cult around the dead soldier, redubbed Juan Soldado. They set up a shrine by his grave and prayed to Juan for justice, for forgiveness, and for aid in diverse semilegal activities. One of the early press articles on the shrine clearly displays a photograph of a plaque in which a worshipper thanks the new saint for getting him out of prison.

Unlike other Mexican cities, Tijuana was disposed to the emergence of this type of alternative Catholic cult. The institutional church was weak. Throughout the 1920s and 1930s, there was only one priest who occasionally provided for more than ten thousand inhabitants. Immigration to border towns like Tijuana was rapid, often temporary, and lacked the extended village networks that characterized movement to Mexico City. The informal sector predominated; working life, which relied first on prohibition-era bars, then the vice industry, was precarious (Vanderwood, 2004, pp. 75–103). Health was poor, and most adults died in their thirties or forties. Only 2 percent lived long enough to die of a heart attack (Vanderwood, 2004, p. 110). And corruption, in both the political and the judicial system, was embedded to an extent that outstripped other major cities. Governors like Alberto Vega Aldrete (1946–1947) and Braulio Maldonado Sández (1953–1959) were repeatedly accused of links to the vice and drugs industries.[15] For the rich and well-connected, judicial impunity was common.[16] Meanwhile, hastily enacted prostitution and vagrancy laws were increasingly used to persecute and extract money from the poor (R. Flores, 1970). The moral economy, that skein of reciprocal expectation between elites and nonelites, which in many cities the Partido Revolucionario Institucional (PRI) had managed to co-opt and reestablish, often ceased to function. Socioeconomic, political, and cultural forces all conspired to generate a powerful popular religious subculture and an alternative intermediary between Tijuana's citizens and the state.

If the emergence of the Juan Soldado cult was a rare occurrence, it was not exceptional. In Culiacán during the 1970s, a similar subculture emerged. According to the myth, Jesús Malverde was a turn-of-the-century bandit—probably originally called Jesús Juárez Mazo—a northern Robin Hood, killed by Porfirio Díaz's rural police in 1909. His body was left hanging from a tree. As it slowly disintegrated and dropped to the ground, locals piled stones on top, forming a small, impromptu grave (Vanderwood, 2004, pp. 211–16). According to local believers, during the 1950s local prostitutes started to worship the dead hero, but in 1970s the cult expanded to include a broader section of society. During that period, the Sinaloa government designed a new statehouse to be built on the site occupied by Malverde's grave. As the bulldozers went to work, thousands protested. Eventually they persuaded the governor to donate a new site near the state building to the grave. And in 1979, they laid the first stones of what would become the official chapel to Jesús Malverde (Flores & González, 2006; Sánchez Godoy, 2009).

For good reason, drug traffickers were some of the first supporters of this cult of "the generous bandit"; it was good propaganda. But it also flourished because it represented the rewriting of the pact between elite and nonelite groups. During the 1970s, the old status quo—the easy, relatively pacific arrangement among political leaders, drug traffickers, drug growers, and Sinaloa's citizens—had broken down. US-backed antidrug campaigns put pressure on the old system, local PRI factions divided, and drug gangs split. By 1977, Culiacán was the most dangerous city in Mexico. Murders allegedly ran at over 1,500 per year. The older generation of drug traffickers, who had established agreements with the state government, like Pedro Avilés Pérez, Eduardo "Lalo" Fernández, Lamberto Quintero, and Jorge Favela, were dead, in hiding, or in prison.[17] In the countryside, the violence was probably worse. Military squads raided marijuana- and poppy-growing regions, burning houses, raping women, and torturing and murdering peasants (Ortiz Pinchetti, 1981). As the narcocorrido singers mourned, "la mafia muere"; the old arrangements were gone. The establishment of the Jesús Malverde shrine represented an attempt to negotiate this new reality, to ensure protection for both licit and illicit activities under the precarious emerging system.

CONCLUSIONS

Over the past two centuries, Mexico's revitalization movements have adapted to deal with multiple elements of the moral economy of individual communities including land, water resources, politics, and ethnic relations. Over the past century, they have left the village church, moved into the cities, and morphed to deal with relations not only between elites and nonelites but also between politicians and citizens. In Tijuana and Culiacán they explained, legitimized, and offered a means of intercession in spaces where both structural and contingent factors had shifted the old rules of the game. The emergence of the Santa Muerte cult around the prisons and poor barrios of Mexico City during the early 2000s contains distinct parallels. Although the cult answers a wide range of pleas, most center on the provision of justice. The central concepts of the liturgy, *amparo* and *desamparo*, protection and loss of protection, have their roots in the judicial world (Roush, 2014; Kristensen, 2015). The popularity of

the cult reveals a perception of decreasing individual security and an ineffective, and perhaps more importantly unreadable, justice system. (Here, there
are clear relations to the cult to Juan Soldado.) In rural areas, the Santa Muerte
cult has stronger parallels with the village-based revitalization movements of
the past two hundred years. Worshippers have erected icons and shrines in
order to bring security to regions afflicted by drug-war violence. Like the hastily erected Christs of the Revolution, they are designed to ensure community
coherence and security in the face of outside threats.[18]

Historical understanding can also inform our reading of institutional relations to the cult. Like the radical heterodox movements of the nineteenth and
twentieth centuries, the Santa Muerte cult has emerged in distinctly underchurched spaces, places where Catholic priests have rarely gone. Here, the
Mexican church hierarchy's opposition to the pastoral and social work of liberation theologians, who worked in deprived urban and rural zones, has played
an important role. By discouraging, removing, or dismissing these priests, the
church has effectively renounced its ability to channel dissatisfaction through
more orthodox symbolic channels (Huffschmid, this volume). At the same time,
institutional and popular reactions to the Santa Muerte cult also have historical
parallels. Church leaders and pious believers have attempted to combat the
cult's influence through the conscious adoption of orthodox church rituals and
symbols. The church has declared the movement a satanic cult and introduced
exorcisms to extirpate "devils" from believers. On the front line on the drug
war in Michoacán, self-defense units self-consciously sport icons of the Virgin
of Guadalupe, bulldoze Santa Muerte shrines, and replace them with shrines
to more acceptable local or national saints. Here, the drug war has morphed
into a religious conflict.

Finally, by comparing La Santa Muerte to other, historical revitalization
movements, we can also start to understand the cult's reach. Most revitalization cults have concerned relations within small communities or between
these communities and the outside world. They represent what Eric van
Young terms the "localo-centric" vision of Mexican believers, who during the
eighteenth, nineteenth, and to a certain extent twentieth centuries viewed the
world in relation to their specific villages (Van Young, 2001, p. 62). La Santa
Muerte is different. Like the Pentecostal movements of South America, the
cult is more individualistic. La Santa Muerte is an intermediary between the
individual believer, or at most the believer's family, and the world. As such,
the cult can travel beyond its home in the barrio of Tepito and to individuals

throughout Mexico, Central America, and the United States (Chesnut, 2012b). Furthermore, unlike previous cults, La Santa Muerte benefits from social media. Blogs and Facebook pages that testify to her miraculous powers have aided her ascent.

NOTES

1. Much of this work explicitly or implicitly follows the assertions of James Scott (1977), Paul Vanderwood (2003, p. 181), Serge Gruzinski (1989), Eric van Young (1986, 1989, 2001), and Jacques Lafaye (1984). See also Villoro (taken from Vanderwood, 2003, p. 167).

2. See works such as William Taylor (1996, pp. 5, 67), Matthew Butler (2002, p. 12), and Edward Wright-Rios (2009, p. 7). Also see works on European Catholicism like Peter Brown (1981), Natalie Zemon Davis (1974, 1982), Thomas A. Kselman (1986, pp. 27–28), and William A. Christian Jr. (1981, p. 8).

3. For discussions of these reciprocal relations or "reciprocal dominance," see Arij Ouweneel (1990, p. 34). See also Arij Ouweneel (1995, p. 756), John Chance (1996a, 1996b, 2000), Stephen Perkins (2005), Nancy Farriss (1984), and Benjamin T. Smith (2012, pp. 26–39).

4. Archivo Parroquial de Santo Domingo Tonalá (APSDT), box 51, vol. 1, Cofradía de la Santa Cruz, 1752–1958.

5. See the works of Eric van Young (1981, pp. 271–342), Antonio Escobar Ohmstede (1998), Michael T. Ducey (2004, pp. 23–59), Rodolfo Pastor (1987, pp. 163–358), William Taylor (1979, pp. 113–52; 1996), and Peter Guardino (2006, pp. 91–122).

6. Archivo del Municipio de Chazumba (AMC), Documentos inéditos, Fundación del pueblo de Chazumba; Archivo Parroquial de Miltepec (APM), Libro de Gobierno, vol. 1, Relación de la parroquia. See also Leonor Rodríguez García, Josué Mario Villavicencio Rojas, and Rogerio Montesinos Maldonado (2004, pp. 61–67), and Benjamin T. Smith (2012, pp. 67–69).

7. Archivo Histórico de la Defensa Nacional (AHSDN), XI, 481.3/2124, Plan of Feliciano Martín, August 2, 1845.

8. AHSDN, XI, 481.3/1964, Informe of José de Jesus Maldonaldo, October 18, 1843.

9. Biblioteca de Oaxaca, Colección Manuel Martínez Gracida, box 58, 1837–1842, "A los feligreses" by a priest of Otatitlán.

10. Archivo de la Catedral de Puebla, Datos historicos referents a la milagrosa aparición de Nuestra Señora de Tzocuilac, 1911–1913.

11. This was obviously not entirely the case. Transnational indigenous communities have maintained a concern for village saints (Stephen, 2007, p. 43).

12. The concept is borrowed from Peter M. Beattie's work on nineteenth-century Brazilian prisons (2015).

13. For histories of the clashes, see Jean Meyer (1973–1974, 3 vols.), Enrique Guerra Manzo (2005), Ben Fallaw (2013), and Soledad Loaeza (1985).

14. Since around 2005, the official Spiritualist Church has been on the decline. It is possible that the Santa Muerte cult has replaced both the spaces and the roles previously filled by this church.

15. Maldonado not only established a vast prostitution racket but also had his wife sell prostitutes' children to adopting parents in the United States through a state-funded orphanage; see Carlos Ortega G. (1961).

16. On the impunity of Maldonado's hitmen, Los Chemistas, who were let off numerous crimes including the killing of investigative journalists, see "Two Men Sought in Mexicali Slaying," *San Diego Union*, September 4, 1956. See also Carlos Moncada (1991).

17. See newspaper articles in the *New York Times*, August 9, 1976; *El Informador*, August 9, 1976; and *El Informador*, August 10, 1976.

18. In Michoacán, there seems to be a separate tradition of La Santa Muerte in Santa Ana Chapitiro; see Alfredo Vargas González (2004).

3 | Dances of Death in Latin America
Holy, Adopted, and Patrimonialized Dead

A colleague witnessed the following scene in the city of Tuxtla Gutiérrez (Chiapas): during a family get-together, an architect friend of his was reluctant to swim in the pool, or even take off his T-shirt, despite the heat of the day.[1] His excuses seemed strange, but after a few beers, and as night fell, others saw him finally get ready to take a swim after someone offered him a full-body swimsuit. When he finally took off his T-shirt, they saw a tattoo on his back with an image of La Santa Muerte. The architect was clearly embarrassed to reveal to his friends and professional companions that he was a follower of the cult of La Santa Muerte and averse to answering questions or justifying his belief, as he would surely be obliged to do when others saw his tattoo. Apart from the others at the pool, he showed it to my colleague, who described it to me as follows:

> It covered his whole back, a tattoo of La Santa Muerte with the legend: "Thank you for what you did for me." A more ornate tattoo adorned his calf: a Zapotec demon. The size was scary, giving the impression that his body was a walking altar. He told me he'd had them done to thank La Santa Muerte for extricating him from a critical situation, but that he didn't profess that faith, or perform rituals or anything like that. But later his wife told me that he was, indeed, a worshipper. (K. Chacón, personal communication, September 30, 2014)

This small but telling account provides material for an analysis of the ritual and devotional practices associated with the figure of La Santa Muerte that goes beyond conventional discourses, which relegate this saint and her worshippers to exclusively marginal areas, rough neighborhoods (*barrios bravos*), jails, or spaces controlled by drug traffickers or others generically called "popular." Analyses from positions colored by the ideological and moral lenses of the market of religious competition in Catholic Mexico do not help much, either, because any attempt to understand the meanings of this devotion must consider the totality and complexity of the practices and profiles of the people who dialogue with it, and pray to it, for miracles, be they large or small.

ALLEMANDE

The following pages present an ethnographic exploration of some imaginaries in Latin American societies in which death is a protagonist, a meaningful agency who appears in relation to emerging figures and cults that strive to incarnate her as their property and patrimony. Based on La Santa Muerte in Mexico, I discuss, compare, and contrast similarities and differences with the cultural patrimonialization of death in other American societies, including the construction of "miraculous dead"—or popular saints—in cemeteries, and the selection and adoption of "anonymous dead," victims of violence in Colombia. In areas of Latin America affected by the irradiations of neo-liberalism and violence, these emerging cults connect with the experiences of followers who are desperate to retake control of their lives in precarious conditions of social vulnerability, abandoned by state institutions and other official structures.

Analogous to the omnipresence of Dances of Death in the artistic and iconographic representations of the early Middle Ages—which announced the proximity and inevitability of death so convincingly spread by the plagues, and the looming end of worldly pleasures, at a time when outbreaks of the Black Death and other epidemics jeopardized the continuity of human and social life, with traumatic impacts on demography and modes of sociopolitical organization and relations—today in Latin America death is once again a protagonist. Here I refer to both condensations of "death" itself and other figures related to death—more idiosyncratic or anonymous—that are highly visible and interact in people's lives; for instance, some "living dead" who enjoy good health and dance in choreographed rituals staged by popular demand in contexts of crisis and situations of permanent emergency.

Instead of an exhaustive and intensive analysis and ethnography of the cult of La Santa Muerte, I have chosen an extensive strategy that involves comparing and contrasting it with other popular cults to miraculous dead or popular saints. My aim is to broaden the focus of study, for I have found meanings that ethnographies centered on the cult exclusively do not reach, or identify, due to their modest aim of profiling and understanding the cult's internal social logic. But I privilege La Santa Muerte, for it is a good example of a multiform, complex emerging but unstable cult in full effervescence and transformation.

Since roughly the turn of the twenty-first century, we have observed the growing prominence and visibility of diverse figures who in different ways condense and incarnate death as an agent with the power to intervene in the daily reality of the living in cities, rural areas, and cemeteries in Latin America. While unofficial and unrecognized by the Vatican, these emerging figures seem to expand the pantheon of popular Latin American Catholicism, while the people who turn to them to solicit favors explore new dealings, agreements, and exchanges. The aim of this text is to analyze these emerging iconographies of death, paying special attention to the processes of popular patrimonialization entailed in the development of such cults.

First, I must clarify what I mean by patrimonialization, since this is a key concept in my argument and analysis. To avoid the risks of essentializing a term so characteristic of nationalist ideologies and of institutional or official attempts to explain cultural heritage, a complex definition like that employed by Gil-Manuel Hernández i Martí (2008, p. 7) is useful. Hernández emphasizes patrimonialization as social construction involving the selection of cultural elements from the past with the participation of diverse social agents in contested symbolic and historical fields. Understood in this way, cultural heritage expresses a historical-cultural identity of the community in question, legitimizes power structures, and allows the reproduction of market mechanisms.

Conventionally speaking, patrimonialization—the action of transforming a cultural element or good into patrimony—is understood as a conscious (voluntary) process oriented toward a future in which a society participates by legitimizing the proposal of an agent, institution, or concrete social group to convert something into an item of a patrimonial nature.[2]

Clearly, cultural patrimonialization functions as a powerful current of cultural differentiation, and of the affirmation of local cultures and identities, but it also serves to revitalize traditions adapted to the demands of contemporary societies in late modernity (Hernández i Martí, 2008, p. 31). Although these processes and actions imagine a "popular" character, format, or essence in these new patrimonial objects, many reveal an intense, evident component of direction by hegemonic groups, institutional interests, and incipient or structured cultural politics; that is, "top-down" initiatives, planning, or direction.

Clear examples of this patrimonialization are UNESCO's declarations of Intangible Cultural Heritage (ICP). The criteria applied to determine what constitutes ICP tend to convert the cultural good or product into a thing, high-lighting its visible, formal, and material aspects while ignoring the processes and strategic relations that led to its production, or the social logic that generated it (Villaseñor & Zolla, 2012, pp. 83–84).

Anthropology and related disciplines provide few studies or critical analyses of the processes of interested invention and legitimation of cultural heritage or, more specifically, of the declarations of UNESCO—the principle multinational agency concerned with "internationalizing heritage"—on the oral and intangible heritage of humanity.[3]

This chapter, in contrast, presents an analysis of processes of *unofficial* cultural patrimonialization, those *not* channeled through expert or political discourse. It focuses primarily on rituals and cults that patrimonialize death but are not governed or planned "from above" or institutionally—although I do refer tangentially to the Day of the Dead (Día de Muertos) in Mexico. Rather, they emerge largely "from below" with protagonists who usually emerge from the popular classes. Today, UNESCO does not take these cults into account and shows no interest in receiving requests for declarations of intangible cultural heritage, no matter how "intangible" the deaths involved may be.

Here, I examine the patrimonialization of death in various Latin American societies, paying special attention to the rituals and myths associated with it, and the "spontaneous"—and successful—modes of popular sanctification and creation of miraculous dead in cemeteries.[4] I characterize these regional figures, complex rituals, and cults as "emerging cults" or "emerging autochthonous cults" (see Marzal, 2002, p. 551), expressions that, despite their broad popular appeal and certain shared features with popular Catholicism, have not received the attention they deserve from social scientists. I prefer to use the term "supplicant" (*solicitante*; see Losonczy, 2001, p. 11, n. 4) instead of "worshipper," "devotee," or "believer" to describe the ritual followers of the various cults analyzed. I feel it is more expressive and precise than those terms normally used, as it brings to the fore the demand for, and the pragmatic relationship and exchanges that people establish with, death or the deceased.

Certain pathways seem to lead us toward a new symbolic and aesthetic order, and also to a broadening and transforming of the pantheon of mystical powers in these societies that share a substrate of popular Catholicism. Everything that these emerging cults and iconographies display as they thematize and exploit death as their resource presents a challenge to social research that forces us to refine our analyses and theoretical proposals.

The subsections of this chapter and their titles are structured as a suite: a compound musical genre consisting of a series of short dance pieces in instrumental form. A suite presents a union of various dances of distinct natures and rhythms into a sole opus: a succession of movements, some slow, others fast. I intend to emulate the dramatic sense of the counterpoint that listeners experienced in the baroque period when this genre reached its apogee.

After the initial *allemande,* the text proceeds with a *courante* on La Santa Muerte in Mexico, then a *sarabande* that offers a panoramic view of miraculous dead in other Latin American societies, followed by a *bourrée* that centers on the unidentified dead in Colombia and a process of "adoption," to finalize with a more fast-paced *gigue* that ponders the nature and existence of these "living dead."[5]

COURANTE: LA SANTA MUERTE
IN MEXICO (VERACRUZ, MEXICO CITY)

In La Santa Muerte, we encounter a cult that constitutes one of Mexico's most notable contributions to the globalized spiritual and symbolic imaginary, a very modern, recently developed emerging cult and ritual practice. Daily experiences with the precariousness of life—socioeconomic crises, violence, personal insecurity—among urban Mexicans, especially in Mexico City and particularly during the critical decade of the 1990s, coincided with an accelerated process that we might call the "sanctification of death."

Taking a path that deviates from what I perceive in research by my colleagues, I delve into the reality of a cult that is widespread in different social sectors, fields, and scenarios; one that shows a tendency toward what I dare to describe as "social normalization," for it has penetrated into certain layers of Mexico's middle classes, as the story narrated above reveals (Flores Martos, 2007, 2008b). I hold that the public rituals, symbols, and practices of this cult coexist with other practices of a more intimate, private character (also marginal and less spectacular) that may in some cases be almost clandestine.

Upon reviewing the profiles of some informants from my fieldwork in Veracruz who were attracted to the figure of La Santa Muerte, who have a small altar to her, or who have solicited favors, I found that they shared a popular Catholicism and social circumstances that were neither destructured, marginal, nor excluded, and that they belonged to distinct socioeconomic segments in the city, from the most popular and humble groups to the middle classes.

In previous studies, I have examined the sociopolitical contexts from which this cult emerged and developed in Mexico City in the 1990s, but here my interest is to reflect on correlations between this cult and Mexico's current reality (Flores Martos, 2007, 2008a, 2008b, 2014). The violence, insecurity, and precariousness of life, and the state's waiving of its most basic responsibilities toward the citizenry, were certainly already present in the 1990s; what has changed is the expansion, displacement, and dissemination of these daily experiences throughout Mexico. These societal shifts parallel the expansion of the cult across the country.

Although it is not my intention to suggest a cause-and-effect relation between the reality of violent death and the emergence and spread of the figure of La Santa Muerte and its devotion among ample sectors of the population in Mexico, attention is certainly drawn by the fact that the vital sociopolitical context in which Mexico has lived in recent years coincides with the diffusion of this cult, not only throughout the national territory but beyond its northern border into the United States. In other words, there is a strong correlation between the increase in violent deaths in Mexico and the growth of the cult to La Santa Muerte. In a student demonstration protesting the disappearance of forty-three Normal School students from Ayotzinapa, one question that appeared on placards—charged with a potency that social scientists and researchers had not yet recognized—read: "What will a country harvest that sows bodies?" (Pomeraniec, 2014).

Despite the scarcity and concealment of data on murders and forced disappearances, we can undertake a tentative approach to this reality based on a 2013 report on public security in Mexico from 2006 to 2012 published by the organization Mexico Unido contra la Delincuencia (Mexico United against Delinquency), which analyzes the records of several official Mexican government sources. For the six-year period (*sexenio*) 2006–2012, when the previous government launched its so-called war on drugs, data from the Executive Secretariat of the National Public Security System indicates that more than 114,000 people were murdered (intentional homicides), while reports by the Secretaría de Gobernación speak of some 26,000 forced disappearances—a total of more than 141,000 victims of violent physical, or social, death. Many of these tragedies are officially classified as "collateral damage" of the war on drugs.

Having briefly reviewed this somber panorama, we can now shift our attention to the figure of La Santa Muerte. In an earlier study, I attempted to delimit the principal features of this complex ritual, arguing that the cult of La Santa Muerte can be characterized as individualist, accessible and utilitarian, and immersed in mercantile logic (Floress Martos, 2008b, pp. 59–62). According to a profile of its supplicants, it is a marginal mestizo cult among the popular and middle classes. But it is also inserted directly into a Catholic cultural and symbolic substrate to which people turn seeking, above all, protection. An examination of its relation to other cults or agencies reveals its "cannibalistic" nature, in the sense that it appropriates and phagocytizes ritual elements of other currents. Its expansion into other countries confirms its transnational character, while its presence in forums, web pages, and Internet communities evidences its emergence as a "virtual" cult.

Although the street altars, rosaries, and multitudes of people who worship La Santa Muerte in Tepito (the infamous "tough" neighborhood in Mexico City considered the birthplace of the cult) are highly visible, the vast majority of ritual acts and dialogues between supplicants and saint take place before figures housed in intimate, private, usually domestic sites, sometimes ornate altars but often very simple representations.[6] The complex, mystical ritual focuses largely on the supplicant. Rituals are magical-religious in nature, and the agent of the cult is the individual, with little or no intervention by any intermediary or ritual specialist. The saint requires a domestic altar—in the supplicant's home or business, if the aim is to protect the supplicant—and the ritual acts contribute to the growth of individual consciousness and the construction and practice of the subjectivity typical of individualism in contemporary urban contexts. According to the manuals (*recetarios*) for rites and prayers—which give easily understood, practical, "do-it-yourself"–type instructions—rituals must be performed by the supplicant alone, in an isolated room or space. There, the supplicant presents a petition and places her or his soul in the saint's hands. Petitions commonly involve practical, immediate objectives (e.g., love, sex, money, success in business or at work, sending harm to someone, overcoming addiction, or being cured of a disease).

Contrary to common conceptions about supplicants of La Santa Muerte, most are not drug traffickers, delinquents, convicts, or prostitutes. They come from groups living in conditions of social vulnerability, of an "irregular" modernity, who use the cult to confront that reality from their structurally weak position (Fragoso, 2007a, p. 45). These are ordinary folk who experience suffering or social trauma and feel increasingly abandoned by the state or the official church. Indeed, informal traders and street peddlers constitute a growing majority in the cult, as Perla Fragoso identified (2007a, p. 53) and Anne Huffschmid described:

> The traumatized are no longer only those most visibly excluded from the worlds of legality and formality, inhabitants of urban underworlds like sex workers, transvestites, illegal substance users, or peddlers. Ever more "ordinary" men and women enter this temporal space, neighbors and business people, adolescents and the elderly, members of the vulnerable, violated classes that, having suffered multiple abandonments, seek new horizons of belonging and meaning. (2012b, pp. 105–6)

In my experience in the port of Veracruz (2007, 2008b), and as Fragoso also recorded (2011, p. 12), most supplicants are Catholics, but their Catholicism is open to new searches and experiences: "We are Catholics, but in a different way," one believer in La Santa Muerte explained to Huffschmid (2012b, p. 103). They also practice what Fragoso calls "multireligiosity," since they may form links to cults and rituals that are in fashion in Mexico City, including Santería and Marian-Trinitarian spirituality (Fragoso, 2011, p. 12). This is an iconography that has enjoyed success, one chosen by groups immersed in a structural situation of social vulnerability (Fragoso, 2007b; 2011, p. 10), by victims of multiple, ongoing abandonments, as Laura Roush accurately records when she writes that protection (*amparo*) and the lack thereof (*desamparo*) are key concepts in the liturgy of the cult to La Santa Muerte:

> [T]he central concepts in the emergent liturgy—amparo and desamparo, protection and loss of protection—have both juridical and religious origins, though many devotees understand them from their use in informal-sector politics. There is a vocabulary of protection that crosses easily from the clientelist politics of survival to otherworldly concerns and back again. (2014, p. 130)

La Santa Muerte thus presents a dual iconographic profile. On the one hand, it reflects life experiences in which death is near and omnipresent. According to Alfredo Hernández, chronicler and student of popular culture in Tepito, La Santa Muerte offers "a domesticated expression of death that is apt for Catholics and families" (Reyes Ruiz, 2010, p. 11). On the other hand, it allows supplicants to contemplate and present themselves through the overwhelming iconography of terror exhibited, the aesthetic equivalent to the "hyper-violence that floods the country" (Huffschmid, 2012b, pp. 102–3).

Part of the success and growth that this cult has attained is due to its pragmatism. It is, above all, a utilitarian cult more devoted to resolving small, everyday problems than to performing exceptional, awe-inspiring miracles.[7] In a sense, La Santa Muerta does the "dirty work" that her many thousands of supplicants request, acting as a kind of "cleaner" (*fontanera*) of micropolitics.[8] In effect, she is one of several "dirty saints" (Huffschmid, 2012b, p. 98) who have broad visibility and power in Latin America. Believers maintain that she is the most "efficacious" saint who concedes favors quickly, and thus she enjoys a competitive advantage over other popular — but official — saints, such as San Judas Tadeo, the advocate of lost causes. Andrew Chesnut (2012a) writes that there were many believers in San Judas Tadeo among his informants, but that they might go for months without receiving a favor from him, while La Santa Muerte quickly answers their petitions and performs "miracles."

"Popular" versus Official Policies

Stanley Brandes (2006, 2007) has critically analyzed how "Mexican" stereotypes of death (of and by Mexicans), the processes of patrimonialization, and national policies of popular culture have defined and modeled "death" as a cultural "good."[9] In the same vein, UNESCO's 2003 recognition of the Day of the Dead as an oral and intangible heritage of humanity has impacted the aesthetic, social — and even ritual — success of death in Mexico's social tissue. This is a deeply mestizo cultural, symbolic, and aesthetic complex (a peculiarly Mexican festival that has acquired hues of a "national fiesta") that in UNESCO's perspective is an "indigenous fiesta," which, as such, can be incorporated in the international tourism calendar and be presented to tourists fascinated by packages that offer "local flavor with spectacle."

The 1980s witnessed an exaltation of the altars and fiestas associated with the Día de Muertos, which, with institutional support, transformed it into a ritual of Mexico's national identity (Lomnitz, 2006, pp. 429, 438–39).[10] Those efforts have nourished the power of seduction that death-as-traditional-fiesta has wielded, and continues to wield, on contemporary minds, whether Mexican or those of tourists, intellectuals, artists, or international analysts. Mexico has become a universal and relevant referent of what we might call an aesthetics and a supposed experience of what is a more intimate vision of death as a cultural phenomenon that enjoys recognition and occupies a key position in the contemporary cultural imaginary (Lomnitz, 2006, p. 442).

The studies by Lomnitz and Brandes, with their emphasis on official and directed processes of cultural patrimonialization and the politics of popular culture of the Mexican state, lead us to problematize—even nuance—the idea that the success and diffusion of La Santa Muerte in Mexico reflects an exclusively "bottom-up" cult and popular movement. It is clear that, despite their distinct intentionality, interests, and logics, these two processes of cultural patrimonialization have areas of mutual contact and influence, fundamentally of "official" cultural patrimonialization, which, I maintain, has a more popular character. In more plastic terms, familiarization with José Guadalupe Posada's *calaveras* and the Catrina as typically Mexican "tastes" produces a fertile nursery for the germination of La Santa Muerte, despite the fact that these figures are symbolically and morally distanced.[11]

All of this, added to the broad diffusion of news of death and reproductions of its images in sensationalist (*nota roja*) newspapers in the context of the country's latent war on drugs, in a social territory that is especially sensitive to them and to the resulting "spectacularization" of death, has produced a sociocultural fermenting that develops and condenses this new "saint," who has earned the trust of thousands who believe in her ubiquitous figure and omnipresent power. In these scenarios, the only sure thing in life, for many, is death.

From a symbolic, iconographic, and historical perspective, devotion to La Santa Muerte was not originally related to celebrations of the Día de Muertos, that fiesta so popular among Mexico's mestizo and urban populations. Recently, however, both the rhetoric with which the media refers to La Santa Muerte, and the emphasis on her content—elements of her symbolic profile, objects of power, and offerings—reveal a process that is fusing La Santa Muerte to death as a protagonist of the festivities of the Día de Muertos, with its altars to the dead and iconography of Posada's Catrina.

For example, in 2007, regarding the notable transformations I have been able to identify in the cult, some newspaper articles spoke of the "assemblage" that emerged between celebrations in honor of La Santa Muerte and the "traditional" altars of the Día de Muertos, specifically in relation to the rituals and *atrezzo* (props) that took place on the first days of November in the "home" chapel of La Santa Muerte in Tepito, where, for many years, people had celebrated September 7 (on the more anodyne, much less spectacular, Fiesta of Santa Regina).

One example of this "catrinization" (i.e., the act of "dressing up" using the iconography of the Catrina) of La Santa Muerte was described in an article in the newspaper *El Universal*—in rhetoric appropriate for speaking in the name of the "tradition" of the altars of the Día de Muertos—that profiled the altar "de muertos" erected in the chapel of doña Queta, underlining its iconography of a "bride" and Catrina.[12]

These public identitary discourses on death and the politics of popular culture that converge in this strange patrimonialization of death and *lo mexicano* seem to have mobilized a popular movement that seeks to sanctify death as an authentic independent agent, "an arbiter without mediators" (Lomnitz, 2006, p. 464), a close and powerful saint present in sites both domestic and public and in workplaces; first among marginal, common folk living in precarious conditions, next among the humble, and now even among middle classes fearful of the chaos invading their cities and their very lives. An elusive, changing—even contradictory—powerful figure who together with the small dead honored in miniature in altars and cemeteries holds such attraction for the middle class, for life experiences of fragmentation, and for curious tourists.

Iconographic Mutations

Since around 2005, the iconography, symbolic values, and aesthetic emphasis of this cult have undergone varied and significant mutations and transformations, among them currents of transformation in Veracruz and Mexico City that we might identify as "re-Indianization," "Marianization," or "Guadalupanization," and hybridization with, and within, Santería.

Although I have not yet succeeded in identifying a clear catalyst or vector, my research in Veracruz has detected, since at least 2007, a current of "re-ethnicization," or "re-Indianization." La Santa Muerte has appeared as a cross-dressed version of Mictlantecuhtli, the pre-Hispanic Mexica god of the world of the dead, even bearing the typical Aztec feathered headdress (a la Moctezuma), clothes, ornaments, and symbolic elements, delving into an aesthetics shared with the religious-identitary movement of Mexicanness.[13]

This re-Indianization of the cult is visible as well in cities like Veracruz, where emphasis on its indigenous, pre-Hispanic origins flourishes, accompanied by efforts to distance it from Catholicism. This transformation of La Santa Muerte has been picked up and amplified by the media and is beginning to impact the nationalist and popular logics that establish a continuity, both symbolic and of belief, between Mictlantecuhtli and La Santa Muerte, now incarnated as heir to the whole "package" of ritual meanings and practices of pre-Christian and precolonial times.

The cult to La Santa Muerte that has been developing in Veracruz since the

1990s gained public visibility in the context of this pre-Hispanic aesthetics. Local newspapers chronicle how an "organization" of followers of this saint, called Mictlantecuhtli, planned a celebration in her honor on dates that coincided with the Día de Muertos, and how Aztec dancers—called *concheros* in the movement and aesthetics of Mexicanness because of their costumes adorned with seashells—danced in public in the city center, followed by a visit to the archaeological site of El Zapotal with its sculpture of Mictlantecuhtli. One newspaper article, in *Notiver*, includes a photo of the saint in her chapel in the Almendros neighborhood, dressed in a tunic with feathered headdress, adorned with Aztec motifs.[14]

But what most impacted me in this polymorphous saint was her singular transformation, her formulae of transfiguration, no longer just of her iconography and meanings associated with the Mexica god Mictlantecuhtli but also with those of the peculiarly Mexican Virgin of Guadalupe. We can speak of processes of hegemony, mimetics, and camouflage that take La Santa Muerte as their protagonist and seek to equate her with the image of Guadalupe. These processes have flourished in paintings and other creations of artists and graphic designers, who somehow hybridize plastically not only their iconographies but also the devotional and practical experiences of broad sectors of the population, with respect to these two "saints." The Virgin of Guadalupe may be coming to form part of the symbolic scaffolding of the construction of the profile of La Santa Muerte.

From a plastic viewpoint, one finds images on the Internet—which will likely soon make the jump to products and objects of merchandising—that fuse the profiles and iconographies of what are today, in all likelihood, the two most revered saints in Mexico. Artists and graphic designers have assembled symbols, forms, and features of both entities; even created a hybrid product of symbolic Mexican "essences" for a peculiarly Mexican devotion. These images are tattooed on gang members (*cholos*) on both sides of the Mexico-US border and appear on T-shirts designed by the Bershka brand of globalized clothes for young people.

Parallel to this current of Marianization, or imitations of Guadalupan iconography, some years ago I identified a second interesting process in the transformation from a "disincarnated" to an "incarnated" iconography; that is, the conversion of the original image into that of a woman with clear white skin and dark hair wearing a tiara or crown and veil—the garments and iconography of a "virgin," or representation of the Virgin Mary (Flores Martos, 2008b). This transfiguration was propelled by the offices of the Traditional Mexican-US Apostolic Catholic Church, supposedly as the result of a dream-vision of one of its believers. The goal was to somehow soften the image of La Santa Muerte as part of this group's application for official registration as a "religious organization" by Mexico's Directorate of Religious Affairs, which would free it from paying taxes and allow it to attract new followers. This new image of La Santa Muerte came to be called the Ángel de la Santa Muerte, or Angel of Death. Instead of a terrifying, intimidating, bony skeleton, it showed a dark-haired angel with mantle, veil, and tiara, styled like a virgin: a figure inspiring peace and harmony. But this change in the image of La Santa Muerte set off a popular reaction by traditionalist followers who criticized the new "look" of the cult that had transformed the original bony skeleton into "a mannequin that resembles a transvestite."[15]

This is where we must situate the fact that the fiesta of La Santa Muerte held by that church initially took place on August 15 (when Catholics celebrate the Assumption of the Virgin Mary) and was called the "official" festival of the Day of La Santa Muerte. That date differs from the days that the media and currents of popular institutionalization of the cult hold as the "true" time for celebrating this saint, namely October 31 and November 1 and 2, precisely the time of the Día de Muertos. This shuffling of dates around key days of Mexico's national ritual calendar contrasts with our knowledge of the first chapel dedicated to La Santa Muerte in the Morelos neighborhood of Tepito, where she was fêted on September 7, the day of Santa Regina, before the change to October 31–November 1.

In the context of the processes of transformation-mutation and transnationalization affecting Santería, Mexico's La Santa Muerte plays the role of protagonist (clearly more strongly in Mexico and Cuba than elsewhere). This goes beyond the fusion and new iconographic version of La Santa Muerte with the stamp and image of Yemayá, also called the White Flower of the Universe (Flor Blanca del Universo), and in Veracruz with the Young Death Incarnate (Joven Muerte Encarnada).

A researcher who has studied Cuban Santería in Veracruz and Mexico City, Kali Argyriadis (2014), identified in Veracruz processes of the digestion and relocalization of Cuban Santería through the cult of La Santa Muerte, urban spiritism, and local healing (curanderismo), or perhaps all three agencies, which appear intertwined in most cases in this urban culture.

This cult found its most effective vehicle of generation, expansion, and transformation in the uses that its followers, product consumers, seekers of orientations and "prescriptions" for the individual performance of rituals and prayers, and suppliers of goods and services have articulated on the Internet and in sections of certain markets and stores that specialize in esoteric goods. This expansion has largely followed the commercialization formulas that Afro-Caribbean (Cuban, Dominican) Santería has applied in the virtual space of the Internet, taking advantage of the diaspora and migration of people from those countries, thereby generating authentic transnational religious networks (see Sánchez-Carretero, 2004, 2005; Argyriadis, 2012; Argyriadis & Juárez, 2005).

SARABANDE: THE MIRACULOUS DEAD

Since the late twentieth century, people in many Latin American societies have venerated the so-called miraculous dead, or popular saints, entities that spontaneously, and outside processes of institutionalization/canonization, are recognized as imbued with a living, though unstable, holiness in an ongoing process of fabrication.

These miraculous dead (a concept we owe to Francisco Franco) are singular individualities exalted by their community after death, incarnations of victims who were out of sync with the existing social or political order (Franco, 2009, p. 212). In these cases, supplicants place, on graves in cemeteries, letters with petitions, or offerings (exvotos; objects related to the person's "life history"), reelaborated in tune with the deceased involved. It is not my aim to present an exhaustive list of these elements but to provide a generic and selective analysis of some ethnographies that focus on these singular, miraculous dead.[16] In what follows I will present a brief hagiographic synthesis of these miraculous dead, all of whom reiterate the theme of "bad death," with corpses that bear the markings of bodily mutilation and extreme violence.

There are several versions of Salomé la Milagrosa's life (Salomé the Miraculous, Bogotá): exploited prostitute, candle vendor in the cemetery, washerwoman, or domestic employee (Losonczy, 2001, p. 12). People say that she lived in the Egipto neighborhood, or La Perseverancia, of Bogotá; that she was often beaten by her husband; and that her children had deeply disappointed her. Her followers attribute her death to different causes: some say uremia, others that she was immolated, still others that she was asphyxiated, drowned, killed by her mother or out of revenge, and mutilated, her body cut open to remove her heart and breasts, then stuffed with sand and stones.

A *cangaceiro* (poor bandit) from northeastern Brazil named Jararaca was wounded and detained by police after a shootout in Mossoró. Then, in the middle of the night, officers hauled him out of jail and buried him alive in the town cemetery. Baracho, an illiterate, two-bit thief who became known as the "taxi killer" after he gave a forced confession to that crime, escaped from several jails before being trapped in a vacant lot in the slums of Natal and executed by eighteen gunshots. Significantly, as he died he was afflicted by thirst (Freitas, 2007).

It is said that Machera, a Venezuelan *malandro* (thug) living in Mérida, was an intrepid outlaw who died when police sprayed him with a hundred bullets after an epic chase during which he disarmed and killed several officers (Franco, 2009). In Catamarca, Argentina, a young woman was sequestered, force-fed cocaine, and gang raped by a group of adult men with links to local political power. María Soledad Morales's body was then thrown onto the street.

A young indigenous woman named Sarita Colonia arrived in Lima as a migrant. She had a rough life there, full of hardships as a domestic worker and street peddler (Marzal, 2002, pp. 554–56; Ortíz, 1990, p. 201). She died young, just twenty-six, and was buried without a funeral in a mass grave in the cemetery in El Callao. After her death, people began to visit her grave to leave candles and flowers, believing that she was miraculous. There are several accounts of her troubled life and how she succumbed: officially, she died of malaria in a hospital, but the most popular story maintains that she was brutally raped and murdered. Sometime later, her followers bought a plot in the cemetery and erected a mausoleum, including a chapel, in her honor. It seems that the stevedores in the port of El Callao were the first social group to venerate Sarita Colonia, but some marginal collectivities, including prostitutes, delinquents, and homosexuals, soon followed suit. Today, there is a strong popular cult to her in Lima, a city where migrants, Indians, street peddlers, and informal traders abound.

The eruption of the Nevado del Ruiz volcano in Colombia in 1985 produced an avalanche of ash and mud that buried the town of Armero. Television and other media transmitted the agony suffered by Omayra Sánchez, a girl barely twelve who died tragically in front of the cameras. No one could do anything to help her as she was sepulchered, soaking wet, for three days in the ruins of her home. At the site where her house had stood, people erected a tomb that has become a place of pilgrimage for thousands every year.

In answer to Eliane Tânia Freitas's question—"Of what raw material is a popular saint made?" (2007, p. 66)—the author summarizes some of the traits that might characterize the social promotion of these dead: the victims were stigmatized in life; they suffered violence (state, intrafamily, sexual, or gender); and long before their physical death many had previously experienced a kind of "social death" due to stigmatization, abandonment, oblivion, extreme poverty, or persecution.[17]

Among the masses of dead in a cemetery, popular sanctifying initiatives focus on what we might call the most public and "unpalatable" deaths, those marked by extreme drama and violence. These dead are reelaborated socially through a process that promotes figures of miraculous dead and popular saints (Freitas, 2007, pp. 66–67). Thus, in some Latin American societies we witness the development of processes and strategies of a ritual and mythical nature that can be interpreted from the perspective of the cultural patrimonialization of death. These strategies and processes appear oriented toward coping with a discontinuous, traumatic memory, and the oblivion and anonymity that emerge from political and social violence. Rituals repeatedly manifest petitions intertwined with a yearning for miracles, which, as Anne-Marie Losonczy points out, are transferred to a class of "emblematic deaths from the regime of family memory toward a ritual record of shared memory" (2001, p. 12). In other words, the meanings and linkages of these deaths extend from a private and family kind of memory to one that is more communitarian and collective.

Expressions of an approach distinct from the relational model based on Catholic patronage and a more vertical dependence on gaining the "favor" of official saints, the relations formed with these popular saints manifest a more egalitarian and horizontal model of exchange—"a more egalitarian companionship"—that supplicants strive to establish with the miraculous dead. In doing so, they adopt the logic of a more direct, agile, and individual kind of access to procuring favors (Losonczy, 2001, p. 20).

In their words and ritual acts, these supplicants establish a pact of egalitarian reciprocity with popular saints. This is one way of bringing the cult to popular saints into focus: they offer paths that allow supplicants to access and recover their "agency" as political subjects, while simultaneously facilitating the emergence of a new type of civil memory, though one still sketchy and under construction. This appears as an attractive option for reconstituting violated social relations by offering people an assay in political access to citizenship (Losonczy, 2001, pp. 21–22). For Freitas, these cults make it possible to "cope with scenarios of public social conflict," as through ritual the local community manifests an "unofficial" reading of history that diverges from what public authorities present—regarding the concrete moment of those deaths—using accounts from the past, or reaffirming present-day miracles (Freitas, 2007, p. 84).

Comparing the ethnographies of these cult figures allows us to identify some shared political—even "judicial"—dimensions of cults and the miraculous dead or popular saints in the cemeteries mentioned above, and the cult to La Santa Muerte in Mexico. In their daily lives, and at critical moments of their life cycles, suppliants turn to these power entities seeking "favors"—some of their letters or petitions are similar to the expository rhetoric of an administrative or official communication—that in reality could be considered services that a conventional state would provide through a popular logic of reciprocity.

Such is the case of another "miraculous dead," Irene del Carmen Iturra Sáez, known as "Little Black Boots" (Botitas Negras), from Calama, Chile. Apparently, Irene was a prostitute whose body—wearing high black boots— was found by miners. It had been mutilated: breasts and scalp removed; no nerves or skin on her face, ears, or hands; and the skin and tendons of her left upper arm and wrist eaten away by animals (Pavez and Kraushaar, 2010).[18] Botitas Negras's grave is used by suppliants as an office or cabinet "of government," as Jorge Pavez and Lilith Kraushaar have analyzed:

> We can see the sanctuary of Botitas Negras as a "government" office that receives petitions (letters) and offerings (payments), and the miraculous saint as a minister of a biopolitical theocracy that dispenses "life protection" and intervenes through miracles to aid subjects who are fragmented and threatened by the "invisible hand" of neoliberal government. (2010, p. 447)

In these narratives, the authors interpret the offerings placed on Botitas Negras's grave as a cycle of exchange between suppliants and this powerful popular saint. But let us look for a moment at how a letter from one Peruvian sex worker broadly synthesizes the working conditions and desires of immigrant prostitutes: the need to obtain legal documents, to accumulate "johns" to earn money to send home to Peru, to meet a marriageable man, to be hired at a prestigious cabaret (like Lucifer's in Calama); and the kind and quality of "miracles" she requests from Botitas Negras, many of which could be channeled through, or attended by, the administrative agencies and social services of an active, really functioning state, but not by the "invisible hand" of Chile's neoliberal government. The following is an extract from her letter:

> Thank you for what I asked for, to be the best *fichadora* [prostitute] and [have] good luck at work, for things to go real well; I ask you to protect me and reveal evil people, and that the guy who stole my cell phone return it. And that when I go to ask for work in the locale of F.'s office they accept me and don't turn me down. Botitas Negras, help me manage my money for the problem I have in Peru with Santiago . . . to get it back and give him his money, so A. stays with me. Help me find a good man who wants to marry me so I can get my papers and my Chilean credential in November, please help me Botitas Negras. Thank you, pretty one, take care of me and bring me good men, not bad ones, so things go well for me. So I can succeed at work to help my mother and siblings. Botitas Negras, I want you to grant me this big wish that Mr. De Lucifer takes me in and gives me a chance to work, please. (Pávez and Kraushaar, 2010)

These popular, miracle-working saints are a substitute for political and judicial actions in contexts and conditions marked by structural violence, insecurity, and impunity, where the neoliberal state is absent and permanently abstains from carrying out its functions. In this experience of daily life and ritual practices, there is no place for anomie; the miracle must resolve the milieu of passions to contribute to a justice unobtainable through law (Pavez & Kraushaar, 2010, p. 484).

Finally, it is important to stress another shared trait of these miraculous dead of emerging popular devotion: the fact that most are "deaths without owners" (that is, no relative arrives to claim the body, identify it, or provide funeral rituals). Despite this, these dead come to be endowed with a history and strong symbolic charge. They are appropriated or "adopted" by a local community that takes responsibility for the burial—or performs a secondary burial[19]—as if the victim were a member of the family (Freitas, 2007, p. 83). And this leads us to examine other deaths, now in Colombia, that experience a certain "familiar" localization and a kind of "adoption," and from whom people seek miracles.

BOURRÉE: ADOPTED DEATHS (NN)

Because my brothers have disappeared, tonight I wait by the riverbank for a cadaver to float by that I'll make my own. Everyone in the port has seen someone taken away, had someone disappear, seen someone murdered, we are orphans, widows. So every day we wait for bodies carried by the muddied waters, among the palisades, to make them our brothers, parents, spouses or children. (Jorge Eliécer Pardo, "Sin nombres, sin rostros ni rastros")

It is an established practice in Latin American societies to render cult status to anonymous, unidentified souls, but this seems to go a step further in Colombia through ritual and plastic expressions that manifest a logic in which those unidentified dead—called NN, from the Latin *nomen necio*, of unknown name—are "adopted" by believers in some towns and cemeteries.[20] As the fragment that introduces this section shows, Colombia's rivers, like the Magdalena or the Cauca, reflect the traumatic reality the country is living, plagued by death, violence, and missing people due to decades of civil war. Rivers are used as improvised mass graves for victims whose executioners seek to wash away all evidence of violent death and of the person's identity. There are few anthropological studies on the reality of NN deaths in Colombia, and those we have take only a partial approach, such as Elsa Blair (2005), Paula Andrea Velásquez (2009), Juana Chaves (2010, 2011), Constanza Vieira (2008), and Gervasio Sánchez (2010), or a journalistic one such as by Patricia Nieto (2012). The best and most complete work is by María Victoria Uribe Alarcón (2011), but there is also the documentary by the Colombian plastic artist Juan Manuel Echavarría (2013), *Réquiem NN*. Since my interest here is to compare the funerary ritual practices and treatment of corpses in two scenarios of postconflict Colombia, I largely follow Uribe Alarcón.

In Beltrán, a village near Marsella, an eddy in the Cauca River gathers many body parts, human remains treated indifferently—even inhumanly—in a way that has become normal and habitual, some even used as play toys by children as they leave school (Uribe Alarcón, 2011, pp. 42–43). Rarely are these remains gathered and taken to the municipal center to be processed, possibly identified, and then interred (Velásquez, 2009, p. 36). Worse yet, it is common practice to erase the identity, even the very existence, of those unknown, unidentified victims. For example, when Colombia's Ministry of Culture declared the cemetery of Marsella as "Historical and Architectural Heritage," the Municipal Ornamental Society (Sociedad de Ornato) ordered more than four hundred NN tombstones to be painted white, thus "erasing" the few bits of data (gender, year of burial) that might one day permit their identification (Uribe Alarcón, 2011, pp. 44–45). The people of Beltrán-Marsella show no concern for the fate of those human remains.

We find an opposite approach in the social formula or protocol practiced by residents of Puerto Berrío—on the banks of the Magdalena River—when handling anonymous NN corpses. People there gather, care for, and "adopt" such remains and "integrate them into families" (sometimes even giving them surnames). This is a vehicle in the process of converting those anonymous corpses into miraculous dead or popular saints.[21] The sociocultural logic activated here merits closer attention. Bodies or dismembered remains wash up on the riverbank, where they are rescued and "adopted" by relatives of other "disappeared" people (also likely thrown into rivers or buried in mass graves) who have not been found. Adoption gives them a new social identity; one reads on tombstones "NN Carlos," "NN Sonia," or expressions of gratitude. Local people may then ask them for favors during life crises or with everyday problems, generating a process of (popular, spontaneous, and from below) patrimonialization of some "adopted" and renamed NN dead bodies. This process of making the recovered cadaver their own allows families to exercise their right to grieve, eases their pain, and cements the memory and image of their own loved ones who disappeared, victims of extreme violence for whom they could never perform appropriate funeral honors or visit in the cemetery. Here, the act of placing a small tombstone allows them to move on with their lives.

Finally, I end with a reflection on the agency of the subjects implicated in these new dealings and "contracts" established by people in Puerto Berrío with NN victims. I do not refer here to a political agency, as Pavez and Kraushaar (2010) do in the case of Botitas Negras, but to a more basic agency that allows people to retake the initiative or, perhaps better, exercise some control over their daily lives. The first step occurs when a believer goes to the cemetery and chooses an NN by painting the word "chosen" (escogido) on the modest tombstone (Uribe Alarcón, 2011, p. 40). This choice initiates the adoption process of the NN and activates a contract in which the parties exchange offerings (called dones): the deceased may grant the favor requested while the adopting citizen promises to maintain the tomb and a ritual dialogue with prayers and conversations for the victim at the grave site. This exchange reduces, or reverses, the normal hierarchical positions occupied by Catholicism's official saints and "believers" who beseech favors, because these saints are not patrons in this relationship; rather it is the supplicant who sponsors the deceased chosen from among the many unidentified graves. It may turn out that the miraculous dead fails to "function" for the person who initially "chose" her or him, and is abandoned, but that deceased person may be chosen a second time by another believer and, given this second chance, prove to be miraculous for the new sponsor (Uribe Alarcón, 2011, p. 41).

This ritual practice and dialogue, with its staged process of adoption, needs to be analyzed more thoroughly from the ethnographic optic and logic of kinship—in this case, the ritual kinship established—and from the formulas that modernity introduces into the processes of transformation of these societies at the micro level of family structure and new formats of relations.[22] Informants and the few studies available emphasize the desire to express, establish, and cement "families-by-choice," or "reconfigured" families, in which NNs are not only "baptized" with their own names but may even be given the surname of their adoptive sponsor.[23] It would be interesting to determine the limits of this insertion into the family by, for example, finding cases in which the adopted NN is reburied in a family grave, mausoleum, or cemetery beside other deceased relatives of that sponsor or the adopted family.

GIGUE: THE LIVING DEAD?

As everyone knows, zombies are hybrids of the living and dead, beings that died, but not completely, who remain in the ambiguous territory of catatonic life: the half-dead. Cultural patrimony behaves like a zombie: it may have good or poor health, but its energy is a product of a life breathed from the present by some live instances interested, for some reason, in rescuing fragments of the past. The patrimonial zombie, a hybrid product as much the child of modernity as of the Promethean monster Frankenstein, thus enjoys an artificial life, one connected to the machine of present urgencies, a modern machine that through diverse administrative, economic, and technical apparatuses extracts rich fluids from the patrimonial zombie in the form of political-identitary legitimation and potentially exploitable merchandise, but that, in return, must receive regular injections of vital liquids, administered bureaucratically and rationally, to keep the zombie breathing. (Gil-Manuel Hernández i Martí, "Un zombi de la modernidad")

The figure that may best characterize the limited and paradoxical quality of cultural patrimony is the zombie, the living dead of modernity. But are these deaths with a capital D, and those lesser or anonymous dead in these societies in the same class as the zombies or dancing figures of our time? What similarities and differences in profile and agency do La Santa Muerte and other miraculous dead or popular saints in Latin America manifest?

To answer this question, we must imagine and map a cartography of supplicants and ritual users of such deaths—La Santa Muerte, miraculous dead, and adopted NN dead—to demonstrate whether they overlap in the field or appear separately, differentiated by some kind of frontier. Probably we will be able to identify how, in those Latin American societies where the experience of spiritual possession by the dead is current (through Santería and Afro-American cults, whether localized or transnationalized), another style of the patrimonialization of death is hegemonic, one that likely traverses a performative, ephemeral-provisional identification with a corpse that is neither of the family nor adopted but that bursts like a torrent or pattern into the identitary nucleus of the person, expressing a plural, unstable format of the subject's identity, distant from the monolithic identity and the body-soul duality elaborated in the Western tradition. The NN adopted dead do not "mount" or possess the sponsors who choose them and demand things of them; they are not batteries of agency that penetrate the subject's body and will; rather, they function as external entities with which a contract and exchanges are established.

In these pages, my concern has been to examine the patrimonialization of culture—popular, from below—that subaltern sectors, but not only them, activate through practices and rituals that are condensed in figures of death and the dead, and certain counterhegemonic logics that allow culture to flourish as a process of disputes over power (Wright, 1998, p. 137). What we have observed are some specifically Catholic cults and ritual practices, since their "users" never stop being Catholics. While perhaps this is a more plastic, malleable aesthetic and ritual complex, one that, as in the case of La Santa Muerte—or the collars of Santería, the discourse of beings of light and "energy" in Marian-Trinitarian spirituality, or the power chains and testimonies of Pentecostalism—allows more transformations and incorporations, the logic and activated substrate are clearly still those of popular Catholicism.

With respect to the profiles of the supplicants and users of these cults and rituals, it is important to emphasize that most share a lifestyle immersed in informality, characterized by precariousness. They are part of a fringe population especially exposed to the physical and social vulnerability generated by a crisis-ridden, ever-changing political, social, and economic context. They suffer intensely from the effects of abandonment by the state—with its neoliberal policies—and from the generation of violences, some structural, others more direct, in basic areas like infrastructure, public safety, justice, and social services. The fact is that many of the petitions and demands they present to dead "saints" could be attended to and resolved by a competent state, and it is surprising that the people who approach these figures plead reiteratively for safekeeping and protection regarding the most basic of issues, exposing, quite literally, a profile of abandonment by state and government institutions.

Supplicants do not necessarily request favors only or exclusively from these figures of sanctified death, for previously they may have "proven" the inefficacy, "deafness," or slowness of responses by other saints, whether "official," like the Virgin of Guadalupe, or popular, like San Judas Tadeo, in Mexico. These new figures offer more accessible, direct communication and attention, free of special or complex mediations. Moreover, they can beseech their mediation rather laxly; that is, without elaborate ecclesiastical structures or the obligation to show constant devotion. People can, and do, approach them only occasionally or intermittently. We are, therefore, witnessing different trials with a model of exchange and reciprocity, of adaptation to a particular modernity; a micro model that can also be read as an expression of a popular process of the recomposition of subjectivity.

The trait that perhaps most vividly connects the cult to La Santa Muerte with the extensive panorama of emerging cults of miraculous dead in other areas of Latin America is that in conditions where the presence and "power of death" is ubiquitous, one sector of the population (the most vulnerable) opts to strengthen its dialogues, treatments, and negotiations with these figures that incarnate death by assuming its emblems and symbols and converting them into its patrimony; even, in some cases, adopting death and integrating it into their families, as with the NN dead in Puerto Berrío. In this apparently paradoxical manner, death is "validated" and activated in its service—even sponsored in the "chosen" NNs in the cemetery—by its supplicants, who are thus somewhat more empowered as agents of their lives, and can block death from continuously threatening and surrounding them and infecting their lives.

It is important to emphasize that in these processes of cultural patrimonialization of death, one shared trait from a micro perspective is the role assigned to "adoption"; that is, the inclusion of the figure of death or the dead in question in a moral-familiar social and economic logic dramatized in the ritual acts and intimate dialogues effectuated in the domestic sphere or before graves in a cemetery. This can serve as proof that we are, indeed, witnessing "bottom-up" processes of cultural patrimonialization.

And this is the basis of the new pact—not with the Devil, but directly with death—that broad population sectors in Latin America are choosing. La Santa Muerte (in capital letters) and those other, "little" dead (in small letters), "chosen" or sponsored as powerful agents and allies for their lives, seem to be coming to life as zombies, literally the living dead in postconflict landscapes and in the face of social vulnerability normalized by the hegemony of neoliberal states, in Latin American societies characterized by a particularly singular modernity. These figures that dance in the imaginaries, ritual practices, and daily lives of thousands of people in these settings bring to mind the dances of death in the Middle Ages that announced the proximity and inevitability of death—so graphically illustrated by plagues and epidemics—and people's awareness of the looming end of all worldly pleasures. Strangely, however, nowadays these figures no longer seem to announce the end, nor do they inspire fear; rather, they have been transformed into facilitators and mediators of life, referents of moral authority and power for a growing number of people in this part of the world.

NOTES

1. This chapter is based on the results of research conducted on La Santa Muerte over a prolonged period of time. I thank the insightful comments of Wil Pansters, Regnar Kristensen, and Nuala Finnegan.

2. "Patrimonialization is a voluntary process of incorporating socially constructed values contained in the space-time of a particular society. It is part of the processes of territorialization that are at the base of the relation between territory and culture. Appropriation and valorization as selective, individual, or collective actions are expressed in concrete acts that permit the construction of durable identitary references" (Bustos, 2004, pp. 18–19).

3. See the studies by Flores Martos (2009), Villaseñor & Zolla (2012), Fernández

(2013), and Dosal (2014). In this regard, Isabel Villaseñor and Emiliano Zolla's words are revealing: "The notion of intangible cultural heritage has been received enthusiastically by the member states of UNESCO, including Mexico. However, there are very few critical analyses of the diverse social, economic, and political phenomena that lie behind the patrimonialization of cultural practices. The new conceptualization of patrimony by cultural institutions is heir to the vices of traditional conceptualization, including the essentialist vision of patrimony, its material and symbolic appropriation by hegemonic groups, an emphasis on the grandiose and spectacular, and the search to conserve authenticity, defined from optics external to those of the subjects that construct said patrimony" (2012, p. 75).

4. Few anthropological works—theoretical or ethnographic—are devoted to studying death in Latin America. See the studies by Cipolletti & Langdon (1992), Ciudad, Ruz, & Iglesias (2003), Flores & Abad (2007), Hidalgo (2011), and, especially valuable, the monographs by Calavia (1996) and Scheper-Hughes (1997).

5. Allemande, sarabande, etc. are all musical movements with different tempos and rhythmic, harmonic, and melodic characters. For a more detailed account, see *The Harvard Dictionary of Music* (Randel, 2009).

6. For a discussion of visibility, see Huffschmid in this volume.

7. In their interesting study of the hybridization of Cuban Santería and Marian-Trinitarian spirituality, Silvia Ortíz and Isabel Lagarriga (2007) identify the development of new "utilitarian cults" in Mexican cities—especially the capital—in the context of an increased concern to reduce the problems of daily life and resolve pressing questions, and a declining concern among believers for the afterlife. Favors include: for children to do well in school, an end to alcohol or drug addiction, success in business, keeping one's job, protection against "black magic" and hexes, not being assaulted or accosted and detained by the police, and paychecks sufficient for people to satisfy their needs.

8. *Fontanera* is used in journalistic and political discourse in Spain. In politics, people often use the word "fontanero" to identify an individual who, from the shadows, resolves issues and problems that require discretion.

9. For an approach to the process of the cultural patrimonialization of death in Mexico and its role in the constitution of Mexican "identity" and uses in Mexican nationalism, the most complete and important book is Claudio Lomnitz's *Idea de la muerte en Mexico* (2006). Also useful are the academic writings of Octavio Paz (1950/1998), Roger Bartra (1987), and Paul Westheim (1985), and literary and artistic works that provide indispensable material, or foundations, for their global extension, including Juan Rulfo (1955) and Malcolm Lowry (1947).

10. Lomnitz's analytical perspective explores how death has become a national totem in Mexico, utilized as a privileged vector in constructing the modern Mexican state and popular Mexican culture: "Rather than imagining a popular culture of

death that precedes the state and then a state that manipulates or creates a false image of that popular culture, we shall explore how the cultural construction of death shaped the state and popular culture" (2006, p. 56).

11. The image of the Catrina depicts a female skeleton elegantly dressed only in a bonnet, befitting the upper-class outfit of a European of her time. The Catrina has become an icon of the Mexican Día de Muertos.

12. "So Mexican. The 'Holy Saint' dressed as a bride, surrounded by thirty-five statuettes all dressed in white. A couple of them, Catrinas, in the style of José Guadalupe Posada. At the foot of the altar they place offerings, as believers are accustomed to doing (apples, roses, tequila, lit cigarettes) and others [typical] of the season of death (bread, skulls made of sugar and chocolate). Perforated papers, *cempasúchitl* flowers and fruits, gave the character of traditional offerings at the altar lit by neon lights and flickering candles. . . . Today, altars in Mexico City's streets are innumerable, where separate celebrations take place. The megacity, however, was a large extension. The annual fiesta of the [saint] was but a dot in the package of the popular tradition of celebrating deaths, and of Halloween." (Arvizu, 2007).

13. The Mexicanness movement is one of the most significant collective phenomena of an identitary, cultural, religious, and political type in contemporary Mexico, though with a neotraditionalist profile. It seeks to revitalize the civilization that existed before the conquest.

14. "Celebrarán a la 'Santísima Muerte' en el puerto," *Notiver*, October 26, 2007.

15. "Hacen primeras misas a la 'nueva' Santa Muerte," *Tabasco Hoy*, August 15, 2007. Retrieved from http://www.tabascohoy.com/nota.php?id_nota=139274.

16. More solid, suggestive ethnographic work in this field has begun to appear, especially since around 2005. Important studies include those by Losonczy (2001), Carozzi (2005, 2006), Freitas (2007), Graziano (2007), Lozano (2007), Franco (2009), and Pavez & Kraushaar (2010).

17. "Most of the miraculous dead are poor, weak, even unknown. Several accounts of miraculous dead say they died alone, with no funeral, hungry, thirsty, without relatives . . . abandoned. Only long after their death are their bodies— according to some narratives, 'only bones'—found by someone who 'charitably' decides to bury them in exchange for a favor. To the degree that their interventions prove to be 'efficacious,' sponsors will spread the word of their miraculous power and erect a 'chapel.' The contaminating power of the dead is thus transformed into one that is protecting and beneficial, thanks to ritual solidarity" (Franco, 2009, p. 337).

18. On the discursive confluence of sexuality, desire, and violence with the resignification of murdered prostitutes as popular saints in mining cities in Chile, recent work by Lilith Kraushaar stands out (2013).

19. Reburials, or secondary interments, may be a feature shared by all miraculous dead, or popular saints, in Colombian cemeteries (Velásquez, 2009, p. 33), as in the

cases of Omayra Sánchez and Sarita Colonia, who are "removed" from mass graves, unhallowed ground, or small graves by believers or people who received a favor, and who may build a more personalized tomb or mausoleum.

20. Anonymous souls are called "little miraculous souls" (*almitas milagrosas*) in Peru (Ortíz, 1990, p. 201); "little souls" (*animitas*) in Chile (Benavente, 2011); "lonely souls" (*ánima sola*) in Colombia (Losonczy, 2001); and "souls of the Guasare" (*ánimas del Guasare*) in Venezuela (Navas Soto, 1997; Franco, 2009).

21. The adoption of NN dead is not only practiced in Puerto Berrío, as we have references indicating its practice in other areas of Colombia; for example, the cemetery in Ríonegro, near Medellín (Antioquia). In 2010, Spanish photographer Gervasio Sánchez observed that "some niches of NN have been adopted by anonymous citizens, perhaps seeking consolation for their own losses. The tombstones are impeccable, the flowers fresh, and immobile angels on Greek pedestals watch over them. One reads: 'N.N. Thanks for the favor received'" (2010).

22. Kristensen (2014) has studied kinship relations and family intimacy as keys to understanding the logic of the cult to La Santa Muerte and its success and dissemination in Mexico. He sustains that it strongly connects with, and strengthens the relations and functions of, the Mexican family. See also his contribution to this volume.

23. "Another man told us he had chosen several NNs, and given them his surname. He visits them periodically and converses candidly with them" (Uribe Alarcón, 2011, p. 41).

ANNE HUFFSCHMID

4 | La Santa Muerte as Urban Staging
Notes on the Images and Visibility
of a Transgressive Performance

SKULLS IN MEXICO: A PREFACE
TO THE VISUAL CULTURE OF TERROR

What comes to my mind when thinking of images and imaginaries of death in Mexico these days is certainly not the Niña Blanca or Flaquita, the widely worshipped skeleton figure surrounded by candles and flowers, but the new and terrifying iconography of "real" and dirty skulls, bones, and skeletons emerging from mass graves, and their counterpart, the disappeared bodies of those who were kidnapped, presumably killed, and literally erased from the surface of the visible. Nowadays, we find ourselves, impotent and horrified, forced to witness the emergence and circulation of a new set of images, among them the face of a young murdered man, one of the victims of the police attack on protesting students from Ayotzinapa in late September 2014, who was tortured to death by having his face skinned. This procedure (nothing new really, for it is a paramilitary technique, trained and applied in counterinsurgency in Central America), did not leave a "clean" skull but sheer flesh, an image beyond disturbing—one I never saw, and did not even dare to imagine, not only because it would have been physically unbearable but also because I reject the role as receiver of its message. But the photograph was (and supposedly still is) out there, communicating actively, as an intended visual strategy of terror, violating both our gaze and our imagination. The tortured face and body of young Julio César Mondragón echo the thousands of tortured and mutilated bodies of women and men exhibited in public places, explicitly to be looked at: a visual culture of terror that began with the slaughtering of young women in northern Mexico and then became generalized, following a similar pattern, all across the country.[1]

This is very different from what Thomas Keenan and Eyal Weizman (2012) came to call "forensic aesthetics," although both relate to the topic of extreme violence: the public presence and presentation of dead bodies, skeletons, bones, and skulls, and their transformation into evidence, the materialization and deliberate visualization (through photographs and other visual devices) of the invisible, a disappeared body and the circumstances of its death. The possibility that forensics might bring the nameless human remains from mass graves back to humanity (though not to life) by identifying and restoring them to their families, contains a dignifying potential that opposes the explicit degradation of the dead by displaying their shattered bodies, victimized once again by their murderers. Both visual modes—dignifying and degrading—are related to the use of extreme violence and strategies of terror intended to communicate unlimited power "over life and death," whether by exhibiting violated corpses or ensuring that dead bodies disappear.[2]

It is interesting, perhaps even necessary, to reflect more deeply on the connections between these images and the aesthetics that emerge in the context, and as markers, of contemporary terror in Mexico and the subject of this book, the culturally empowered skeleton. For purposes of this chapter, I must clarify and emphasize the enormous difference between (1) the notion of *excess* (in the sense of *excessive* or transgressive violence) generated in the context of an emerging visual culture of terror in Mexico that has site-specific communication purposes as well as impacts on global image circulation (whereby decapitation and on-camera torture were associated with Mexican drug cartels, at least before the Islamic State came along); and, (2) the public performance of *visual* excess and transgression related to La Santa Muerte. It is the latter, with its possible meanings and place-making capacities, that I discuss in the following pages.

WAYS OF LOOKING AT A "NEW SAINT IN TOWN"

In contrast to most of the contributors to this volume, I do not look at Santa Muerte devotion from within but turn to the long-term anthropological fieldwork of expert scholars who provide ethnographic insights and in-depth knowledge on the social relationships and affective economies involved in the worship of this saint, and the complex exchange relations that constitute the practices and daily and family life routines of its devotees (Kristensen 2015). Regnar Kristensen identifies the "familial character" of this saint, capable of assuming several roles in the family: child, sister, mother or godmother (*madrina*), soulmate, even wife. In order to overcome the simplifying binary distinction between the "evil" saint associated with criminals and the trend that seeks to "beautify" La Santa Muerte as a "good" spirit, Kristensen (2015, pp. 3–4) insists that her "ambiguities" be taken into account, for in the micro-social network of troubled families, she operates in ambiguous ways, providing (or expected to provide) both protection and punishment; solutions, but also revenge. In all these roles she appears as a clearly feminine figure, though one that defies the stereotype of the powerless, self-sacrificing (*abnegada*) housewife through an empowerment accorded to women as stalwarts who are responsible for "holding the family together."

Findings of this nature involve the "inner social world" of Santa Muerte devotion and provide invaluable anthropological knowledge that precludes simplifying and exoticizing projections. In contrast, an outward-looking approach like that proposed here focuses on La Santa Muerte as a spatial and visual experience. It is framed by three conceptual filters: an explicit interest in the *urban* (spatial, public) character and visibility of this saint, a focus on her specific visuality and semiotic implications, and an analytical awareness of competing social frames, semantizations, and imaginaries.[3]

To begin with the latter point: there is, of course, no way to simply approach and observe La Santa Muerte as such, one's mind blank, objectively recording pure, located interaction. Instead, and inevitably, our initial gaze, and that of all agents involved, is framed by current images and narratives circulated by the mass media, organized religion (with intentions all too clear), and state officials, perhaps even by social activists, all of whom relate La Santa Muerte, in one way or another, to spheres of illegality (drug dealing, narco-folklore, the protection of criminals) and—not the same thing—the macabre imagery of narco-Satanic rituals (necrological inclinations, cruelty, sadism) or supposed nihilism, a symptom of spiritual decline or loss of values, of a universe with inverted common or "natural" values. These narratives create an effect of Satanization, both literally and metaphorically. In visual representations (films, photographs), the fancily dressed skeleton that is La Santa Muerte often serves as a marker that "indicates a dangerous place" (Roush 2012, p. 185).

This pejorative stereotype coexists with another semantization, less stigmatizing but still simplifying, that of cultural continuity: La Santa Muerte's supposedly ancient, pre-Hispanic roots, opposed to Catholicism and vaguely associated with a sort of autochthonous resistance. In fact, what distinguishes

Mexican visual culture from others is a certain familiarity with skeletons and skulls due to their visualization and materialization in Mexican archaeology and the country's pre-Hispanic heritage (see also Flores Martos, this volume). But from a different perspective, the cult appears as a permanent, though discontinuous, blending of diverse cultural (re)sources, of high esoteric hybridity, not so much in terms of religious syncretism but of voracity, as Piotr Grzegorz Michalik (2011) puts it, a sort of strategic eclecticism that is penetrated by New Age semantics and commercialization with its inherent banalization.

Nevertheless, in my perspective, a closer reading and understanding of this voracious or "cannibal" cult cannot reduce La Santa Muerte to fragmentation, vulgarization, danger, or her supposed cultural autochthony. Instead we must focus, first of all, on her utility and meanings for a growing number of devotees who are searching not so much for origins but for social effects and functions. One crucial framing, related to a culture of illegality and growing insecurity, appears to be the notion of *amparo* (protection), as a counterpart to the notion of abandonment. Another key idea noted by scholars is this saint's particular effectiveness or efficacy in granting wishes or fulfilling specific desires: not so much promising miracles as performing favors (*paros*) in the context of a moral economy based on exchange and reciprocity, if you will, though not to the extreme of a purely material instrumentalism of giving and receiving (Michalik, 2011; Roush, 2009). So, which narratives of La Santa Muerte will allow us to provide a broader picture without reducing her inherent complexity?

A second filter relates to the aesthetic qualities of La Santa Muerte as spectacle, appreciated by literally looking at and capturing aspects both visual and material. This perspective focuses on visual strategies and (self-)representation based on the assumption that the *image* (materialized in statues and statuettes, depictions or pendants) and a specific setting or stage (a public service or an altar) play a constitutive role in her performative power and impact. What are the key elements of this spectacular visuality of La Santa Muerte and their relation to the social visibilization effect?

A third layer involves a special interest in urban landscapes and topographies, such as informal marketplaces, public squares, and chapels or other places of worship, which are appropriated, reconfigured, or created through cultural or religious practices and stagings. This perspective was conceptualized by the international, transdisciplinary research project Global Prayers: Redemption and Liberation in the City, which dealt with the emergence, incidence, and place-making capacities of new urban religiosities in Africa, Europe, Asia, and the Americas.[4] In order to explain my focus on the Santa Muerte phenomenon, it might be useful to present part of this initiative's conceptual framing. It set out from a conceptual "blind spot" in urban studies and theory, in both mainstream approaches and (post-)Marxist analyses, concerning the links between religious agencies and modern cities (Lanz, 2014, p. 21). Despite the undeniable empirical facticity of the decline of mainstream Catholicism and the boom of Pentecostal churches in Latin American and African megacities; the rise of Hindu nationalism in urban India; and the growing importance of religion for subaltern identities and politics in the Middle East, Africa, and the Americas, for a long time research in cities did not systematically incorporate religion as a factor in urban transformations.[5] And when scholars later began to tout the "return of the religious," it was often in association with fundamentalist threats and antiurban eruptions in formerly secular and potentially emancipatory urbanities, as Mike Davis (2006) suggests in *Planet of Slums*. According to Davis, when God disappeared from the industrial cities of the North, his resurrection was witnessed in the postindustrial megacities of the South, where religious agents are supplanting progressive movements by seducing and manipulating the urban poor.

Against this rather apocalyptic view, and the general assumption of urbanization as an inevitably secularizing process, the Global Prayers project worked from the assumption that the religious never actually disappeared from the city, for even in the most industrialized regions modern cities have always "served as laboratories for religious innovation," ranging from conservative charities to social gospel and Afro-American churches (Lanz, 2014, p. 19). Often conceived as a symptom of urban backwardness, urban religion is better considered a constitutive element and driving force of the—tangible and intangible—production and transformation of the everyday life of cities. One intellectual pioneer in postcolonial urban studies, Abdou Maliq Simone, strives to consider the yearning for "the miraculous" as a productive factor in the generation of social and urban spaces, since it facilitates "the possibility of those who have 'no part in anything' to become 'anyone at all'—that is, to come to the *stage*, be *visible* as an ordinary life in the city" (quoted in Lanz, 2014, p. 27, emphasis added).

Because the Global Prayers framework is interested in religious practice as *material* urban culture (B. Meyer, 2012), it focuses on material aspects, although it also ponders affective and sensorial forms, and spatial and social dimensions. This interwovenness demands expanded notions of methodology and research that incorporate not only ethnographic field research but also visual and artistic studies in order to open up the two channels considered crucial in the process of the construction of knowledge under conditions of complexity: first, reflections on subjectivity, the positioning of the gaze, epistemological attention, and points of view; and, second, the focus on what I call the "aesthetic interrogation of reality," which includes visuality and mediality, materiality and performativity.[6] In this way, cultural researchers and research-oriented artists approached a whole range of religion-related "urban imaginaries, infrastructures and materialities, cultures, politics and economies, forms of living and working, community formation, festival and celebration," all of which contribute to (re)production and urban life (Lanz, 2014, p. 25). A guiding hypothesis is that the religious and the urban are constantly interacting and mutually transforming each other. The city, a scene of/for unexpected experiences, otherness, conversions, and conflicts, not only offers a setting proper for religious experience but "belongs to the basic constituents from which such experiences . . . are generated" (Lanz, 2014, p. 29).

In this sense, emergent urban religiosities, conceptualized as "the practice of mediation between everyday life and spiritual experience," are, on the whole, neither fundamentalist nor emancipatory (Lanz, 2014, p. 42). Rather, they consist of an ambivalent and contradictory range of urban-religious configurations that involve the dynamics of conversion and (temporary or permanent) appropriations and sacralizations of secular structures or spaces (e.g., movie theaters, industrial architecture, public spaces), and the creation of new religious hot spots and pilgrimage destinations. Indeed, one witnesses the emergence of hybrid expressions of spiritual techniques of self-governance, a melting into urban youth and subcultures (e.g., evangelist funk in Rio de Janeiro, adolescents taking over burial rituals in Kinshasa, or youngsters converting traditional religious celebrations into rave-like techno parties in Mumbai). These new configurations may also take the form of "self-made religions," analogous to informal, self-made urbanism, akin to favelas and other informal settlements. Finally, there is the blurring between political and religious claims and practices, the public performance of a religious right to the city embodying new forms of citizenship and community, as practiced and demanded by political Islam in the streets of Tehran, or by urban movements supported by liberation theologians in the barrios and public places of Latin American megacities.

MEETING LA SANTA MUERTE

The encounter with La Santa Muerte that occurred during one of the two case studies I conducted—in Buenos Aires and Mexico City—was framed from the very beginning by these conceptualizations and assumptions.[7] The issues were what urban territorialities are produced and performed in the specific case of La Santa Muerte, and in what sense can the cult be considered a mediation between secular and religious authorities, or between urban life and spiritual needs. I addressed La Santa Muerte from a clear-cut urban studies perspective, even delimiting it spatially to a particular spot in Mexico's capital city: the Tepito neighborhood, where the figure of the saint "crossed our path"—without us looking for her—under circumstances that I shall now explain briefly.

Our starting point was not La Santa Muerte, but a more general research question concerning current religious preferences, practices, and beliefs among the urban poor in Latin America in the aftermath of liberation theology, which had once—from the late 1960s to the 1980s—played a significant role not only in rural areas but also in impoverished urban zones. So-called Third World priests (*sacerdotes para el Tercer Mundo*), of Marxist or Peronist inspiration, played a crucial role in the social organization and resistance of the urban poor during the military dictatorship in Argentina, especially in Buenos Aires, where the prominent liberation priest Padre Múgica engaged in the defense of one of the poorest inner-city enclaves before being murdered by a paramilitary commando unit in 1974.

In Mexico, with its peculiar form of sophisticated authoritarianism that draws on selective repression and co-optation, the "preferential option for the poor" came to mobilize around a hundred clergymen and a dozen bishops. In the poorer quarters of the Mexican capital, liberation priests supported urban popular movements in their struggles for land, urban infrastructure, and the legalization of informal settlements. They also founded cooperatives and hundreds of base communities (*comunidades de base*), thereby socializing and politicizing religious experience. This methodological innovation enabled a new kind of communitarian space that mediated between the inner life of individual believers and the public domain of society and the world of politics.

Ethnographic observation, a review of the literature, and interviews with experts in a dozen districts in Buenos Aires and Mexico City allowed us to trace the legacies of this socially engaged Catholicism against the background of the general decline of mainstream Catholicism, and to discover diverse responses to these changes. Without delving too deeply into the specific findings at the district level, it was interesting to note not only a conceptual diversification toward ecological, indigenous, or feminist theology combined with pastoral work with migrants or youth, but also a semantic shift in the agenda from the notion of oppression—as capitalist exploitation—toward that of repression by police and security forces, as well as the incorporation of concrete social work and a certain culturalist turn that often replaced existing political categories.[8]

Some priests lamented an individualistic turn in society and a general depoliticization promoted by the evangelical churches, which openly compete for the religious preferences of the poor. Others recognized the need to innovate and make the church more attractive and inclusive, especially for younger believers, while some even considered the possibility that they might learn something from the most popular Pentecostal formats, which are quickly gaining ground in Latin American cities, including Mexico City, especially due to their capacity to mediate between spiritual and material needs, and to incorporate emotions and pragmatism, in contrast to the more discourse-based spirituality of leftist Catholicism (Semán, 2004).

Clearly, contemporary urban religious landscapes offer a wide range of religious options, due to the diversification not only of Christian beliefs but also of popular saints. In the case of the well-dressed skeleton of La Santa Muerte, we find a figure that seems to compete, at first sight, with the widespread presence of two other leading ladies of Mexican popular culture: first, the Virgen de Guadalupe, the mestizo version of the Virgin Mary, an image omnipresent as a "secular saint" on nearly every corner of the megacity, a description often attributed to the late Carlos Monsiváis; and, second, doña Catrina, the deceased heroine of the annual Fiesta de los Muertos, less common but still a key figure in Mexico's visual canon and popular imagery.[9] According to the Mexican chronicler and expert on La Santa Muerte Alfonso Hernández, this feminized skeleton, often with colorfully decorated skulls, represents "the domesticated appearance of death," humanized and gendered; a figure—despite her inherent eroticism—suitable for family consumption (taken from Reyes Ruiz, 2010, p. 11). La Santa Muerte, in contrast, embodies the end of recognizable human features; she is beyond domestication, even beyond sexuality.

But how did this androgynous Santa Muerte become an urban saint? The first traces of Santa Muerte devotion in Mexico City date to the 1950s, although at that time she was kept and worshipped discreetly in living-room altars, a sort of spiritual family secret, sheltered from malicious gossip and misunderstandings. It was in the mid-1990s, during the economic crisis in Mexico known as the Tequila crash, that La Santa Muerte began to circulate more publicly, first appearing on religious stamps, badges, and pendants, and printed on T-shirts. Later, as anthropologists and other researchers have documented, her image began to spread massively in prisons and youth detention centers, where it had been present, rather latently, since the late 1970s. Jailed youngsters received her spiritual power from their older relatives, mostly mothers or grandmothers.[10] Indeed, it was largely in jails that the bizarre saint acquired her most persistent manifestation, as her image was often tattooed on bodies, emerging to compete openly with Catholic inscriptions (see also Perdigón & Robles, this volume). "For a long time, young males in prison would have the Virgen de Guadalupe tattooed on their backs because, obviously, no one would stab the Virgen," Laura Roush explains (personal communication, October 2010, April 2011). But with the growing crisis of insecurity in the 1990s, more and more prisoners had a Santa Muerte etched into their skin as well, "just to be sure."[11] These expressions gradually led to a perceptual shift as the image of death as a holy figure, long seen and in a sense tolerated as a sort of religious "misunderstanding" of the poor, became associated with conditions of illegality and criminality.

Going Public: The Tepito Stage

Informal structures, including religious ones, usually challenge statistical pretensions. José Gil Olmos (2010, p. 18) estimates that there are some 1,500 public and private shrines and altars in Mexico City, perhaps associated with an astonishing three to five million devotees. These figures are not necessarily farfetched, but it is hard to find reliable empirical evidence. Kristensen (2015, p. 8) offers a much more modest estimate; based on his survey of some three hundred sidewalk shrines in Mexico City's metropolitan area (in 2008), he estimates that at least thirty thousand devotees pray monthly in public spaces. According to these cartographies, the areas with the greatest presence of street altars also manifest a marked density of "legal trouble" (police, lawyers, courts, prisons) as well as informal and illicit economic activities. This urban configuration determines the "unpredictable" nature of power relations, especially within and around prisons, not only for inmates but also for their families (Kristensen, 2015, p. 11).

Whatever a realistic number of devotees may be, the most famous of all the Santa Muerte sanctuaries is, without doubt, located in the aforementioned barrio of Tepito, an urban territory characterized by a high degree of informality though at the same time one that is highly organized. While limited in terms of physical space (barely forty blocks with thirty to forty thousand residents), it is huge in terms of urban legends and mythology. The self-defined *barrio bravo* (fierce neighborhood), once made famous by anthropologist Oscar Lewis's study of Mexico's so-called culture of poverty and located less than one kilometer from the city's colonial center, constitutes an urban universe of its own, with various churches, two soccer fields, and a travel agency, the first in Mexico to specialize in trips to China.

Tepito's most distinctive and well-known feature is a huge open-air market that covers much of its topography and is considered one of the largest informal markets in Latin America. In more than eight thousand stalls distributed along thirty-five streets, literally everything is available: original and pirated merchandise (depending on the size of the customer's wallet), the latter including locally adapted brands such as Armandi and Versánchez. Informality there traces its roots back to the early twentieth century, and in the 1930s it was a red-light district that offered gambling and *pulque*, tobacco, and sexual services to the rest of the city. Later, local workshops (*talleres*) were established and a self-made economy arose, not entirely legal but a useful outlet for the booming capital city. This was considered Tepito's "golden era," as local crafts and recycling activities thrived and streets occasionally turned into dance floors and playgrounds for children. Urban celebrities had their boots and suits made there. Boundaries between the street and the yards of the *vecindades* (tenements) were blurred, creating a flourishing street and barrio culture, a perfect stage for cultural performances of all kinds.

Street trading from roofed stalls took up more and more space as all attempts at regulating it failed. Things began to change in the 1970s with the arrival of *fayuca*, goods smuggled in from all over the world that flooded local markets, pushing out local handicrafts. Tepito was soon a commercial center supplying contraband goods to the city. But the devastating earthquake of 1985 destroyed many talleres and colonial-era buildings, which were replaced by shoddy housing. At that point, pirated products provided lucrative sources of income, attracting people from all around the city. The barrio was invaded by new traders and economic agents. Current statistics suggest that only one-tenth of local street vendors actually live in Tepito.[12] Unsurprisingly, in the 1980s, along with fayuca, stolen goods and illegal drugs began to enter the district. Today the barrio is not only perceived but also experienced as a local hot spot for small-scale drug trafficking, and—as even the proudest *tepiteños* must admit—weapons are an everyday sight. Although its appearance and features have changed dramatically over recent decades, there is still a living myth of *cultura tepiteña* that defies the negative semantization of the barrio as a dangerous place and narco-barrio "populated by lower and alienated classes," as Wikipedia accurately sums up the dominant imaginary.[13]

The fact that Tepito has been associated with notions of cultural defiance is undoubtedly related to its recent cultural history. During the 1970s, when local culture still coexisted peacefully with the new contraband economy, Tepito was considered a fertile ground for all kinds of cultural and religious missionaries. Underground artists and art collectives, as well as base communities and liberation priests, all found their way into Tepito. Among them was a young clergyman from the United States named Frederick Loos, better known as Padre Federico, who ended up in Tepito more or less by chance in 1967 when, following the express wishes of the pope, recently ordained priests from the United States swarmed south of the border because, according to Rome, clergymen were in short supply there. This particular young American priest remained in Tepito—which he remembers as a "Mexican Harlem"—for seven years, becoming active as a social entrepreneur and setting up cooperatives, a district newspaper, and base communities (inspired by liberation theology), and working with local young people, the so-called *chavos banda*.[14] When interviewed in 2010, he recalled that his move in 1974 had been difficult for him, even though the evangelization of marginalized youth constituted the very spirit of liberation.[15]

Nowadays, hardly any traces of liberation theology remain. As in other Latin American megacities, religious life has diversified radically. Most popular among the more than sixty traders' associations in Tepito are Pentecostal churches, but there are also Catholic chapels, shrines devoted to the Virgen de Guadalupe, and *santeros*. Nevertheless, it was the presence of this young priest from Michigan that led to the unexpected encounter with La Santa Muerte.

According to a well-known and widespread local legend, the (literal) coming out of La Santa Muerte occurred one day in September 2001. A local trader, Enriqueta Romero, known as doña Queta, who had worshipped La Santa Muerte for decades within the confines of her home, received a life-size figure from one of her sons, which she immediately placed at the entrance to her home, visible and accessible to fellow believers. This act initiated a spontaneous street ritual and public place of worship *en crescendo*. At first, mainly fellow devotees from the neighborhood met there, laying down flowers and votive candles. Later, believers from farther away began traveling to this sidewalk altar in Tepito. Then Queta decided to invite devotees to celebrate the Day of the Dead (Día de Muertos) on October 31, and that festive occasion established her altar as a street sanctuary.[16] Ever since, celebrations have been held on the first day of every month, as people gather for a rather freely adapted rosary service held before the sidewalk altar at the entrance to doña Queta's home and led by a member of the Romero family. Every October 31 — the day considered the saint's anniversary — the congregation bursts into an enormous "birthday" celebration. It was in 2010 that we first witnessed La Santa Muerte as a collective street performance.

Some Clues for a Reading

As mentioned above, the objective of my research project was to incorporate an aesthetic interrogation of this field that focused on its visual, performative, and media-related features. This required both a self-reflexive attitude and the possibility of dealing with narratives not necessarily purely textual in nature. To better understand the traces of "liberation spirits" in Latin American megacities, photographers joined our field explorations and turned — in the case of my own "taking pictures" — to the use of photography as an observational device.[17] This visual approach, together with my ethnographic presence, conversational interaction, and archival research, facilitated the identification of significant visual and spatial markers and constellations by producing images that may be connected, in analytic readings, to circulating imaginaries and discourses. On the other hand, photography allowed — even obliged — us to reflect on our (visual) subjectivity; that is, "to map our reflexive engagement with the research field," including questions of point of view, expectations, affective dispositions, proximity, and distance (Emmel & Clark, 2011).[18]

More than a conclusive reading, the following paragraphs present a loosely tied series of field observations with some initial readings, the first results of what I like to call "associative research," consisting of the free (but by no means arbitrary) association of visual, spatial, corporal, and affective observations and "qualitative data." It is not meant to be an exhaustive ethnography but hopefully will point out some of what Michael Agar (2006, p. 64) calls "rich points," understood as the "raw material of ethnographic research" and a "signal of a difference between what you know and what you need to learn to understand."

As a starting point, it might be useful to recall the remarkable gap between

FIGURE 4.1 Young woman with Santa Muerte statuette, Tepito neighborhood, Mexico City, March 2013. Photograph by Anne Huffschmid.

FIGURE 4.2 Young man with Santa Muerte statuette, Tepito neighborhood, Mexico City, November 2010. Photograph by Anne Huffschmid.

FIGURE 4.3 Enriqueta Romero in front of her Santa Muerte shrine, Tepito neighborhood, Mexico City, March 2013. Photograph by Anne Huffschmid.

FIGURE 4.4 (*left*) "Coordinator of La Santa Muerte" during monthly rosary, Tepito neighborhood, Mexico City, March 2013. Photograph by Anne Huffschmid.

FIGURE 4.5 (*right*) Tattoo of church in flames on lower leg of young male Santa Muerte devotee, Tepito neighborhood, Mexico City, November 2010. Photograph by Anne Huffschmid.

FIGURE 4.6 Group of Santa Muerte statuettes, Tepito neighborhood, Mexico City, November 2010. Photograph by Anne Huffschmid.

media images of La Santa Muerte as an exotic, somewhat gruesome mass performance by criminal or even diabolic forces that, despite our pretensions to anthropological objectivity, configured our expectations and what we experienced in situ. What we saw, lived, and recorded during these gatherings, and what we learned from (visual) field notes and photographs, in no way corresponded to the dominant media images of a frightening underground aesthetics.[19] Therefore, I think it is useful to propose a conceptual difference between visuality, sometimes conceptualized as hypervisuality (meaning the saturation of media images in the digital universe), and visibility, that is, the "visual construction" of social existence.

Hypervisibility

What we witnessed and experienced was a carefully prepared, public staging performed proudly by individuals clearly aware of the fact that they were being observed, with a perceptible need and longing to celebrate and share their devotion with fellow believers and to exhibit this shared devotion in front

FIGURE 4.7. (*left*) Tattoo of Santa Muerte with scythe on back of young female devotee, Tepito neighborhood, Mexico City, November 2010. Photograph by Anne Huffschmid.

FIGURE 4.8 (*right*) Enriqueta Romero touching glass case of her Santa Muerte statuette during "chain of force" ritual, Tepito neighborhood, Mexico City, November 2010. Photograph by Anne Huffschmid.

FIGURE 4.9 Young woman with small Santa Muerte statuette, Tepito neighborhood, Mexico City, November 2010. Photograph by Anne Huffschmid.

FIGURE 4.10 (*left*) Boy with elaborate Santa Muerte image, Tepito neighborhood, Mexico City, November 2010. Photograph by Anne Huffschmid.

FIGURE 4.11 (*right*) Girl with small Santa Muerte statuette, Tepito neighborhood, Mexico City, November 2010. Photograph by Anne Huffschmid.

of others, visitors and outsiders alike, including journalists and anthropologists. The congregation emanated an amazingly peaceful mood, a cheerful atmosphere like that of a street festival where strangers do not feel out of place but are welcomed into a scenario of bizarre figures and outfits mixed with friendly faces. In general, their behavior was considerate and respectful. There was nothing morbid in the air; at most, a floating existentialist melancholy.

The "bizarreness" consists in the superimposition of signs and layers of various visual codes and cultural or aesthetic repertoires, including pre-Hispanic iconographies, urban subcultures, and globalized repertoires, with repeated motifs such as a scythe and globe, a clock, and a set of scales. What might be conceived as a religious palimpsest is the overlap with Catholic liturgy: the rosary and Lord's Prayer, the sign of the cross and blessings, the gesture of moistening the statue's mouth with "holy water"—on this occasion replaced by mezcal—and the format of the religious procession itself, with some pilgrims sliding toward their saint on their knees, at least over the last few meters. In addition, there are elements borrowed from other creeds, the charismatics' "chain of energy" for instance, or pre-Hispanic incense used for spiritual cleansing replaced, in this urbanized version, by cigar smoke that envelopes the statuettes.

There is an astonishing presence of family groups: father, mother, children of all ages, little boys and girls flitting through the crowd on their own, seriously involved in Santa Muerte rituals, holding mezcal bottles or cigars, and posing for visitors with their depictions of La Santa, holding skeleton women up to the cameras as if fulfilling a mission.

Among and in addition to individuals who might be categorized at first sight as belonging to "subcultural" or underground groups, their bodies densely tattooed and shaped by somewhat out-of-the-ordinary or otherwise conspicuous aesthetics, was the notable presence and participation of men and women with no visible eccentric features; one would vaguely consider them lower-middle class, clearly not spectators, but active participants. The negative publicity, media reports, and official warnings about the supposed "satanic" activities of devotees, far from diminishing the cult's popularity, are likely to have propitiated its public defense, even by people who up to then had worshipped the saint in private but who now go into the streets in growing numbers: "Families who had previously never taken their icons out of their homes felt the time had come to stand for their reputation" (Roush, 2012, p. 186; Roush 2009). Observations of the Tepito congregation suggest that participants are staging some kind of counterperformance, based on a strategy of visual excess, or transgression, to confront stigmatization and diabolic visual semantization. They display themselves, posing before eyes and cameras with a defying self-consciousness of constituting a—however temporary—community, devoted not only to La Santa Muerte but also to each other, with nothing to hide. This notion of "nothing to hide" was strengthened by the decision to move the entire ceremony, which until a few years ago took place close to midnight, to the afternoon hours, celebrated in full daylight, accessible to families, literally lightening up the image.

Regulation, Spiritual Exchange, Community Building

It is a widespread and accurate observation that Santa Muerte devotion has no formalized rules or liturgy, no recognized authorities or obligatory canon. But as we know from studies on urban informality in relation to housing or commerce, informal arrangements by no means imply a lack of regulation or organization.[20] On the contrary, most such activities are highly organized and regulated, just not by law or statute. And nowhere is this more evident than at the Tepito sanctuary, an informal place of worship but one configured by a series of effective rules and norms. For example, in what she considers "her" territory, doña Queta does not tolerate any Santería, that is, witchcraft or healers. As she explained, this is to avoid potential confusion with black magic. Nor does she allow excessive dancing on "her" street corner, or any commercial trading (the only exception being her own small family-run shop, which offers devotional articles). This is why, despite the market-like atmosphere, none of the objects—amulets and bracelets, pictures, and candy—that people carry on their bodies or use to adorn their altars, are actually for sale. Booths with such merchandise are set up at a certain distance, beyond the spatially delimited celebration area. Within this range, there are no sales, only ongoing exchanges of small devotional objects from hand to hand or basket to basket. These exchange practices constitute a sort of spiritual gray area that Barbara Rühling (2013, pp. 43–45) calls an "ambulant cult," since it is situated in the broader gray area of informal or street trading in the Tepito market.[21] During these festivities, a part of Tepito's informal market territory is transformed into an informal sanctuary, focused not primarily on economic activities but on symbolic values and economies. It is not only the exchange of material gifts but also "shared worries" that constitute this "relational space" (Roush, 2012, p. 186).

With respect to spatial regulation, several men wearing T-shirts with the inscription *Coordinador* (Coordinator) *de la Santa Muerte* may ask believers to walk a little faster or stand in the correct line. This carefully employed coordination of behavior is accompanied by a certain degree of tolerance of transgressions of official regulations: for example, public consumption of alcoholic drinks, which is strictly prohibited in Mexico City, and the unmistakable smell of marijuana filling the air. But there were no hard drugs or police in sight, giving the appearance of a zone of tolerated self-regulation.

Despite the obvious centrality of Queta's figure of La Santa Muerte, an interesting process of decentralization is taking place. The ritual is clearly not only about this queen- or mother-like skeleton in Queta's showcase but about all figures and depictions, of all sizes and appearances, that devotees bring from their private homes to display on the street so that they may be "recharged" with the energies emanating from the main figure. They carry them in bags and rucksacks, close to the body, even cradled in their arms, arranging their richly adorned saints carefully on the pavement, one next to the other, in a friendly, never hostile competition to determine the "most beautiful one in town." At the end of each ceremony, everyone is asked to hold up his or her figure in the air, "the moment when they are most conscious of being photographed and filmed," not just the spiritual climax but a moment of maximum visibility (Roush, 2012, p. 186).

Here, the boundaries between the intimate and the public, the individual and the socialized, are blurred. During the service, most participants are in a visibly introspective mood (marked by closed eyes, for instance) as they cultivate their own spiritual transaction with the Santa, implore favors (*favores* or *paros*), or make pledges (*mandas*) that are fulfilled as a sign of gratitude. At the same time, the gathering produces a temporary and precarious sense of spiritual bonding, an acting out and exposing of collective emotion. Toward the end of each service, the notion of connection materializes as all those present hold hands as a voice comes through the loudspeaker beseeching them not to break the *cadena de fuerza*, the energy chain. Finally, everyone stands for several minutes, eyes firmly shut, hand in hand with relatives and strangers.

Religious Rivalry

It may come as no surprise that this new cult, which openly appropriates and adapts Catholic liturgy to a "heretical" ritual, is perceived by institutionalized Catholicism as competition. In addition to nationwide ecclesiastical campaigns warning of supposed religious alienation, some years ago local church authorities adopted an offensive strategy in Tepito by erecting a small chapel devoted to the Virgen de Guadalupe, the principal figure of popular Catholicism, right across the street from doña Queta's shrine. But what began as a spiritual challenge ended up in a rather peaceful coexistence, as many devotees of the Santa do not turn their backs on the Virgin and take care not to defy essential elements of the Catholic faith in their own adapted liturgy. They insist that Jesus remains the highest authority, while La Santa Muerte is primarily a mediator. The prayer leaders at the monthly ceremony are deliberately not called "priests" and avoid the expression "(Holy) Mass," claiming their service to be a rosary. "Somos católicos pero de otro modo" (We are Catholics but in a different way), one older woman explained.

The strategy of downplaying the cult's anti-Catholic potential so as not to defy ecclesiastical authorities is accompanied by a more aggressive subtext: that of a "war of cultures and religions," as one young man commented while proudly pointing to his lower leg, tattooed with an image of a church in flames. During this interesting encounter, the young man amicably invited me to visit his personal Santa Muerte, which turned out to be a small figure decked out in Aztec-style feathered ornaments, a colorful poncho with black veil, countless necklaces, miniature knives, and even a small Virgin around her neck. Clearly, an "awareness" of the many roots of Mexican culture was important to this young believer, as he confirmed. In our conversation, twenty-six-year-old Jorge told me about his daily life as a shop owner at the other end of the city, how he tries to come here every month, on occasion bringing his young son. What most attracts him to La Santa Muerte is her lack of prejudice and her impartiality. "Whatever I do, she will always give me her blessing," he said. "Even if you commit a crime?" I asked, "even a murder?" "Even then," he responded, smiling, "even then La Santa Muerte will hold her hand over me to protect me. *La Santa no me juzga*" (She does not judge me).

This absence of judgmentalism is likely one of the core elements of the saint's attraction for urban devotees: her unconditional accessibility. Unlike at Pentecostal churches, here there is no need for purification before acceptance; all manner of sinners are welcome; no one has to renounce anything, swear loyalty, or promise exclusivity. La Santa Muerte is more generous than others and provides protection "from dangers [devotees] cannot discuss with priests" (Roush, 2012, p. 183). Whereas the Virgen de Guadalupe is expected to perform miracles, La Santa Muerte is more "down-to-earth," concerned with providing solutions to everyday problems. As stated above, these are not limited to purely material issues but include, in times of "shared worries," the need and yearning for consolation and forgiveness.

OPENING-UP: A SAINT FOR
THE TROUBLED AND TRAUMATIZED?

It is interesting to note that during the monthly Tepito celebration, followers dedicate their prayers to a wide range of *absent* people—the sick or drug addicts, migrant workers in far-off places, fugitives, and, of course, those in prison. I argue that it is precisely this connectivity between those who are "different" (from dominant or mainstream social norms, although pluriform among themselves), who share a variety of more or less "extreme" troubles but one expression of "extreme" faith, and its constant crossing of the boundaries between the sacred and the secular, the private and public, that constitutes La Santa Muerte's genuinely urban character.

Kristensen (2015, p. 22) stresses the communitarian character of La Santa Muerte on the level of the family network as core community: "La Santa Muerte becomes the iconic representation of the ambiguous Mexican family, with no clear distinction between good and evil, formal and informal, love and hate" (see also Kristensen, this volume). I would suggest expanding this metaphor of a complex, troubled family to a broader urban community, one by no means stable or closed, not similar to a sect or church but based on a sense of union and togetherness that, while ephemeral and noninstitutionalized, is effective. It may not be sufficient to attain religious *communitas*, but it does make for a "temporary emotional space" (L. Roush, personal communication, October 2010).

In addition to, and inspired by, the notion of the production of religious space, there is an obvious place-making quality to this public staging of La Santa Muerte. It involves creating both a concrete pilgrimage destination and a spatial productivity in a broader sense, whereby the temporary sacralization of the street, as the urban stage par excellence, and the coming together as spatial, corporal, social, and devotional practices and experiences, seek to alleviate the existential tensions of the lives of the unprotected. This temporary community invoked by La Santa Muerte might be considered a collective longing for relief, or at least containment, for those constantly troubled (by legal persecution, for instance) or traumatized (by sudden losses), but also for those who find themselves burdened by increasing social and economic pressure. At this point, we must widen our focus beyond Tepito, even beyond the boundaries of the Mexican capital. "The troubled" are no longer located only on the spatial or social margins of formal society, that is, the most visibly excluded (imprisoned drug dealers or consumers, sex workers, or criminals). Rather, ordinary people from all layers of society, though mostly the floating middle classes, also feel increasingly betrayed by church and state authorities and equally threatened by the specter of ending up in dire straits. Therefore, in general terms, the cult to La Santa Muerte can certainly be read as a symptom—a condition shared with booming Pentecostal churches and other congregations—of Catholicism's growing loss of cohesive power and popularity and, especially, of how the official church is shrinking as an "option for the poor," a tendency that might eventually be slowed by Pope Francis. More specifically, when understood as a mediator between everyday life and religiosity, a kind of spiritual troubleshooter, La Santa Muerte might be read as a symptom of the precariousness and growing informality of economic and social conditions in Mexico, in the face of reduced state welfare benefits, the widening exclusion of people, and a generalized sense of a lack of protection amid Mexico's current humanitarian crisis.

Understanding La Santa Muerte as cultural and urban practice thus far transcends the image and imaginary of the stereotyped narco-saint. Nor is it just another folk saint emerged from Mexico's long, rich tradition of autochthonous saints, or, as a more benevolent reading might suggest, a reincarnation of liberation spirits as patron saints who care—or fight—for the urban poor in this precarious modernity. These instant spiritual communities and their specific social visibility do not fit the language or rhetoric of politics, much less those of revolution or the logic of collective action or social movements. But they can and should be read as one of many responses to the perception of crisis, insecurity, spreading violence, and collapsing institutions (family, church, state).

So this is not about good or evil, as not even protection is necessarily to be seen as a valuable social good in and of itself, for it depends on who is seeking protection and from whom or what, like, to give but one example, hardened criminals invoking immunity. To understand the specific attraction of La Santa Muerte in its broader context requires focusing on the visual, performative, and spatial strategies that devotees mobilize to confront what they perceive as the existential fragility of their troubled lives. The notion of insecurity or trouble can no longer be limited to marginal or separate spaces or territories (such as prisons or marginalized neighborhoods), but has become a generalized, vital experience of despair and vulnerability. To confront this perception of losing control over one's life, the nonface of death, materialized and familiarized though still ambiguous, might seem the perfect ally.

NOTES

1. For a reading of femicide as communication and spectacle, see the analysis by Rita Segato (2007); also, Mariana Berlanga (2015).

2. A new research project I am exploring examines forensic anthropology as a form of cultural and social intervention in different scenarios of violence.

3. I refer to "imaginary" in the sense developed by Latin American anthropology, especially related to urban imaginaries, conceived as a collective imagination that articulates social desires and subjectivities, discourses, and narratives and that has a direct impact on the social tissue and behavior. For more detail, see Huffschmid (2012b) and the volume edited by Abilio Vergara Figueroa (2001).

4. Global Prayers (2009–2014) consisted of a network of academic and artistic field studies conducted in more than a dozen cities around the world using an experimental comparative strategy and step-by-step conceptualization. It was begun by metroZones, a Berlin-based independent center for urban research

(metroZones.info), and conducted in collaboration with a wide variety of universities and cultural institutions. For more details, see the website globalprayers.info and three edited volumes: *Urban Prayers: Neue religiöse Bewegungen in der globalen Stadt* (metroZones, 2011); *Faith is the Place: The Urban Cultures of Global Prayers* (metroZones, 2012); and *Global Prayers: Contemporary Manifestations of the Religious in the City* (Becker et al., 2014).

5. On the general decline of the popularity of Catholicism and the rise of evangelical cults, see, among others, Pablo Semán on the Latin American poor (2004).

6. See Huffschmid (2012a, p. 165) for an understanding of research as a constant "procedure of exploration and discoveries . . . between knowing and not-knowing."

7. In both cities, the study was conducted by a small research team consisting of a local researcher, myself, and a visual artist or photographer; the team in Mexico City was accompanied by a local photographer, Frida Hartz.

8. For a more detailed report on the outcome of this research, see Huffschmid (2012b, 2014).

9. On the debate on images of death in Mexico as a national and global cultural heritage, see Flores Martos (2008a).

10. See also the reference to the video installed by the Argentine visual artist Lia Dansker (2012), who examines the precarious presence of La Santa Muerte in prison and how young male inmates revere her.

11. Concerning the urban manifestation and spatial connection among prisons as devotional hot spots, and the material urban presence of La Santa Muerte, Regnar Kristensen (2015, p. 11) identifies a significant overlapping of the increasing prison population, the urban areas where inmates' relatives/families reside, and the proliferation of public street altars or street rosaries since around 2005.

12. Like other assessments and estimates concerning the life and history of this barrio, these stem from conversations and visits with local experts Alfonso Hernández and writer Primo Mendoza in 2009 and 2010. See also the chronicles by Mendoza (2009) and the numerous essays and contributions by Hernández, director of the local Centro de Estudios Tepiteños (CETEPI), published at www.tepiscompany.blogspot.mx.

13. Consult https://en.wikipedia.org/wiki/Tepito. One example of the cultural vitality and attraction of the barrio is the interactive theater play *Safari in Tepito*, developed in 2015 by the Mexican actor Daniel Giménez Cacho in collaboration with residents of Tepito, as a mobile theatrical exploration of Tepito culture in situ; see http://www.cultura.df.gob.mx/index.php/component/eventlist/details/15390-safarientepito.

14. Some years after his Tepito experience, Loos translated episodes of the Bible into the subcultural code of Mexican youth culture (*episodeo del evangelio con sabor*

a banda), with Jesus represented as the *jefe machín* (macho boss). Loos was one of the rare representatives of liberation theology who engaged deeply with youth subculture and also with new popular religiosities, such as the San Judas Tadeo cult in Mexico City. See also http://www.vice.com/es_mx/video/el-evangelio-para-la-banda-frederick-loos.

15. At the time of the interview, the retired priest lived a secluded life in the countryside outside Mexico City.

16. With respect to the date of the Day of the Dead, Stanley Brandes (2006, p. 6) has stated that "in colloquial speech it has come to denote not only November 2, but also, and more usually, the entire period from October 31 through November 2."

17. For a reflection on visual research related to intangible topics such as faith and memory, see Huffschmid (2012a).

18. In my recent monograph *Risse im Raum*, I propose a tentative list of what I consider photography's genuine potential and contribution to cultural and social research: to record field density, capture simultaneity, focus on spatiality, reconstruct gazes and (the affective quality of) encounters, edit visual narratives, and reflect on research expectations and, most importantly, the limits of what can be seen—the blind spots and the invisibilized (Huffschmid, 2015, pp. 410–26).

19. This chapter is accompanied by a selection of my own photographs. The photographs taken by Frida Hartz are published in Anne Huffschmid and Ingrid Spiller (2011) and are accessible online at http://issuu.com/globalprayers/docs/mirar_creer/1?e=0.

20. For an anthropological study of informal regulation in Mexico City, see Emilio Duhau and Angela Giglia (2008).

21. Another interesting analogy drawn by this author involves the patronage relations between street traders and their respective leaders and those between believers and La Santa Muerte, who is interpreted as a kind of spiritual broker (Rühling, 2013, pp. 46ff.).

REGNAR KRISTENSEN

5 | # Moving In and Moving Out
On Exchange and Family
in the Cult of La Santa Muerte

INTRODUCTION

Since the turn of the twenty-first century, the cult of La Santa Muerte has grown rapidly in Mexico and the United States. Today, tens of thousands of people share a somehow uniform approach to La Santa Muerte. They widely agree on approaching death, in the form of a generous Catholic-like saint, through popular forms of vows (in Spanish called *mandas*), by attending public rosaries and Masses at street altars, and by constructing and maintaining home altars. But how did this worship take these largely popular Catholic approaches to saints and combine them in a mostly uniform body of religious practice? And why has the cult not yet developed into an organized congregation with a central authority and approved doctrines, given that so many regularly meet and worship the same image in similar ways?

In this chapter, I tap into the popular Catholic nature of the cult and explore the whys and wherefores of this religious uniformity and lack of organizational coherence from the *inside*. Instead of confirming the common tale among devotees that images of La Santa Muerte were brought out of the cupboard and into the street in 2001 after decades in hiding, I argue that the popular image of her instead moved simultaneously *out* into the streets and *into* devotees' homes. This exploration is principally ethnographically driven but draws also on classic and newer anthropological research on exchange (Sahlins, 1974; Lomnitz, 2005b; Graeber, 2011) and popular Catholicism (Foster, 1979; Gudeman, 1988; Coleman & Eade, 2004; Mayblin, 2010; Lebner, 2012; Bandak, 2017).[1] The main finding of this exploration is that the dyadic exchanges between devotees and saints, practiced throughout Latin America in popular Catholicism, have developed into an unusually strong family commitment within this cult.

I suggest that this popular Catholic "socialization" of the saint into the family has also extended to the organization of the cult, distinguishing it from other saint cults. The familial form that devotees have built their centers of worship on also entails family conflicts that split these centers continuously, only to blossom into similar centers of worship elsewhere.

By focusing on the cultural dynamics of this familial "moving in and out," I add a layer to the studies on La Santa Muerte, which have thus far mainly focused on the historical and social topographies and motivations of the people attracted to this saint (Lomnitz, 2005a; Fragoso, 2007a; Flores Martos, 2007, 2008b; Chesnut, 2012b; Roush, 2014; Martín, 2014; Kristensen, 2015). These scholars, myself included, normally end by connecting the cult's current success to the darker sides of neoliberal capital flows and dysfunctional state practices in Mexico. Rising corruption and violence, the worsening of prison conditions, and the increasing dispossession of larger groups of people doubtless give perfect meaning to the cult's rapid growth. While there is much evidence pointing in this direction, I find that the shared hardship of the common devotee does not fully grasp the cultural dynamic of the cult. Nor does an analysis of neoliberal constraints give us an exhaustive insight into why the devotion conserves its rather stable practices despite lacking central institutions. To grasp the special organizational economy at stake in this cult, I find it useful to reverse the analytical flow and start by analyzing the intimacy of the devotional units.

THE TWO COMPETING SHRINES

This anthropological exploration of the cult begins at the turn of this century, when a series of street altars to La Santa Muerte began to pop up in greater numbers in Mexico City.[2] At that time, two distinct places of religious worship for La Santa Muerte started to attract the attention of budding devotees. Each of these places of worship became, in its own right, a favorite of both scholars and journalists. One was that of padre or Monseñor David Romo Guillen, head of the independent church Iglesia Católica Apostólica Tradicional México–Estados Unidos. In addition to accepting this saint in his parish, David Romo was well known for a long series of provocations of both politicians and church leaders from 2003 until his arrest in 2011, when he was sentenced to twelve years of imprisonment for participating in a kidnapping ring. Another of the journalists' and scholars' darlings was, and still is, the emblematic Enriqueta

Romero, former street vender of quesadillas widely known as doña Queta. She is the head of the main street altar to La Santa Muerte, erected in Alfarería Street in Tepito, a short distance from Romo's independent church. She was the first to arrange street rosaries to La Santa Muerte and is seen by many as being opposed to the more boisterous and self-asserting Romo. Unlike him, she denies her own importance to the cult ("soy una devota más"). Her image as a stern, fighting mother, grandmother, and great-grandmother has turned her into an exemplary follower of La Santa Muerte for many devotees.

The tone between the two leaders has often been described as antagonistic, and doña Queta and David Romo have collaborated in this perception by talking badly of each other (Chesnut, 2012b; Martín, 2014). What few know is that Romo and doña Queta started the street ceremonies together in October 2001 only to split shortly after and continue separately. Doña Queta's street altar was, from the beginning, the more popular of the two, yet for the first couple of years there was little difference in the numbers of devotees passing by. That changed gradually over the next few years. By 2005, doña Queta's altar was attracting thousands while Romo's was attracting hundreds. Doña Queta's uphill and Romo's downhill move accelerated further in 2006 when Romo decided to change the church's skeleton image of La Santa Muerte for a mannequin named the Angel of Death (Ángel de la Muerte). By the time Romo was arrested in 2011, little remained of his or his church's former powers of convocation. Numbers of devotees would, however, be too simple a measure of their respective influence over the cult's development. I shall therefore tap into the history of the people who provided the religious ceremonies at the street altars in Mexico City and the neighboring city of Puebla. Specifically, this involves a select group of fifteen to twenty people who have had a major influence over the devotion and who still do.

Doña Queta has never wanted to tell me why she invited David Romo to conduct a religious ceremony in the street in front of her newly erected altar in autumn 2001. My guess is that she thought he would be the correct person to conduct such a ceremony, being a Catholic priest and knowing that he accepted the devotion in his parish.[3] This collaboration lasted no more than a few months before she dismissed him, apparently because he wished to ask the growing number of devotees for their cooperation in constructing a basilica to La Santa Muerte. Doña Queta has since mentioned that she did not believe that La Santa Muerte had come to Romo in a dream to request he construct such a basilica. Controversially, she claims that if La Santa Muerte had wanted such a thing, she could have told her directly and not Romo. The consequence of this clash was that she then invited a dentist, Jurek Páramo, to conduct the street ceremonies. Much points to the fact that Jurek reconstructed the ceremony's liturgy during 2002, building it up in the Catholic rosary form. He wrote the current prayers and the five mysteries that are read aloud between the Our Fathers and Hail Marys. Doña Queta's affiliation with him was more lasting, but, in the summer of 2004, it broke down, and she invited instead a shoemaker and street vendor, Jessie Ortiz, to take over the ceremonies. This time, the collaboration lasted nearly three years before Jessie was forced to serve time in jail; doña Queta then persuaded a former inmate, Chucho, to continue. As of December 2015, Chucho was still in charge of the rosaries, which have changed little since Jurek initiated them.

Alongside guiding the main ceremony in Alfarería, David, Jurek, Jessie, and Chucho began to offer religious street services for families who were erecting new street altars. David Romo was the first and keenest to take advantage of this opportunity "to enhance the Christian evangelistic work," as he told me when we first met in November 2002. He had been experimenting with transforming rosaries and religious services inside his church for some time, including prayers to La Santa Muerte during Mass. Now, realizing the potential of moving the evangelizing work out into the streets, he started to promote the rather unusual practice of providing Catholic Masses in the streets. He quickly involved half a dozen of the parish's priests in order to keep up with demand. Soon, nearly all new street altars erected to La Santa Muerte in Mexico City offered regular religious street services to the public. Clerics from Romo's church led most of them. Only Jurek and Jessie (the latter from autumn 2004 on) offered an alternative to his church's ceremony during the first years of the cult's public life, apart from the more occult rites of magic that devotees had practiced clandestinely for decades. With time, people began to copy and conduct the street services themselves. In my census in 2008, a little less than one-third of the street ceremonies in Mexico City and Puebla had connections to Alfarería (Jurek, Jessie, and Chucho), a little more than a third had connections to Romo's church (Victor, Noé, Juan, Carlos, and others), and the last third were carried out independently by locals, largely copying the previous two.[4]

Whereas the street ceremonies moved the devotion into the streets and made it public, Romo also started another distinct tradition in 2002 aimed at promoting the cult inside people's homes. He circulated six pilgrim saints who shared many aspects with the Catholic cult of Niñopa in Xochimilco.

The traditions surrounding the *santo niño peregrino* in Xochimilco date back centuries and consist roughly of passing an image of the Jesus child around among private homes, changing families every year. The selected families take care of the image. They accommodate the image in its own room, give it clothes and toys, and talk and pray to it. This culminates in the host family (*mayordomía*) being changed at the yearly Fiesta de la Candelaría (February 2). The six pilgrim saints Romo put into circulation followed many of these traits. The host families provided their pilgrim saint with a space, dressed it, talked to it, and prayed a rosary for it every night for nine nights. When the family's turn came at an end, a new host family would come to the old host family's house, together with a cleric from Romo's parish, who gave a Mass before handing over the pilgrim saint. Romo considerably sped up the process compared with the traditions around Niñopa. Instead of changing a single pilgrim saint's host family once a year, the six images of La Santa Muerte changed host family every nine days. To facilitate this speedy process, Romo designated *mayordomos* (Gabriela, Guadalupe, George, and others) to each of the pilgrim saints. These were trusted devotees from his church who helped him find new host families. These mayordomos prayed with the families and often participated in the final ceremonies given by the priests.

The growing interest in both home and street altars to La Santa Muerte was also reflected in popular magazines published over these years. In 2003, two competing magazines (*La Santísima* and *Devoción a La Santa Muerte*) began to publish fortnightly on La Santa Muerte. They were displayed next to other popular religious magazines in newsstands across Mexico City. *La Santísima* quickly lost the competition to *Devoción a La Santa Muerte*, perhaps because it focused more narrowly, as did most popular religious magazines, on "professionals" (*curanderos* and shamans) interpreting the paranormal phenomena people had experienced. The journalists and photographer who produced the articles in *Devoción a La Santa Muerte* broke with this quasi-professionalism, since they were from the beginning aware of the cult's intimate connection with people's altars.[5] They gave more importance to people's own appropriation of the images in the newly erected street altars. And they visited large numbers of devotees in their homes, took photos of their altars, and interviewed them. This lent a nonprofessional structure to the articles, in which devotees first described how they came to know La Santa Muerte (how they met her, what favors she granted them); what their altars consisted of (the meaning of the shape, colors, and accessories of the figures); and what their caretakers did to please their *santas* (offerings, rituals, prayers, music, food, or whatever they found she liked most).

When I interviewed the journalists and photographer in 2006, they told me that they were constantly being asked to include more information on devotees' altars, despite the fact that this was already primarily what they focused on.[6] They also commented that devotees often copied the approaches toward this saint described in their articles (thereby mimicking others). Two years later, one of the journalists complained about the magazine's editorial line demanding that all stories have a positive tone, preventing him from following up on his desire to visit jails and interview inmates. This positive angle was not a coincidence but a clever strategy by the editors; it was also my experience that devotees preferred to read the "positive" information provided by fellow devotees rather than negative stories about how someone had been harmed. The novelty of the rapidly growing cult was, at this stage, not the image's darker powers but her "saintly" ones.[7] By 2013, the demand for this kind of information seemed to have peaked. Originally published fortnightly, *Devoción a La Santa Muerte* was now only published once a month. This decline in popularity may reflect the fact that information on how to make La Santa Muerte a home (and feel at home) was now more accessible. It might also be related to the fact that the two journalists and photographer left the magazine to pursue other goals.

Whatever the reason, faith in La Santa Muerte and the devotion's connection to street and home altars had by 2005 already been established as a crucial feature of the cult's modus operandi. David Romo's attempt to build up a central organization for the cult failed, however. His pilgrim saints stopped circulating in 2005–2006, and almost all of the collaborating priests and mayordomos left his church during these years. Many started their own centers of worship. Most notable was the separation of Señora Blanca and the mayordomo Martín George Quijano. They established a far-reaching center of worship just some blocks away from Romo's. Some have argued that the change Romo made to La Santa Muerte's image in 2006 was his primary mistake (Martín, 2014; Roush, 2014). This probably did alienate him further from the common devotee; however, his church had already lost its attraction for many even before this change of image. Most devotees simply started out on their own. But what did they take with them?

THE MASS AND THE ROSARY
TO LA SANTA MUERTE

Despite the fact that David Romo's church was not recognized by the Roman Catholic Church, he did largely follow the order of a Catholic Mass in his parish, starting with the introductory rites, followed by the liturgy of the Word, the liturgy of the Eucharist, the communion rites, and, finally, the concluding rites. La Santa Muerte was merely mentioned now and then along with God, the Virgin Mary, Saint Peter, Saint Jude, and other Catholic saints often inserted in the chants when asking the saints and the Virgin for protection. Many devotees asked Romo to include La Santa Muerte more in the Mass, a request he normally refused, except in the readings and prayers dedicated more directly to her. The charismatic priest did, however, gradually include more on La Santa Muerte over the years, in particular in his readings, in which he beseeched devotees in strong disciplinary terms to abandon their more demonic practices with the image (e.g., giving it their own blood as an offering).

When I first met David Romo in 2002, he told me that he used La Santa Muerte to attract prostitutes, drug addicts, and assassins to the house of God. He insisted that, by accepting La Santa Muerte into his church, he and his fellow priests could introduce outcasts to the Christian catechism. An important part of this evangelizing project was to gradually transform the image of La Santa Muerte. He also explained that La Santa Muerte originated from both the Aztecs and the Bible but that she was mistakenly approached in popular culture (and by the Roman Catholic Church) as an entity that solely brought destruction and suffering. He saw it, therefore, as his task to correct this erroneous approach, in particular the practices surrounding the novenas. La Novena is a collection of prayers that offer guidance to people on how to approach La Santísima Muerte in case of emotional problems. In the old pamphlets, people were advised to recite different prayers for nine consecutive days in order to create emotional attachments (*amarres*) to a named person (for more on this, see Kristensen, 2016a). To facilitate his moral project, Romo wrote prayers that removed this understanding of death as a slayer. He circulated them among his mayordomos, who helped "ignorant" devotees follow the right track by reciting these prayers with them for nine nights. The modified prayers ended, now symbolically, with the priest's arrival on the ninth night, fulfilling the wish to bring them closer to the Word of God. Romo thus already had an elaborate strategy behind his rewriting of the prayers in the novenas known from popular culture. He also allowed devotees to erect an image of La Santa Muerte in his church to facilitate his evangelizing project. From August 2003 on, devotees could bring her tequila and cigarettes as offerings, although he told them "not to open the bottles."

The same restrictions were not applied to the street ceremonies led by Jurek at doña Queta's altar. When Jurek performed the rosary, the skeleton image in Alfarería Street "drank" its tequilas. Even here, however, there was also a moral limit on what was considered correct. She could not, for example, be dressed in black. Like Romo, Jurek also drew heavily on popular Catholicism (and, to a lesser extent, spiritualism) in his ceremony. He insisted that it was a rosary and not a Mass, and it followed from this that he had the authority to give it, even though he was not a Catholic priest. Laura Roush discusses the Catholic nature of the rosary in detail and argues forcefully that "[t]he positive gestures and prayers included in the Alfarería Street services must be understood as performances given in contradiction to the representations and personal uses of La Santa Muerte that Enriqueta has chosen to exclude" (Roush, 2014, p. 137). I agree with Roush that doña Queta had, and still has, a strong drive to present a "cleaner" and more "virtuous" version of La Santa Muerte to the public. Doña Queta shares the rejection of the popular novenas with Romo and endorsed Jurek's popular Catholic take on the ceremonies (Kristensen, 2016a, pp. 418–19). Like the editorial line of the magazine *Devoción a La Santa Muerte*, she applauded any attempt to speak positively about La Santa Muerte, but whereas Roush seems to relate this take predominately to a strategy of contrasting with the mass media's dark image of the cult, I find it more inward pointing. Like Romo's disciplinary corrections of devotees in his Masses, doña Queta also sternly corrects devotees who ask her for advice on how to curse someone. They are normally told harshly that they have got the wrong end of the stick, that the novena is for ignorant people, and that La Santa Muerte is not meant to harm.

The "Catholicization" of death was thus more than simply a clever response from doña Queta and David Romo to the outside "demonizing" of the cult in its earlier years. It was also directed toward devotees' own popular use of La Santa Muerte when calling on her darker powers at night to castigate a failing lover, an enemy, or a bullying neighbor. The street rosaries, Masses, and home ceremonies (the pilgrim saints) have to be seen as crucial elements of this cleaning. Indeed, the very altars to La Santa Muerte surged as part of these efforts to draw the image away from the witch-marked economy to a more acceptable popular Catholic practice. And the efforts seem to have worked. Today, the mass media have changed their initial critical focus; at least, many journalists now portray the cult positively. Scholars have also discussed her in more positive tones (Fragoso, 2007b; Chesnut, 2012b; Roush, 2014). But most importantly, tens of thousands of new devotees have erected home altars to La Santa Muerte. They have fully embraced the more virtuous, Catholic version of her. In a longer conversation with me in 2008, Jurek reflected on the Catholic nature of the rosary. Minutes after claiming the copyright of most of the prayers and the two most important segments added to the traditional rosary form, he criticized the very same rosary for its Catholic nature and lamented its success among devotees:[8]

> I have wanted to change [the rosary] many times. Once a Catholic priest asked me: "If you know she is not Catholic, why do you pray to her as if she was?" He was right, because we always complain that the Church discredits us but in the end we must be aware that we also provoke it by praying a Catholic rosary. It made me think a lot, and once I re-wrote the rosary and gave it at a place where I felt a lot of confidence. The answer of the people attending was: "It was beautiful, you are a great speaker, but we liked it better before." The rosary has stayed that way because people want it so, they have become accustomed to it and feel confident with its actual form. (J. Páramo, interview, June 2008)

When I recorded the above statement, Jurek was tracing the origin of La Santa Muerte elsewhere (pre-Columbian gods and New Age energy flows), which was also why he lamented the fact that devotees by and large preferred the Catholic rosary form. In the same interview, he also criticized their ignorance when they brought mariachis with them to the ceremonies. He could not help complaining that, sometimes, devotees requested the musicians to play "La Guadalupana," as if she were a virgin. The point I want to make is not, as Jurek suggests, that these devotees were ignorant. Like him, however, I am also puzzled at how well the Catholic-inspired Masses, the street rosaries, the circulating pilgrim saints, and the home altars managed to touch a religious nerve of the time. Whereas most anthropologists have looked elsewhere to explain this religious nerve (the history of death practices in Mexico and the current violence), I find it more fruitful to explore this strong demand for a Catholic-like approach in the popular practices of exchanging favors with saints.

Mandas

Vows (mandas) are common in popular Catholicism throughout Latin America as a way of exchanging favors with saints and the Virgin, although they are also considered a manipulation of God or a blackmailing of the divine (Gudeman, 1988; Lebner, 2012). Many Catholics criticize this practice, arguing that one should not barter with God. The Roman Catholic Church in Mexico nevertheless accepts these practices despite their potential for deteriorating into a kind of extortion of the divine. The famed shrine to the Virgin of Guadalupe is, like other shrines in Mexico, a gathering place for people seeking help or looking to repay their mandas. Devotees of the Virgin walk long distances, many barefoot and some through the last streets on their knees. They put themselves through this ritual to show their gratitude for favors granted or to plead with the Virgin to grant them one. Local employees at the shrines assist the pilgrims to swear an oath (*jurar*) in the presence of the saint or Virgin, providing the swearing party with a printed contract bearing an image of the saint.

The most quoted anthropologist on this phenomenon is George Foster, who, in his classic monograph *Tzintzuntzan* (first published in 1967), dedicated a chapter to analyzing the dyadic contracts between patron-client and the social relations of compadrazgo (1979, pp. 212–43). The dyadic contract was, according to him, an implicit agreement between pairs of "contractants," bound together of their own free will. These voluntary contracts between individuals were essentially noncorporate, since social units such as extended families could not be said to enter into contractual relationships of this kind. The special credit Foster has in regard to the themes taken up here is that he also argued that the practice of making vows to saints was a special kind of voluntary contract between humans and supernatural beings (Foster, 1979, pp. 235–41). This practice of making one's saint a promise in return for receiving a favor is probably where the devotion of La Santa Muerte comes closest to other popular worships of Catholic saints and virgins in Mexico. Devotees of La Santa Muerte also make vows and go on pilgrimages, climbing the last part of the journey to the street altars on their knees to show their gratitude for a favor received. However, I find that the practice of making vows among the devotees to La Santa Muerte goes further than Foster noted among his informants. The following story, told by a devotee, serves as a case in point:

> They say that his brother had a big image of La Santa Muerte in his
> house and that he had promised to give her a box of candles, flowers,

and wine every month. A time of abundance came to him afterward. Every week he was *padrino* at some fifteen-year-old's birthday, wedding, baptism, or other party. He had everything, but the money started to run out. Yet, his momentum still lasted some time. In the beginning, the candles were left out each second month, and so on, until one day he removed the image from his house [altar]. They say she responded forcefully. He was left without a job; his friends left him, and his wife, who had to work, suffered a critical accident. In the end the person who had given him the image told him, "You wanted to commit yourself to her, it was your promise; so fulfill it."

This devotee, like many others, had made his santa a manda. A time of abundance came to him, but, in the long run, he did not fulfill his promise and was castigated for his neglect. The story, as such, targets the classic Fosterian dyadic contract between devotee and saint, or rather the lack of the devotee's fulfillment of such a contract. It nevertheless contests the noncorporate nature of the contract. The devotee's wife also suffered from her husband's neglect, as she had probably also gained from his promise. There is thus a socialization of debt at stake. At least in this case it includes the close family. There is also another layer in the story that contests Foster's model. Rather than a time-restricted contract that terminates when the saint is repaid, the story exposes a long-term relationship that more closely resembles a marriage than a short-lived, commercial-like contract. The devotee made a particular kind of economic contract that, besides conceding him money, obligated him and his santa to socialize: drinking wine, receiving flowers, and providing candles every month are characteristically social acts. This socializing aspect of the contractual promise was also underscored by the punishment of the devotee. In spite of his longer neglect, he and his wife were first punished when he removed his santa from the house. The turning point was not the contractually defined lack of payment but his failure to maintain the social relationship that emerged from the nature of this contract.

My summary of countless hours talking with devotees points to a picture in which street and home altars are related to repaying the saint in gratitude for a favor received or to persuading her to grant them one. The street altars and the ceremonies were often initiated because the street altars' owner promised their santas they would do so in return for her help. Most of those bringing mariachis would also describe the act as being their way of showing La Santa

Muerte their gratitude for helping them with a concrete and often desperate problem (often related to sickness, prison, unemployment, infidelity, or death). Roush (2014, p. 143) describes at length the circuits of exchange going on alongside the prayers in the rosaries at Alfarería Street. She also mentions that the gifts given on these occasions are one way of repaying La Santa Muerte for particular favors or of showing one's appreciation for her overall protection. And, once again, I find that Roush could push her analysis further. Whereas she argues that the exchanges at the ceremonies are a tacit recognition between devotees "within a shared frame of difficulties, shared stigma, or shared perspective on the dynamics of fear," I suggest that the exchanges form a vital part of an ongoing socialization process between the devotees and the home images they worship (Roush, 2014, p. 144). The act of cohabiting with their images while waiting takes on a special significance for them. Devotees may very well bring their images (santas or santitas) with them to the rosaries to fulfill a vow, yet they often describe this act as part of cohabiting with her. It simply means something for them to keep their image happy. At the rosaries, the santas they bring with them meet with other santas. Here, they and their owners exchange gifts (such as sweets, apples, or more labor-intensive carvings) and pass time together with the crowd of santas as well as with the "mother" image in the street altar. On some occasions, they celebrate the street image's birthday (the day it was erected) with mariachi music, tequila, and cake. When the rosary ends, devotees and their santas return to their homes, and the gifts received are placed on the home altar. The whole process thus resembles a couple (or a family) going out to enjoy themselves, returning home happily afterward.

The particularly strong intimacy of the social space created between the devotees and their santas is underscored in the popular books that guide devotees on how to become devout. This process starts by buying an image and constructing her altar. One such book recommends: "You need to give La Santa Muerte a place in your house so she always dwells at your side. She will hear your supplications, regrets, and complaints but also your thankfulness and devotion" (Cruz, 2006, p. 60, my translation). Another book recommends: "The more private the place for the altar the better" (Goodman, 2006, p. 7). One important aspect of taking care of an altar is to feed and dress the image. In this respect, the images of La Santa Muerte are distinct from those of Saint Jude and the Virgin of Guadalupe, who do not normally "eat," "drink," or "smoke." The importance of this aspect for the intimacy created should not be underestimated. One often finds that devotees speak to their santas as if they were family members or close friends. They often call their image their "child" (*mi niña, mi nena*), "sister" (*manita*), "mother" (*madrecita*), or "godmother" (*madrina*). This family approach to the saint has its pitfalls. It is no easy task to commit oneself in a family-like manner as this also becomes demanding, living in a household with children, sisters, brothers, mother, father, husband, wife, and godparents. Visits, flowers, food, birthdays, chatting, and cleaning all take their toll. It simply takes an effort to be regularly present in the lives of others.

UNITING CONFLICTING THEORIES
OF EXCHANGE UNDER THE SAME ROOF

The manda's transformation into a social obligation now raises a classic theoretical question concerning the credit/debit dyad (for a review, see Peebles, 2010). What kind of reciprocity is at stake when devotees give La Santa Muerte a family in return for a favor? Drawing on Marshall Sahlins's classic theory of exchange, we might ask if the exchanges so far discussed are governed by *generalized* (putative, altruistic, yet accounted), *balanced* (economically accounted), or *negative* reciprocity (theft or exploitation) (1974, pp. 193–95). Sahlins's main argument is that, the further one goes in this continuum from generalized to negative reciprocity, the further the social distance between the stakeholders, ending with an antagonistic relationship (theft). I have so far argued that, when devotees beg La Santa Muerte for a favor, it is perceived as forming a relationship in which faith and loyalty are stressed through a family commitment. This points toward a generalized reciprocity. Yet we have also seen that they promise her something concrete in return for a favor, which points toward a more accounted kind of reciprocity resembling an economic relationship. This is potentially a dangerous economy, as an irritated devotee once clarified, stating: "She is death, *güey*; when she comes, it is over." This sensation of dealing with a powerful and at the same time benevolent as well as dangerous woman is widespread. "Better her friend than her enemy" is an often heard phrase. "Take care, she is jealous," is another. Some devotees, and many nondevotees (often neighbors or family members of devotees), maintain that if you do not keep your promise, La Santa Muerte is vengeful. She will take your life or the life of a loved one. She may therefore require a return much higher than the favor could possibly be worth (what favor is worth one's death?). And this violent gathering of debt can even be projected onto another, close-standing person (e.g., one's own child). The logic of the exchange now points toward negative reciprocity.

Many devotees will deny this demand for reciprocity and make the counterclaim that La Santa Muerte is pure giving (*es todo dar*). They will contend that it is a misunderstanding to attribute La Santa Muerte a punishing role. As doña Queta once told me: "La Muerte will not punish anybody. It is you that punishes yourself for being loud mouthed, promising her more than you know you can keep." Señora Blanca, another of the leading personalities around the cult, explained it in further detail: "She does not have to charge you, because she does not sell you anything. If you approach and ask her for a favor, it is your own responsibility if you promise her something; she does not need any promise or offering. Why should she castigate if you approach her with faith and devotion? She is not made to castigate. Only God can carry out divine justice. If you voluntarily offer her a flower, an apple, or such-and-such a thing, it is your decision, not hers."[9] Despite doña Queta's and Señora Blanca's clarification that La Santa Muerte is not punitive, they hint at the same time that there might, in fact, be a social relationship established that could potentially provoke castigation. Their point is that it is not necessary to promise La Santa Muerte anything in return for her favors. Devotees basically punish themselves and those closest to them when they are too loud mouthed and exaggerate their promises; and yet, once made, the promises are irreversible. This sounds as if there were opposite approaches to exchange at stake (free versus nonfree favors); however, the boundaries between obligatory relationships, exploitation, and altruism are easily crossed, even in the space of a sentence. Most devotees would agree with doña Queta and Señora Blanca that favors from La Santa Muerte are free of charge and yet still choose to promise her something in return. They are also inclined to continue maintaining their altars once their promises have been fulfilled. So what starts as an economic transaction (a manda) ends up being a family commitment, which if neglected might provoke the ultimate castigation (death).

If we turn to more recent anthropological literature on exchange, I find it remarkable that Claudio Lomnitz and David Graeber, on different occasions, draw on the family figure to clarify inconsistencies in Sahlins's and Marcel Mauss's theories of reciprocity. Lomnitz challenges Sahlins's classic model on exchange, arguing that there is not necessarily a growing social distancing at stake when reciprocity moves from generalized (altruism) over the balanced (more economic) to a negative form (exploitation). He draws here on the family figure when he argues that social intimacy and violence can be juxtaposed, as in coercive marriage arrangements (*matrimonios a punta de pistola*), which are built on exploitation and cultural forms of dominance and yet are still considered social relationships that involve some kind of intimacy (Lomnitz, 2005b, p. 323). Graeber draws likewise on the family figure to contest Mauss's idea that a gift should always be theorized as a social act involving a demand for a counter-gift (Graeber, 2011, p. 99). He argues that reciprocity can only take place between more or less equals and uses the mother-child relationship as an example of this logic of exchange that has nothing to do with exchange, because the whole idea is that the mother always gives and the child always receives. Rather, it is a social relationship that follows a nonreciprocal logic that he calls "mutuality" or "communism," since it operates on the principle of "from each according to their ability to each according to their need" (2011, pp. 102–3, 99, 94). The irony is that Sahlins also draws on the family cluster when he exemplifies generalized exchange. He described it as "voluntary food-sharing among kinsmen — or for its logical value one might think of the suckling of children" (Sahlins, 1974, p. 194).

My point in drawing on the different theories of exchange of Sahlins, Lomnitz, and Graeber is not to discuss theoretical inconsistencies or contradictions. Rather, the way they exemplify their theories (the family is a recurrent figure in all three) serves to stress the ambiguity and tension of the family cluster. When Lomnitz comments that the testing of tenderness and mutual affection in violent matrimonial relationships is part of specific social and cultural forms of dominance, and when Graeber describes love as an important feature of nonreciprocal exchange in a mother-child relationship, I suggest that, from different sides, they exemplify a structure of exchange incorporating tense internal contradictions similar to those found in the cult to La Santa Muerte. On the one hand, this saint is the kind mother who loves her children and demands no return (like the Virgin Mary). On the other, she is also the wife who can be exploited if the devotee is not too "loud mouthed," promising her too much in exchange. And yet this wife demands, for her part, an indefinite constancy in return. If one's promise is not fulfilled, La Santa Muerte castigates the devotee's family like the all-taking child, by requiring irreplaceable returns (one's death or a child's death). This family cluster (the very platform of the devotion) somehow embraces the entire range of exchange discussed by Sahlins, Lomnitz, and Graeber, including forms of nonreciprocal logic such as altruism and pure exploitation. I wonder, therefore, if the ambiguity of this cult's political organization does not have more to do with the ambiguities already existing within the popular Catholic family unit in Mexico than with a particular form of resistance or cohabitation with neoliberal violence. To explore this, I will shift the focus from the nature of devotees' exchanges with her to the familial practices inside the two centers of worship.

THE CULT'S UNSTABLE POLITICAL PLATFORM

By 2015, David Romo's church was a shadow of its former self, and doña Queta's street altar was attracting only half the number of devotees as during the peak years between 2005 and 2008. An attempt at uniting the street altars in Mexico City had also failed. The cult was, however, now spreading more strongly than ever to innumerable homes elsewhere in Mexico and in the United States. Why?

The mayordomo Gabriela left Romo's church disillusioned. When she first came to him, her daughter had recently committed suicide. Romo received her as an emotionally supportive father, embracing her and giving her emotional relief. She was deeply grateful for his fatherly affection and worked long hours with him as mayordomo. During this work, she often had to defend his more "human" attributes. "I told my people [her group of devotees in her housing complex] that he was as human as us. You know he is married, don't you? He also has the right to a family." Romo's marital status was, however, not always easy to defend. "Once, one of my people gave the santa standing in his church a collar and some rings and, two weeks later, she saw that David Romo's wife was wearing them. That was not right." His wife was also his secretary, and Gabriela commented with contempt that "she dressed up in hot pants and always had a deep cleavage." Gabriela was liberal of mind and it did not trouble her that he later divorced this woman, but she again felt that he had overstepped a moral line when he announced weeks later that he had married another woman. As she said: "We Mexicans are reactionary [retrógadas]; this does not sit well with us. That was what made us leave." Her support simply died after being repeatedly confronted with Romo's failure to behave as a trustworthy family man. But not only did he break her trust as a father; he was also greedy:

In the end padre David was charging 9,000 pesos to give a service, and yet when I started with him the sacerdotes only charged for the taxi expenses. After only two months, David told me, "Gabi, let's charge 200 pesos for a service." I agreed but people started to complain. I told them that priests also need to dress, eat, and they suffer from sickness. That was OK but then the price rose to more than 1,000 pesos. And he forced us to pay for his services and his votive candles. Even the tips people gave, he demanded. (Gabriela, interview, July 2008)

The fragile balance between an economy of need ("priests also need to dress and eat, and they suffer from sickness") and one of greed ("the price rose to more than 1,000 pesos") was a recurrent issue when I spoke to devotees. It seemed hard for Romo to be both a trustworthy Catholic padre, charging moderately in the name of the divine, and a father-like figure giving his love to his "children" generously. Romo was far from the only one whom people suspected of making business out of their faith. Devotees also widely suspected that doña Queta was benefiting economically from the cult. They found that she had bought new teeth and her children new cars. Most of this talk was rumor, yet she has surely benefited from the shop she put up next to the altar. Doña Queta was, from the start, acutely aware that this income was a source of envy, and this is also one of her reasons for redistributing much of it by arranging rosaries, inviting mariachis, and redressing the effigy in ever more spectacular ways. She also returns the apples given to her image (they are put in a basket next to the altar to take for free), and she has, for more than a decade, offered devotees bread and atole at the monthly rosaries. Still, it has not been enough to dispense with the suspicion that she benefits enormously.

The conflict between how faith relates to humility and opulence is of paramount concern among Christians, with a particularly strong significance for Catholics. Andreas Bandak (2017) has argued that this tension is fundamental to the vigor of the Roman Catholic Church, and Maya Mayblin (2010) argues that the imperfect nature of human lives is a part of the vitality of Catholicism in rural Brazil. I am inclined to interpret devotees' suspicions in line with the views of these authors. The classic tension between humility and opulence seems, nevertheless, to gain another layer inside the cult due to its intimate family-like organization. Rather than focusing on the tension between a leader's humility and true faith, and his or her personal gain from an organization's budget (a question of leaders' moral corruption), the dilemma (and within that also the vitality of the faith) now becomes a question of what makes a trustworthy family member. David Romo was not an ordinary Catholic padre. He was married. His wife was part of the cult, and at least one of the priests was his uncle. Some devotees also suspected that the image of the Angel of Death was in reality a sculpture of his wife. Gabriela defended Romo's needs by referring to his similarity to others ("he is a human like us") but found his frivolous life morally untruthful, not least because it threatened her whole idea of what faith and family ought to be. Her disillusionment with him was exacerbated by his disrespect for her as a family member. He had embraced her, been there when she was grief stricken; they had worked closely together; and then, suddenly, he started treating her with utter disrespect, such as on one occasion when he blessed her with beer instead of water, or when his wife wore the offerings one of her group of devotees had given to the saint. In her eyes, he had failed as a family figure and as a Catholic padre.

I find it striking here that doña Queta also failed as a family "mother." Jurek and Jessie were both adopted by her as close family members, and both were abandoned brusquely. Knowing that Jurek was like a son to doña Queta, I was astonished when he was suddenly no longer giving the rosaries. I asked doña Queta why. She did not like the question and told me off, informing me that Jurek had been too harsh on the devotees. Years later, Jurek told me his version of the painful breakup:

> At first she told me and the journalists who came to the rosaries that I was her son. I started to gain confidence and when journalists asked me if Queta was my mom, I told them yes. There was nothing bad about it. Contrary to all the *cariño* we felt for each other, it felt real. However, her real son Chucho is out of jail now and is giving the rosaries. (J. Páramo, interview, June 2008)

Jurek explicitly felt a familial kind of affection until he was abandoned for doña Queta's "real son." What Jurek did not know is that Chucho is no more her son than he is. Chucho has no blood or affine relation to her, even though he tells people that his surname is Romero. Queta also calls him her son (*mi hijo*); however, none of her sons or daughters call Chucho their brother. On the contrary, one of Queta's daughters has the bad luck that her jealous husband is convinced Chucho is her lover. Another daughter corrects her children when they call Chucho's children their cousins. It is therefore one thing that Queta has verbalized the ceremonial leaders as family but quite another as to how the commitments resulting from that familial figure are fulfilled.

What is clear is that trustworthy mothers and fathers do not abandon their children. This is a capital sin for almost all devotees. Nor do they force their "children" into a balanced or exploitative kind of economy. Gabriela did not find her trust and friendship reciprocated properly when she was forced into an economic exchange that threw into doubt the loyalty and love of her master. Something similar happened to Jurek. He assured me that he had given the rosaries on Alfarería Street because he wanted to. Doña Queta was of the idea that she did not want to owe anybody any favors, and so she started to give him 300 pesos on each occasion. That hurt his feelings as a "son," but he accepted it after his wife had an accident. I shall not delve further into this long and complicated story due to space constraints. Nor shall I elaborate on the equally complicated story of Jessie's family-like affection for doña Queta and its brusque ending. Suffice it to say, the familial economy that Jurek, Jessie, and Gabriela were engaged in became increasingly tense over the years, only to break down eventually. Gabriela started her own center of worship after that. Señora Blanca and Martín George Quijano are another example of a ritualized mother-son relationship that emerged after they separated from David Romo. Jessie and Jurek separated from doña Queta but continue giving rosaries at street altars in Mexico City, now competing with each other, alongside Chucho and the former priests and mayordomos from Romo's church. They are, in many respects, familiar but no longer in "family."

If we return to the initial problem of understanding the rapid dissemination of a mostly uniform cult during its first epoch-making years, a broader picture of the cult's political platform surfaces. When a family center of worship becomes important, the cluster tends to split and reproduce itself elsewhere, just as families split when the children leave home to create their own families. It is not a ritualized split, though, but rather a tough and painful outcome following many considerations and wearisome fights. As the first centers of worship, David Romo's church and the shrine on Alfarería Street had a great deal of influence in forming this political platform. The familial form around which they built the centers of worship has split multiple times only to blossom into similar centers of worship throughout Mexico City, many of them competing with each other. This dynamic may also be prevalent outside Mexico City and Puebla. Señora Blanca has connections in California, while Romo's congregation used to have connections both in the United States and in cities elsewhere in Mexico. Moreover, leading individuals running their own centers of worship in the United States and Mexico have visited the altars in Mexico City.

I am not in a position to say whether these new leading individuals have also taken with them the familial dynamic of the two centers of worship discussed. If they approach La Santa Muerte through the same familial logic and offer her a family in return for a favor, there is a good chance that some of that dynamic will be reproduced. The devotion will then somehow be socialized into the wider family and possibly also assume some of the tensions this unit entails (juxtaposing conflicting forms of reciprocity). Not that this "homeliness" is radically different from what is found in other popular Catholic worships. The devotions to the Virgin Mary and Saint Jude show many similar facets (Orsi, 1996; Christian, 1972/1989). Indeed, the cult to Saint Jude has since the mid-1990s developed strikingly similarly in Mexico City. However, the Virgin and Saint Jude are not as intimately adopted into the family cluster and therefore not as familiarized with this juxtaposition of different forms of reciprocity under the same roof. It is a question of degree of familiality, not of kind.

CONCLUSION

Whereas most scholars have focused largely on the Santa Muerte cult's relationship to current insecurity and death practices in Mexico, I find that a different story surfaces by focusing on the cult's more popular Catholic qualities. A story of the difficulties that emerge when uniting clashing forms of exchange in an intimate cluster, such as the family, has materialized in this analysis. The cult's vitality is here connected to socially and culturally hard-pressed Mexicans' failure to operate as an ideal family more than to violence as such, albeit the family also includes its share of violent relationships. But the more violent schemes of reciprocity are not *exclusively* presented in this cluster. They are juxtaposed under the same roof with those of love or of a more balanced gift-economy. This analytical viewpoint stresses the need for scholars to reevaluate the focus on La Santa Muerte as a death cult, a perception that is principally driven by the violence in present-day Mexico. It also stresses the importance of not separating La Santa Muerte radically from other popular Catholic cults (e.g., the cult to Saint Jude) but rather seeing it as an ingenious assembly of popular Catholic practices that has given birth to a full-blown cult reaching deep into popular culture in Mexico.

The irony is that the select group of devotees who facilitated this creation at the turn of the century have veered from the Catholic approach. Jurek, Jessie, David Romo, and doña Queta have all flirted heavily with Cuban Santería, and Chucho is today deep into Palo Monte, another Afro-Cuban belief system based on the veneration of spirits and natural powers. Shamans and curanderos, drawing more on their interpretations of pre-Columbian versions of death, are also largely getting a stronger foothold in the cult, offering, for a fee, professional spiritual guidance to solve people's concrete problems. The temptation to leave the hard-won saintly character of La Santa Muerte behind to take advantage of her more destructive powers in magic sessions has been an intervening issue from the start of the cult's public life. The ceremonial leaders dismissed any such use of death in the early years as based on economic thinking rather than proper faith. Yet, with time, they have also ventured into the darker sides of death's nature, perhaps desiring a "stronger" favor than they could readily ask the virtuous death for. They forgot, however, that the boom in the cult was due to a morally positive approach, and that a great number of devotees were much more confident of inviting a saintly death into their house than a pre-Columbian, Santería, or Palo Monte one. Only time will tell if devotees in the future will maintain their more popular Catholic images of death in their houses. Doña Queta has indeed moved the Santería paraphernalia that was piled up in her home altar into the room next door in order to give La Santa Muerte the place to herself. Hence, the more virtuous, Catholic death has moved *in* again in the very first place from where she moved *out* into public space. At least, for the time being.

NOTES

1. In 2008, I conducted a full year of ethnographic fieldwork at the street altars to La Santa Muerte in Mexico City and Puebla, and, in 2013, I returned to conduct another full year of ethnographic fieldwork with one family devoted to this saint. The ethnographic material presented here is, however, mainly based on unpublished material collected in Mexico City between 2002 and 2007 in cooperation with my wife, Claudia Adeath Villamil. It is as such situated in the very first years after this cult went public.

2. For a historical discussion of the Santa Muerte cult's more occult life before 2001, see Claudio Lomnitz (2005a), Katia Perdigón (2008a), and Regnar Kristensen (2016a).

3. Because his congregation was never accepted by the Roman Catholic Church, Romo was, technically speaking, not a Catholic priest. However, in this chapter I follow his own view and that of the devotees who addressed him as a priest/padre.

4. Devotees not only imitated the popular Catholic liturgy and the rule of

repeating the ceremonies every month on the day the altar was erected—they also imitated the way in which the altar's image was celebrated on her anniversary (inviting mariachis and offering food), her regular redressing, and the offering of sweets, fruits, alcohol, and cigarettes. They also largely imitated the practice of carrying the home altar's image with them when attending the public rosaries, and to a lesser extent of exchanging small gifts among themselves.

5. *Devoción a La Santa Muerte* was published by Mina Editores. This same publisher had, in 2007, also published four smaller books and eight special editions fully dedicated to stories about altars to La Santa Muerte.

6. From personal conversations with Gerardo Cabrera and Fernando Sandoval, who wrote most of the articles published in *Devoción a La Santa Muerte* from 2004 to 2009. Very few would have a broader and more profound knowledge of people's home altars than these journalists.

7. The more demonic image of the saint was not new. The picture of her on the prayer book *Novena: La Santísima* had by then been sold for half a century at the Sonora Market in Mexico City, famed for its popular religious merchandise, as a remedy for people seeking to curse a failing lover or husband, or a bullying neighbor (Lewis, 1963; Kristensen, 2016a; see also Roush, 2014, 137–42, for the mass media's take on the image's more demonic side).

8. These being the collective blessing of the images and the *cadena de la fuerza*, both detailed as discussed by Roush (2014, pp. 135–36). Jurek did not mention, though, that he had copied some of the prayers from elsewhere. Roush comments in this regard: "Elizabeth Juárez of the Colegio de Michoacán identified several lines of prayers as having been adopted from 'Universal Souls,' used in yoga circles, and from the '33 Taos' used by spiritualists" (2014, p. 131, n. 2).

9. My translation of a transcript interview published in Álvares et al. (2007, p. xlvii).

JUDITH KATIA PERDIGÓN CASTAÑEDA
AND BERNARDO ROBLES AGUIRRE

6 | # Devotion That Goes Skin Deep
Tattoos of La Santa Muerte

INTRODUCTION

Popular religiosity enjoys a broad range of forms in Mexico, as people deeply devoted to Catholicism develop and practice their own ways of worshipping, celebrating—and beseeching favors from—saints, Christs, virgins, and angels. Particularly visible displays of this phenomenon are the dances that take place in atria and temples, and the act of dressing devotional sculptures in the attire typical of different regions of the country, such as the Virgin Mary clothed like the Nahuatl women of Cuetzalan, Puebla (Zárate, 2007, p. 8; Perdigón, 2015a, p. 166). Another expression is seen in the mixing of beliefs from ancient indigenous cultures with those of Catholicism, as in the invocations of traditional Nahuatl healers (*curanderos*) from the hilltops of the northern sierra of Puebla (*tiemperos*) to ensure abundant harvests. Following José Luis González Martínez, we understand popular religion

> from the dialectics of cultural, social and institutional marginalization. Throughout history, different social subjects situated in such a position who also profess the Christian and Catholic faith have elaborated their own systems of symbolic religious meanings that allow them to under- stand the world, their lives, and their sociocultural and ecclesiastical situation. In short, we can say that all popular Christianity is nothing more than a fundamental nucleus of Christian meanings re-interpreted from the conditions of marginality. (2002, p. 109)

Practices like dancing, singing, praying, performing "cleansings" or "exor- cisms" of the human body, participating in pilgrimages, processions, fiestas, and initiation rituals, or accepting a commission (*cargo*), are all common expres- sions of popular religiosity in Mexico, reflections of the relationship between ordinary people and their divinities. While the Catholic Church recognizes some of these activities as part of the pastoral liturgy, Mexico's high clergy does not always see them in that light.

Popular religiosity is thus understood as actions taken by ordinary folk, marginalized people who express the feelings they hold toward the objects of their devotion. Although discourses calling for tolerance and respect for (religious) diversity abound, reality often differs, for in some cases the multiple ways in which popular religiosity is exercised have come to focus on saints not approved by the church, the so-called *santones* and popular saints. These are not true saints because they have not been officially canonized. They are not accepted, recognized, or admitted by the institutionalized Catholic Church. However, common people experience them as powerful and persist in turning to them. Examples abound: El Niño Fidencio, Jesús Malverde, La Santa de Cabora, Juan Soldado, and Pancho Villa. But one of the most polemical is La Santa Muerte, a popular saint who has come under strong attack by both Catholic ecclesiastics and Protestant churches. Father José de Jesús Aguilar Valdés, for instance, has denounced the cult to La Santa Muerte as a product of ignorance, superstition, and idolatry. Since its origins, however, the Catholic Church has implored believers to live "in grace" so when their final hour arrives they will die free of sin—a "saintly death." The church has declared that people are using this phrase to deceive the faithful into believing that it has *always* venerated La Santa Muerte (Aguilar Valdés, 2007, p. 180).

The figure of La Santa Muerte is a skeleton-like allegory of popular devotion that began in Mexico but has spread beyond its borders into nations of Central and South America, the United States, and Canada, as our interviewees recounted. This is due primarily to the heavy flow of Central and South American migrants to the northern reaches of the continent. Studies by Katia Perdigón (2008a) and Andrew Chesnut (2012a) have verified the high number of devotees among migrants, who have successfully introduced devotion to La Santa Muerte into North American popular culture. Chesnut (2012a, p. 217) found La Santa Muerte in Virginia, New York City, Los Angeles, and Phoenix, while believers also spoke of altars in Europe, although we have no reliable documentation to support the cult's presence there, or in Asia or Africa.

La Santa Muerte is identified by a series of well-defined attributes: she is dressed in a Greco-Latin-style tunic (an iconographic element that bestows purity), her divine nature represented by a halo. To these basic elements people add various accessories: a balance (to symbolize justice), a scythe (representing the Grim Reaper), an axe (the administration of justice), a globe (the fragility of the world), or an owl (an emblem of carnal desire), among others. While this skeletal figure is normally dressed in the style mentioned above, believers may modify her costume according to their own beliefs (Perdigón, 2015b).

Although recognized as having an ambiguous nature, La Santa Muerte is regarded as a spiritual entity who will come to the aid of those who are trying to "progress" or "get ahead" (*salir adelante*). Free of prejudices or value judgments regarding sexual preference, social condition, age, or economic status, she offers support in all circumstances: economic, work-related, sentimental, health; in short, any kind of problem. Believers are prone to say: "If you have faith and believe, anything is possible!" (Perdigón, 2008a). There are no specific formulations or religious leaders to tell believers what to do or how and when to worship this figure, so devotees are free to develop their own style of veneration.[1] In addition to prayers, they adorn altars with whatever they have at hand, though it is said that La Santa Muerte has a penchant for apples, tobacco, tequila, chocolate, and cigarettes. Of course, flowers, water, and candles are omnipresent.

When people ask La Santa Muerte for a favor, or after she performs a miracle, they offer flowers, make her a new dress, or adorn her with jewelry. Women may cut off some of their own hair to make her a wig, while others share the joy of a "miracle" by giving away candy, apples, flowers, or stamps bearing the Santa's image. But when they sense that such acts fall short of expressing their thanks, devotees may be moved to offer more, to sacrifice something deeply personal, unique: their own body, which is transformed into an altar, a blank canvas upon which they display their gratitude in the form of tattoos. It is in this sense that, once tattooed on the believer's body, La Santa Muerte becomes a symbol of protection; emerging from the soul, she finds expression on the body.

OBJECTIVES AND METHODOLOGY

To better understand the meaning of venerating and living with La Santa Muerte, we undertook qualitative-descriptive research on the meanings of the tattoos. Our interviews with several people bearing tattoos with her image were complemented by conversations with tattoo artists whose careers include experiences of this type. On the basis of the information gathered, we analyzed the features of these tattoos and sought to determine if there are differences in type based on the image of the saint (i.e., form, color, and technique, among others). We asked the artists to observe a series of photographs of tattoos and tell us how they would classify them. Finally, we examined the responses given by the interviewees to construct a provisional categorization of tattoos.

Information was gathered largely using two techniques: in-depth interviews and participant observation; that is, ethnographic research understood as "the descriptive study (graphos) of the culture (ethnos) of a community, or some of its fundamental aspects, from a comprehensive perspective. In this way, ethnography describes other cultures in all their grandeur and dignity" (Baztán Aguirre, 1995, p. 4). Armed with the information from our observations and interviews, we were able to describe the different representations of people with tattoos on their bodies and the meaning of La Santa Muerte in their lives. Here, we made use of social representations, which are "systems of notions, beliefs, orientations and attitudes that social groups express with respect to a given social reality, and which synthesize historically determined ideological and cultural meanings."[2] Anthropology interprets social behavior by studying the mental representations of subjects. Therefore, "all interpretation is the product of intuitive work and obeys a personal criterion that varies with each researcher's point of view" (Sperber, 1989, p. 142).

In this study, we speak of social representations because, "as intellectual constructs at any level (scientific ideas, theories, and opinions), they manifest social identities of some type at a certain historical moment" (Uribe Iniesta, 2000, pp. 124–25). Here, our intention is to describe how a group of people identifies with La Santa Muerte and determine if there are reconstructions of the body and ways of representing it through the tattoos etched into them. Our work does not aspire to generalize the problematic under study to all tattoo artists or people who decide to get tattoos. Our objective is to approach the reality of the specific group of people chosen as subjects for this study.

The interviews functioned as a tool for acquiring knowledge of the social life of this particular social group. They were semistructured and in depth, required several face-to-face encounters with informants, and were designed to provide an understanding of the perspectives on their lives, experiences, and situations, expressed in their own words (Taylor & Bogdan, 1996, p. 101). This approach allowed us to record the authentic experiences of tattoo artists and the people they tattooed and so construct and interpret the importance and transcendence of La Santa Muerte in the lives of the devotees. In defining the framework of the study, we had to ensure that the tattoo artists had several years of experience so as to learn how they identify with the tattoos they apply, and describe how they understand themselves as tattoo artists. A second criterion was that they had applied various tattoos of La Santa Muerte, for we wanted to determine what types of images clients request, if there are specific categories of tattoos, which are the most common designs, and how are the social characteristics of their clientele best described. We were able to interview three male tattoo artists aged thirty-five to forty-five, each of whom said that they had over ten years of experience in designing, modeling, and making tattoos, and that this was their main occupation. With respect to the devotees of La Santa Muerte—men and women, young adults and older people—the only requirement for inclusion in our research was having one or more tattoos alluding to La Santa. The study population was heterogeneous: we interviewed six people—four men and two women—aged thirty-three to sixty who have worshipped La Santa Muerte for more than fifteen years. In their daily lives, they performed diverse roles: student, homemaker, tradesman, and spiritual leader.[3] Added to this sample were testimonies from thirty other devotees, also dedicated to various activities, trades, and jobs, gathered over the past twenty years at various altars on the streets of Mexico City.[4]

FROM THE CONCEPT OF THE BODY TO THE BODY OF THE SANTA MUERTE DEVOTEE

The body manifests emotions, pleasures, likings, and pain; and therefore it "is constantly present for the person as the ordering centre of the totality of experience" (Aisenson Kogan, 1981, p. 20). In this view, the body is everything, the space where we feel, live, create, and experience; it is total existence.[5] The body is a participant because we live inside it: not a receptor of data but an active presence. Hence, the body cannot be conceived as an object, for it is the result of our social, cultural, and biological organization. According to Rosa María Ramos Rodríguez (1989, p. 112), "[people] modify and determine their social organization in relation to the conditions of life and components of the group in which they live and develop," because human groups are molded and manifested through the social significations of the world in which they live their corporality. All alterations they construct out of this are transformed into means of communication that exteriorize their meaning in daily life (Ramírez Torres, 2000).

The body is personal territory, and through it we capture and appropriate the experience of our surroundings and of the group in which we are raised. Feeling is an essential part of being human, for it is through feelings that people share their milieu with others, with their space, and with all the beings around them. Our senses include not only sight, smell, touch, taste, and hearing but also perceptions of heat and cold, pleasure and pain, kinaesthesia (i.e., the sensations detected by our muscles, tendons, and articulations) and synaesthesia (visceral sensibility)—that is, interior well-being or malaise. Thus, corporal experience brings awareness—perhaps clear, sometimes blurred—of reality and of the existence of each of us; it bestows identity. The body allows us to express ourselves and provides the fears, pleasures, joys, and terrors that construct us as bodies among bodies (Laín Entralgo, 1989).

La Santa Muerte presents, manifests, and re-creates herself in the full context of that which is human, the corporal and the sociocultural. This allows us to identify her devotees as unique and with a specific identity. In this context, we understand identity as "the idea we have of who we are and who others are; that is, our representation of ourselves in relation to others. This entails, therefore, making comparisons among people to encounter similarities and differences" (Giménez, 2009, p. 11). Identity has four key elements: it possesses permanence in time as a subject capable of action; it is conceived as a unit with boundaries; its boundaries distinguish it from all other subjects; and it requires recognition by those others. From the perspective of individual subjects, identity can be defined as "a subjective (often self-reflexive) process through which subjects define how they differ from others (and from their social milieu) by attributing to themselves a repertoire of frequently valorized cultural attributes that are relatively stable over time" (Giménez, 2009, p. 12).

MY BODY, MY SAINT, MY DEVOTION

During our study, we found that the devotees interviewed conceived of their bodies as a space with its own language, a text dedicated to the devotion of La Santa Muerte whose principle passage, they avowed, consists of breathing life into their veneration and hence allowing the Santa to appropriate their bodies for a specific goal. These groups identify among themselves by sharing similar codes, signals, images, habits, and customs that reflect their symbolic religious capacity with its implicit aesthetics related to each individual's tastes. In this sense, Martín George Quijano observed:

I can say that within spirituality, within the cult, the devotion, my body is a temple, a place, a site I maintain, an altar where I store all my beliefs . . . principally in a true God, a creator, all spiritual deities and La Santa Muerte. It is a place, a site where I owe her such respect.

Blanca González Guerrero considered that the body is a vehicle of God, although individuals can do with it what they believe to be in their best interests, according to their own criteria: "It's something God gave me, that I can use according to my own criteria . . . something that I treasure, love, and respect." Manuel Valadéz and Alberto Rodríguez Costabella maintained that body and spirit are related as one sole being, a work of God that, as such, must be cared for and respected:

It's a gift that God gave me thanks, of course, to my mother and father, who gave me the opportunity to be in this earthly world. . . . Obviously, my body is sacred to me, it's unique, every person is unique. . . . I think there are some little people out there who believe that the body is just skin, hair, nails, but it also has to do with the spiritual. (Valadéz)

The body is very delicate, it's something sacred you need to care for, you know God gave it to you [so] it's something you must return just as it was given. (Rodríguez Costabella)

These comments reflect the belief that it is people's nature to symbolize everything, even their own bodies; each area, each place, has a meaning for others and for oneself. Believers in La Santa Muerte who were brought up in Catholicism from infancy refer to the body as part of God, a temple, a sacred place that deserves respect.

In this regard, we concur with David Le Breton (1991), who observes that people are subject to the set of values that govern their society but who emphasizes that these are human interpretations, since all descriptions of the world are symbolizations made up of meanings and values. Hence, the body is the result of social and cultural reproduction, a malleable reality that depends on the specific society studied. Analyzing it, therefore, requires entering its social, ecological, and cultural milieus. Finally, we therefore understand the body as "a symbolic structure that subjects construct according to their social and cultural context determined by their personal history" (Le Breton, 1991, p. 97). This became all the more clear when the interviewees explained what their bodies meant to them.

Martín George maintained that all parts of the body have a direct relation with God because they enable direct communication with him and allow the spirit to connect and be extended to one's relatives:

The hands [are] agility, action, kindness, giving, and receiving. The eyes: the power to see far beyond, not only through natural sight but with the spiritual mind. The power to transcend, fly, travel and, obviously, like I said, the spiritual power to know God though we cannot see him, and the deities and the beliefs to which you are deeply attached. The back is part of a defense, of the [reality] that if you didn't have a back you wouldn't have a front; I mean, the back can be . . . something . . . a protection . . . of your sight; it could be your sight, the part that lets you see behind. The thorax holds the heart, strength, grandeur, self-devotion, giving of yourself, having the power to confront things naturally. The legs are for advancing. The arms allow you to extend yourself . . . to obtain what your family . . . your loved ones . . . need, to spread spirituality, the cult, devotion, offerings, and to embrace. That's why, if I may continue, I'm not going off topic . . . just a comment. . . . That's why in this sense priests open their arms to receive people, perform the consecration, and conduct rituals during mass; to extend themselves [and] the power to protect, embrace, a broad fraternity, perhaps an imaginary universality . . . the power to be able to offer this receiving, see? To receive it with love and attention. The feet are for advancing, stability, being steadfast in what you're searching for, what you wish for, and what you desire. Steadfast, standing firmly.

Valadéz stated that the body is an agent that only receives stimuli, that makes one feel but does not feel; that allows expression but does not express. Thus, he conceptualizes the body in a simple, utilitarian way:

One touches, feels with the hands. The eyes are for seeing, visualizing, observing people. The back is the body's strength; the thorax protects our vital organs. The legs give us the mobility to be able to move about and the power to do things. The arms are the body's strength. The feet allow you to stand firmly wherever that may be.

These fragments reveal that each interviewee structures the representation of the body somewhat differently; its social, biological, and cultural attributes are defined and re-created, cemented, and materialized on the basis of their experience, translated into the body. It is their limit, their only continent, all things included and represented in it to construct their unique corporal existence.

AND IN THE BODY, WHERE DOES LA SANTA MUERTE RESIDE?

The body is the continent of our sensations. We live, suffer, love, and die inside and outside it. We are subject to, and molded by, history, society, regimes, and ideologies (Barthes, 1985). Le Breton (1995) considers that the body only has existence when it has been created under the gaze of human culture, the social construction of the body of each of us. The body becomes the frontier that marks, precisely, the difference between one person and another. In this sense, each one of our interviewees manifested that the specific place on their body they had tattooed was not only important but actually conveyed a message and meaning, perhaps gratitude or an imploration.

Blanca told us that the tattoo of La Santa Muerte on her legs is meant to keep her on the straight path and guide her actions: "I decided to get it on my legs because they're my guides; maybe I want to go somewhere but my feet take me someplace else." Mónica Sánchez Chávez and Luis Valadéz, in contrast, got tattoos on both their right and left arms, where they say they can see, touch, and feel the Santa.

> I carry her on my arm. I like the left side because that's where the heart is; I preferred the front, not the side so that she goes by my side and I don't feel alone. She accompanies me. (Sánchez Chávez)

> On the right arm because I have more contact with her there, I can touch her, kiss her, contact the tattoo, but the one on my back, well, not so much. But with the one on my right arm I have more. (Valadéz)

In contemporary Western society, speaking of the body means referring to the anatomical-physiological knowledge of modern medicine. However, today, subjects "have only a very vague knowledge of their body" (Le Breton, 1995, p. 84). In popular wisdom, in contrast, the body is not disassociated from the person, as in biomedicine, for it is joined to the world. This has consequences for the body and how it is represented and constructed. In this sense, each body is structured, represented, and interpreted in relation to each individual's personal history and sociocultural context.

In *Los usos sociales del cuerpo* (The Social Uses of the Body), Luc Boltanski (1975) develops a critique of sociological research on the body in which he argues that the precepts of distinct analytical approaches have fragmented the scholarship on the body and corporal behavior. Arguing that we must consider the "plurality of its facets," he emphasizes two key points of construction: the relations that exist among the corporal behaviors of a group, and the conditions of the group's existence. Boltanski holds that the interest and attention that social groups attribute to their bodies (features and physical sensations both pleasant and unpleasant) intensify according to the "social class" to which they belong, such that social groups share subconscious codes concerning the body that reflect the "norms and values that govern the relations that individuals in each social class maintain with their bodies." He adds that the body transmits the norms that govern the relations between the individual and her or his own body and among the people who form a particular social group. These norms are molded to the "somatic culture" of those who perform them, because the body is a sign of social position whose symbolic meaning gains importance when we consider that it is often not perceived as such and can never be separated from the person to whom it belongs (Boltanski, 1975, p. 106).

It is, therefore, important to observe how devotees of La Santa Muerte recognize each other and form a brotherhood that offers mutual support and assistance, through which together they can recount their joys and misadventures. Those with tattoos show them to one another, some boasting of how well done they are, others bragging about how they bore the pain as the ink-filled needle penetrated their skin; they might share information on tattoo artists. The stories flow because La Santa Muerte offers help and the hope that doors to better things will open. In a special issue on tattoos of the magazine *Devoción a La Santa Muerte* (2005, p. 29), the testimonies of believers and the editors render the following picture:

> During each meeting, the search for people tattooed with images of
> La Santa Muerte is filled with excitement. . . . Surprising, difficult, but
> the interview with Héctor surpassed our expectations. We didn't have
> to talk much . . . he rolled up his right pant leg and invited us to take
> pictures. We had never experienced anything so easy and surprising.

These individuals are interlinked by a common sense of belonging as they share symbols and social representations. They can think, speak, and operate as members or representatives of this sense of belonging, thus creating a collective memory (Giménez, 1997).

TATTOOS: PROMISES KEPT FOR FAVORS RECEIVED

Tattoos are modifications of skin color that create images, figures, or texts by means of needles that inject ink or some other pigment under the epidermis. The use of corporal signs like tattoos first appeared in ancient tribal societies in association with rites of passage or moments of change, especially involving young people. They were important elements in the construction of collective identities, always possessed symbolic value, and expressed a certain relation with the sacred (Alcoceba Hernando, 2007, p. 79). Tattoos are also a way to express feelings, ideologies, or beliefs, and therefore they are imbued with special meaning.

Tattoos are distinguished by three criteria: the significant symbolic importance that serves to construct bonds of community; their social function, which implies interpersonal and/or group relations with an identitary function; and decorative expressiveness, associated with fashion and existing considerations or patterns of beauty influenced by the mass media (Vergara Figueroa, 2009, p. 11). During our interviews, we found that the tattooed devotees satisfied these three criteria, for they narrated that while being tattooed with the image of La Santa Muerte, they kept the following aspects in mind: the design had to be etched into a specific part of their body; the image had to be pleasant to look at; and it had to reflect something they had dreamed or imagined at the precise moment they decided to get it. We further observed that they respected cultural matrices that incorporated local expressions and autobiographical inscriptions to make a permanent record of some particularly intense event, signs to circulate in the global symbolic marketplace, and images found in magazines or other media. Hence, their tattoos are much more than simple adornments obtained to beautify the body.[6]

We found that the tattoos of La Santa Muerte are individual identitary marks, but that the personal histories they narrate are also histories of community, for they are retold in a complex circuit of devotees who are also tattooed. For these individuals, tattoos are signs of their valor and their faith, although observers from outside this mystical-religious knowledge see them more as icons or symbols of transgression. Under the influence of Mexico's alarmist press, in society these "marks" are often associated with marginal, excluded, and dangerous groups.[7] What is certain is that the majority of such tattoos have no connection to prisons, because the people who have them done are just ordinary folk who wish to display their gratitude for a favor granted or who are seeking protection. A tattoo displays this implicit symbolism on the body.

Tattoos thus construct, symbolize, and transform. They produce symbiotic mechanisms that represent the positive or negative aspects of societies. And this is not only because they are polysemic but also due to the distinct circumstances that lead people to seek them, including pain, grief, loss, devotion (*mandas*, protection), love (maternal or erotic), memories of family or friends, fashion (something seen in a movie), taste ("just because I wanted to"), identification with communities, groups, countries, ethnicities, and so on, or perhaps a desire to exhibit virility by withstanding the physical pain inflicted. Although not necessarily visible, these inscriptions are always important for those who bear tattoos (Vergara Figueroa, 2009, p. 15).

As mentioned above, these are cases in which La Santa Muerte's divine protection is invoked through an image etched into the skin; that is, tattoos as abstract representations of the positive pole, images that incite individual and collective memory and that transit between the past (when the event occurred) and the future:

> They seek to eternalize an event reborn in each version, a new version for each new audience, though perhaps renewed as well by the tattooed teller who, while narrating his tale, speaks of—and with—this figure. This figure may be perceived as all that will endure, and for this to happen, paradoxically, each version must clothe it as the interlocutor or interpellant imagines it. (Vergara Figueroa, 2009, p. 20)

We also observed that tattoos carry a very special religious weight among our interviewees, who consider that being tattooed is a way of rendering homage to La Santa Muerte for a favor received or for her protection from something or someone. Alberto Rodríguez Costabello told us that the three tattoos he has inked on his body are a means of demonstrating his devotion after a tragic experience he managed to survive:

> The three tattoos reflect different circumstances. The last one I had done—the red one—was out of gratitude. The other two were to show faith and devotion to the deity. . . . The first two were out of faith and devotion, the third to give thanks for a miracle. . . . I was kidnapped.

And, what do you know? Desperate, I beseeched her to end it, in any way, for good or for ill. There in the shadows, 'cause you're blindfolded and everything, I saw her image. That day I slept and when I woke up they told me: "Go on, get out of here" . . . well, not exactly in those words, they were really foul mouthed, but I was out! They left me on the bypass to Saltillo.

This narration tells us that Alberto was kidnapped, but while sequestered he saw La Santa Muerte in a dream. Alive after the episode, he interpreted his dream as a sign of such importance that he needed to have her image tattooed on his body. Later, he told us that he'd had the third tattoo done after another dream in which the Santa appeared:

The image I have on my back . . . well. I had dreamed about her once, then she appeared again in a dream; that's why I had the tattoo done on my back. I wanted to get something more or less the same for the third tattoo, showing her being carried away by the wind, because she always appeared to me that way . . . like she was floating away . . . her tunic all torn.

Another aspect to emphasize is that all the interviewees mentioned the importance of the pain experienced during the tattooing procedure. They consider this an integral part of their devotion, a way for them to repay the attention, care, and companionship they had received from the Santa in their lives.[8] As Alberto put it:

The last tattoo really hurt . . . you know, I almost fainted. I believe the pain is part of the gratitude, see? It's . . . like a manda, that you have to fulfill. Now see, I have two tattoos that didn't hurt, the only one that hurt was this one, but I think that was part of the manda, right? Like what I was offering to the deity was my pain.

As these extracts show, when tattooed devotees of La Santa Muerte are questioned, they actualize their narratives. Miracles emerge and supplications are emphasized. Also, an identitary relationship appears between believer and tattoo, in the sense that the body is seen as a sacred space, beliefs are updated, and people feel protected, as if someone were watching over them. According to Edgar Morín (2009, pp. 42–43), this occurs as well with people who get tattoos of different types of crosses, crucifixes, virgins, sacred hearts, portraits of Christ, or even the scene of the Last Supper.

In this sense, La Santa Muerte represents protection, like the deity or deities of other religions or Catholicism itself. Regardless of their particular style, designs of La Santa Muerte become known through the mass media, but if someone wants to be original, a unique design will be made.

With respect to this, our interviews led us to understand that when a devotee is contemplating getting a tattoo, it is because she or he has a specific purpose in mind, perhaps to seek some kind of favor—be it sentimental, economic, or health related, to mention but a few—or to express gratitude for a miracle; or for La Santa's intercession in resolving a particular problem, such as surviving a risky surgical procedure, settling legal troubles, working out an inheritance, or facilitating the return of a loved one from abroad, among many others. Having determined the purpose for getting the tattoo, the next step is to select the design. This may come to the devotee in a dream, reflect her or his tastes or likes, bear a relation to the aesthetic aspect of an image, or be inspired by a supernatural phenomenon associated with the apparition of La Santa Muerte at some important moment in life. Once these aspects have been resolved, the individual has to choose the place on the body that the image of La Santa Muerte will occupy, first deciding whether it will be done on the right or left side of the body.

When believers implore or ask for a favor, they are expressing something they desire, hoping that doing so will make it happen; that is, they ask the divinity for grace or a gift (*don*). The most common petition among believers involves protection, so they have the tattoo of La Santa Muerte done on an area of the body that symbolizes what they wish to protect: a tattoo on the back, for example, defends against betrayal, while one on the right arm may signify strength, especially if the person is right handed. Whatever the case, what really matters is that this is a way of thanking the Santa for a miracle and/or a means of protecting one's person or family. Some time ago, a parent explained that "a tattoo doesn't mean you're a convict, thief, or drug addict; it's a form of protection. When the person who has it done is a head of household, it provides protection for everyone." We know of several cases in which heads of households got tattoos to protect their children, even going so far as to have their names or initials, or those of their wives, incorporated into the design. In sum, a tattoo and a scapular fulfill the same function: to protect. The difference is that a tattoo is permanently imprinted on the wearer's skin, thus forming part of the body until death. It is a form of requesting protection in addition to daily prayers (Perdigón, 2008a, pp. 88–89).

The act of giving thanks, of feeling and wishing to show gratitude for something received, is known colloquially as *pagando una manda* (keeping a promise). This is a kind of tribute that a devotee offers to La Santa Muerte for a miracle performed or a favor granted, serving as a lifelong reminder that the saint helped when the devotee most desperately needed her intervention, whether the individual tattooed was the one who received the favor, or a spouse, or some other family member. The case of Miguel Sánchez Marceliano is emblematic: Miguel prayed for a couple of favors that he knew only she was capable of granting. When things later worked out in his favor, he felt that the best way he could express his thanks was by getting tattoos:

> At the altar on Alfarería Street I promised "the Skinny One" [*mi Flaquita*] that if my wife got pregnant I would show my thanks. When my wife brought the news that she was expecting a baby, my faith grew stronger and I thanked her by getting a tattoo; the other one, the one on my back . . . I got it because she helped me get my health back and find a job.

Once the devotee decides to get a tattoo (for whatever reason), she or he visits a tattoo artist. Usually, believers bring a model, or various designs, but they may also ask to see the specialist's catalogue and choose an image from there, or perhaps one from the Internet. Generally speaking, tattoo artists ask their clients to choose, but sometimes they suggest modifications to the design. And some people create new designs. During her interview, Sol Chicahuatzin explained that her experience as a tattoo artist allows her to advise her clients so that the emblem is placed in the best area with the best colors, depending on the specific motif, size, and degree of difficulty involved in achieving the finished image.

> I think that when people come they've already pretty much decided what they'd like and where they'd like it, right? Sometimes we change the model for aesthetic reasons, or to make sure the tattoo flows anatomically with the form of your body; like I might recommend they change . . . say . . . the angle of the drawing, or include some other element in the composition to make the space look pretty . . . but . . .

well, that's where communication comes in, how good you are at persuading [people], to enhance the idea or modify it so it "fits" the body better; it's subjective, like an artist.

TATTOO TYPOLOGIES

During fieldwork, we observed diverse types of tattoos. Variation depends primarily on who did the work (what type of tattoo artist), because the products of different tattooers can be recognized by their quality. Some of the tattoos we saw were clearly made by tattooers who had learned the trade in prison; they are called the *canero* type. These artists usually work out of their homes or in marketplaces. Their work is normally inexpensive; their designs show little creativity and are structurally limited and rather crude. Other tattoo artists have stalls in flea markets (*tianguis*). Few of them have studied the art of tattooing (by acquiring a knowledge of techniques or formal training), and they began to work out of necessity or interest, with tattooing eventually becoming their full-time trade. Their work is not expensive, and most of their designs are based on images from the mass media.

The final group includes tattoo artists with formal training. Their work is the most highly valued because it has the best aesthetic quality. These artists enjoy prestige among their colleagues. Also, they are continually actualizing their techniques and designs; some even participate in international expositions. For a tattoo to be considered of fine quality, it must be well designed, taking into account functional, aesthetic, and symbolic aspects. It also has to form part of an idea that is sketched out before being materialized according to a specific technique on a selected area of the body. Finally, the elements of color, texture, and size need to be taken into account (García Olvera, 1996).

These true tattoo artists are knowledgeable in diverse techniques of the plastic arts—aquarelle, graffiti, calligraphy, pointillism, and aerography, among others—and have developed great dexterity in handling tattooing equipment. Their mastery is reflected as well in their ability to combine colors and control line thickness, shadows, and contrasts of tones of grays. Their tattoos are usually well proportioned in relation to the area of the body where they are drawn, regardless of skin type.

When tattoo artists discuss designs, they speak of "traditional" or "classic" models, the ones they have been drawing for years. Often called "typical" motifs, these include images of birds, hearts, flowers, anchors, mermaids, tigers, dragons, and skulls, among others. Another type is called "commercial" or "in style." This category includes specific tattoo designs that are borne by well-known singers, athletes, or actors, that are replicated hundreds of times by noncelebrities. One example of this category is the meteor shower, a symbol of infinity.

Tattoos of the "religious" type feature representations of the Virgin Mary, Christ and Christian saints, Yoruba gods and motifs, and Hebrew and Muslim symbols and calligraphies, to mention but a few. In the specific case of La Santa Muerte as a religious entity, one may see hyperrealist forms (with a 3-D appearance), or true portraits (realistic representations based on photographs), although these may reflect ethnic features (e.g., pre-Hispanic elements) or popular culture, especially those adapted from posters, cover art from rock music CDs, or designs from the Internet, as we explain below.

For our study, we chose to develop a classification of tattoos based on the comments of the devotees we interviewed and iconographic research. Applying this twofold approach allowed us to isolate three key categories of design: one historical, a second media related, and a third that reflects creative invention. In what follows, we clarify the observations that led us to this classification system. Regarding the historical element, we found images that have emerged with the evolution of humankind, motifs from diverse Western cultures (including iconographies seen in tombs and at religious sites), and decorations observed in architecture and greater and lesser art forms. Some well-known motifs in this category are danses macabres, *ars moriendi*, memento mori, the tree of life, death, and the triumph of the cross over death. The media-influenced rubric includes skeletal representations extracted from historical contexts that were transformed in the twentieth and twenty-first centuries into album covers, posters, and the wide world of Internet images. Finally, the category of creative invention refers to embellishments of images in the historical and media categories that reflect the particular tastes and likes of the devotees who have them done and of the tattoo artists who do them.

Although the diverse images recognized in commercial circles as representations of La Santa Muerte differ markedly in size, color, and materiality, many have been transformed and adapted to the techniques of tattooing. The devotees we interviewed told us that they can distinguish the following basic images: imperial, traditional, warrior, winged (angel), wind, apocalyptic, portrait, and mixed (invented). Variation depends on what the best place on the body is for the classic emblems of this deity. For example, the design features and impact of the imperial image are best suited to the back. Based on the testimonies gathered and our own observations, and respecting the aforementioned classification, we categorized the tattoos we studied as follows.

Tattoos of the imperial image reflect the antecedent of the Empress Death from medieval times. Usually she is shown seated on a throne, although in the twentieth century this image was transformed by two social phenomena: the introduction of the horror fiction cinematic genre and the emergence of heavy metal music. Their influence explains how La Santa Muerte came to incorporate elements intended to produce fear and amazement. Some of these components have been taken up by artists like the Swiss painter and designer Hans Ruedi Giger (1940–2014) and two Americans, authors Howard Phillips Lovecraft (1890–1937) and Stephen King (1947–). Others have been appropriated and incorporated into the stagings of heavy metal groups like Iron Maiden, Death, and Sinister (to mention a few), in which the figure of death has been dressed in feathers and placed in frightening scenarios, such as floors replete with corpses, and scenes with fallen angels or gargoyles perched on the backrest and arms of a throne.[9] According to comments by spiritual leaders we interviewed, other images include the inverted star and the crow, although these do not pertain to the original design of La Santa Muerte and introduce a distinct esoteric meaning.[10] Finally, some variants of the imperial design feature additions like skulls or long bones, depending on the tastes of individual clients.

Tattoos bearing a traditional or classic image are based on the archetypal design of La Santa Muerte, which began to circulate commercially in the mid-twentieth century (Perdigón, 2008a). They may show the complete body or just the torso of a skeleton dressed in shawl and tunic, carrying a globe, scythe, and scale, sometimes accompanied by an owl or the moon. In contrast, the "warrior" image is an effigy of death wielding a scythe, depicted to show movement, with enlarged eye orbits and a grimace instead of a smile. Occasionally, this figure may have fangs, which is why people outside the cult perceive it as malevolent or vengeful. Devotees said that people who tattoo this image are either angry at life or want to present an appearance of toughness. This icon has been adapted by artists like Melvyn Grant, Derek Riggs, Luis Royo, Andreas Marschall, and Jim Warren, who often illustrate album covers for heavy metal groups like the ones mentioned above. All images of this nature date from the 1970s.

Known as the "Angel of Death," the winged image is a design more often

FIGURE 6.1 Man with tattoo representing "Santa Muerte of the Wind," September 2010, Tepito neighborhood, Mexico City. Photograph by Jorge Salgado Ponce.

FIGURE 6.2 Man with tattoo representing La Santa Muerte as empress, September 2010, Tepito neighborhood, Mexico City. Photograph by Jorge Salgado Ponce.

FIGURE 6.3 Woman with tattoo representing winged image of La Santa Muerte known as "Angel of Death," July 2010, Tepito neighborhood, Mexico City. Photograph by Jorge Salgado Ponce.

FIGURE 6.4 Man with tattoo representing La Santa Muerte as warrior, July 2010, Tepito neighborhood, Mexico City. Photograph by Jorge Salgado Ponce.

requested by women, curiously enough, according to the information we obtained. It also has historical antecedents in religious art and is often seen in funerary settings in Europe. This particular design became popular after it appeared in the cemetery scene with Tom Riddle in the film *Harry Potter and the Goblet of Fire.*[11] Since then, extensive marketing has led devotees to develop a penchant for this image, which shows La Santa Muerte's skeleton with shawl and tunic but adds wings and, perhaps, some of the prototypical elements described above.

There are other images as well. The one called the Santa del Viento (Saint of the Wind) may depict death with a shawl and tunic or wearing a monk-style habit, the lower part rippling as if "the wind were blowing over it." This representation may carry some of the iconographic elements listed earlier; it may have wings, and it is often shown walking over skulls. The image that devotees call "apocalyptic" portrays La Santa Muerte on horseback in a motif clearly adapted from ancient Western art, specifically the Four Horsemen of the Apocalypse (described in the first part of chapter 6 of the Book of Revelation). This biblical passage mentions a scroll held in God's right hand that is sealed with seven seals. Jesus opens the first four seals to release horsemen mounted on four steeds: one white, one red, one black, and one pale. According to the exegesis, they represent, and are allegories of, conquest, war, famine, and death, respectively, although only the fourth is designated as such. We have seen numerous images and drawings associated with album covers, television series, North American comics, and Japanese manga. Another variant of the Santa is known as the "opener of paths." This image is sought especially by believers who see or feel that their "path" (toward health, money, love, etc.) is blocked or closed off. This figure of death is dressed in a tunic or monk's habit, but its face is hidden from view. Only its hands are visible, and its posture suggests a reaping motion. We were told that when she "moves" the scythe, often with the moon shining on her back, she is showing her "disposition to help open the supplicant's way, always in search of good."

Tattoos of the "portrait" type are often based on ancient Mexican sculpted images of the kind associated with burial mounds, or on Easter Friday processions that represent the cross's triumph over death. Specific reference can be made to the figure housed in the museum at the archaeological site at Yanhuitlán (Oaxaca), or another at a family shrine in Tepatepec (Hidalgo).[12] In our view, these are representations of what art historians call trompe l'oeil, a technique that seeks to "create the illusion that the spectator is attending the event exhibited" through a painted image that takes the place of reality (Pérez Sánchez, 1992, p. 40). Their value consists in creating the illusion that one is in the presence of the original; in other words, they personify portraits of sculptures using a series of plastic conventions that highlight their nature as three-dimensional icons (Amador Marrero & Díaz Cayeros, 2014). Believers with this type of tattoo desire substitution: they have the genuine miraculous, ancient image inked on their skin as protection. One of our interviewees said: "It's as if she's there with me in person," while others commented that their tattoos were "true portraits."

Not surprisingly, some images are composed by the "free will" of devotees or tattoo artists. These often include various iconographic elements seemingly chosen at random, or perhaps due to aesthetic preferences or even inspiration. They reproduce some of the prototypes mentioned previously but fuse them with other designs: for example, a combination of the winged and imperial figures, or the warrior depicted with wind or with pre-Hispanic elements, to mention a few. On the Internet—but not yet in our fieldwork in Mexico City—we found tattoo motifs showing a symbiosis of La Santa Muerte and the Virgen de Guadalupe, a graffiti-style design created by Chicano artists visible on city streets in the United States and along the US-Mexico border. Clearly, this is an attempt to fuse two of Mexico's most iconic religious entities, despite their distinctive origins and meanings. This design likely aims to strengthen people's belief and concentrate iconic power in one sole essence. Here are two dominant symbols with values considered ends in themselves that interact in the same context, both with equal efficacy (Perdigón, 2008b, p. 61).

Other models of tattoos may well exist, perhaps designs derived from small sculptures found in commercial circuits that represent piety, or representations of bikers surging out of a grave, or imagined images based on stories and tales. However, we have not seen these motifs in the altars we visited in Mexico City. Posters are another element. In some cases, images adapted from posters carry words or short texts, often simply the legend "Santa Muerte," someone's name (Esteban, Jesús, Dulce, Urbina) or nickname (Cheque), a phrase alluding to the devotee ("Devotee forever"), or simple initials (M.S.L). Other believers include a fragment of a prayer or poem, for example "Muerte querida de mi corazón, no me desampares con tu protección" (Dear Death of my heart, do not leave me without your protection). The calligraphy may be small or large in relation to the tattoo and the area of the body where it is placed. Lettering shows various styles reflecting the client's taste or, perhaps, the tattoo artist's dexterity.

A way of projecting the body onto the social world, tattoos form part of an individual's image. After all, human beings are characterized by change, influenced by fashion, religion, morality, technological novelties, and new forms that reality assumes. Tattoos are, therefore, personal marks that express people's deepest feelings.

CONCLUSIONS

While tattooing is now in vogue, these images inked into the skin are much more than simple decorations or embellishments of the body. The fact that a devotee of La Santa Muerte decides to get a tattoo dedicated to this entity derives from a need to show gratitude for a favor received or a miracle performed, and/or to beseech La Santa Muerte to protect the body or soul of the bearer or some member of the family. It is important to clarify that all our interviewees—believers and tattoo artists alike—told us that this entity is an intermediary between the devotee and God who can grant favors or perform miracles. As a symbol, La Santa Muerte lives in the everyday world of the individuals who believe in her, bring her offerings, and pray to her. She is nothing less than a part of their way of life and of their situation in the world; in short, part of their very existence. La Santa Muerte must thus be read from two poles: comforting or perturbing, according to the nature of the spectator and the messages and emotions that the tattoos transmit. She is an integral part of a cultural practice of the twenty-first century imprinted for life on the individuals who get tattoos. Tattoos of La Santa Muerte are designed specifically for each area of the body. By getting tattoos, believers seek to give meaning to a veneration, a belief, or a devotion, or to display their gratitude for a petition granted. As a result, the design, creation, and presence of tattoos go beyond the body as objective reality and come to be identified as lived reality.

These marks are representations that not only identify the subject who is tattooed but that are also registered, lived, and configured within their social group of reference. Tattoos may be maps showing the paths each individual has traveled; gifts to recognize prayers answered; or implorations that have been heard and transformed into fortunate solutions. Each tattoo is a particular history that is molded by experience and that transforms the bearer's life. Some believers come to feel such an intense need to exalt La Santa Muerte that they consider most typical offerings (flowers, food, clothes, jewelry, incense, etc.) insufficient. Because the body is the greatest treasure they can offer, they choose to get a tattoo, selecting the design in accordance with three basic factors: a scene that appeared in a dream, an apparition, or personal taste. Then they select the area of the body where the tattoo is to be applied. All our interviewees also alluded to the pain they experienced during the process. Some considered this excruciating but necessary to demonstrate their devotion. Others, however, found it so difficult that they vowed never to go through it again; they said that the experience had been so intense and exhausting that they could hardly bear it. But these devotees commented that La Santa Muerte knows and understands this. We agree with Anabella Barragán Solís and Omar Ramírez de la Roche's observation that "[t]he experience of pain also has to do with the intensity, origin, duration, and meaning attributed to it [and] with social and individual factors among which the most important are family teachings, the gender and character of the individual, the body part(s) affected, religious affiliation, education, occupation, and emotional states, among others" (2014).

During our research, we observed that there are multiple ways of seeing, feeling, identifying with, and worshipping La Santa Muerte. Some interviewees held that the tattoo was an extreme form of giving thanks and that the only way to truly achieve this was to reach the limits of one's pain threshold. What they seek to transmit is their gratitude for a favor received, for protection, or for a benefit. In this sense, it is important to add that several devotees mentioned having rather low pain thresholds, but that because La Santa had granted their supplication, they felt the need to thank her by tolerating the physical pain caused by tattooing. In other cases, we spoke with believers who felt that the benefit received was so great that the only way they could show their gratitude was by getting more tattoos, even though it meant crossing the limits of tolerance. Often, they begin with small, discreet images or designs, but as additional—and perhaps more significant—prayers are answered, they feel that they must choose larger and more intricate motifs. All our interviewees, however, agreed that tattooing is a form of retribution, a show of devotion, and a source of deep satisfaction, for they believe that once they have the image of La Santa Muerte etched graphically on their body, her power of healing, protection, support, and care will be maintained throughout their lives.

NOTES

1. Despite this particular form of organization, Regnar Kristensen argues that a relatively uniform set of devotional practices has emerged over time (this volume).

2. We understand social representations following Serge Moscovici, who postulated them as interpretations of the social life that one lives. He considered it important to distinguish the commonsense meaning from that of scientific thought, and to study subjects as processes in which mental representations are analyzed by the researcher and then interpreted and described as public representations (taken from Osorio Carranza, 1994, p. 8).

3. In all textual citations, we respect the interviewee's lexicon. Because they allowed us to record these talks, we were able to make exact transcriptions of the discourse, though only excerpts are included. (*Translator's note*: an effort has been made to reproduce this lexicon in the English translation.)

4. The combination of a limited number of in-depth interviews and dozens of (informal) conversations and encounters with devotees enables us to construct a detailed and valid description of the cultural attributes of a specific social group.

5. Experience is understood as all the individual events that produce impulses and sentiments in us. Thus, "all that which dominates us, such as customs [and] uses, and which we live every day during general co-existence and which acquires tradition, is founded within our vital experience" (Dilthey, 1998, p. 43).

6. It is worthwhile observing that the choice of particular tattoos and of tattooing particular body parts is conditioned above all by religious or spiritual experiences.

Among popular classes, tattoo visibility is hence much less influenced by allegedly negative external perceptions. This is also related to the fact that in Mexico, as elsewhere, the general stigma attached to tattoos has disappeared.

7. For an interesting analysis of the role of the media in framing the Santa Muerte cult, see Roush (2014).

8. Anabella Barragán Solís and Omar Ramírez de la Roche (2014, p. 7) write: "Anthropological research demonstrates that pain and illness are phenomena of the human; [they] form part of the world of life, so it is indispensable to contextualize them in their sociocultural situation, which entails recognizing that they are subjective experiences situated in a cultural milieu that conditions perception; that is, sensory experience."

9. Imaginary animals and monsters appear in the religious art of the Middle Ages as symbols of strength or images of the demoniacal, draconian underworld, but later as vanquished prisoners subjected to the power of a superior spirituality. This is indicated in the hierarchy in which they always appear subordinated to angelic and celestial images, never occupying the center; see Cirlot (1991, p. 214).

10. The crow is one of the most important universal symbols. It can be imbued with different meanings. On the one hand, it is considered maleficent, but on the other beneficial. It is an image of the devil, due to its black color and strange habits, but also a beneficial animal when it is shown carrying food (usually pieces of bread) to various saints (Cabral Pérez, 1995, p. 97).

11. The fourth film based on the famous series of novels by J. K. Rowling and directed by Mike Newell, the film debuted in November 2005.

12. For more information on these images, see Perdigón (2008a).

7 | # Afterword
| *Interpreting La Santa Muerte*

There has been substantial new ethnographic research on La Santa Muerte since the topic began to gain broad media coverage in the early 2000s, and indeed since the publication of my work *Death and the Idea of Mexico* (2005). Here, I posited that this development in Mexican popular religion was "a symptom of Mexico's second secular revolution—the nation's increasingly tenuous connection to the state," and that its principal sociological innovation was that, within the cult, death, rather than the state, "is in the place of the ultimate sovereign" (Lomnitz, 2005a, p. 491). There has been much additional research since I wrote those lines. Moreover, the Santa Muerte cult has grown and become widely known. Alongside some serious ethnographic work and copious—though often superficial—media attention, the contours of the cult have morphed, attracting new devotees even beyond Mexico's borders. As Wil Pansters shows in the introduction to this volume, the essays collected here allow for a reframing of the subject. I would like to use my closing remarks to sketch what I believe are some key elements of such a reconceptualization.

MANAGEMENT OF STIGMA

The chapter by Juan Antonio Flores Martos leads with an image of a middle-class professional who does not want to bare his torso and enter a swimming pool in front of his friends because he is reticent to expose the fact that he has a large Santa Muerte tattoo. Flores Martos uses this anecdote to make the point that the Santa Muerte cult is no longer relegated to prisons, prostitutes, and the criminal world but rather touches sectors of society whose livelihood can be characterized as precarious. Indeed, all the essays in this volume concur in identifying the community of Santa Muerte believers as a population characterized by living with high degrees of uncertainty and vulnerability. They recognize the Santa Muerte cult as founded first and foremost on transactions and exchanges that prominently feature requests for protection, and secondarily interventions to secure love or achieve various other desires.

Thus, there is, first, protection, and second, desire. And indeed both protection and the ability to access objects of desire are critical for people living in uncertain conditions, including members of the insecure middle class, for whom access to love objects and status commodities can be positively required for consolidating a class position. There is, however, another aspect of this opening example that deserves consideration, namely that the Santa Muerte cult can be analyzed as "stigma." Stigma, as Erving Goffman discusses, can be both a visible or at least discoverable individual handicap, and an exalted sign of "tribal" pride (Goffman, 1963/1991, pp. 105–25). Indeed there is often a connection between stigmata and the sacred: the mark of personal suffering becomes a sign of allegiance with that which cannot be profaned.

The centrality of tattooing in the Santa Muerte cult suggests a process wherein a social or personal stigma is willfully transformed into a physically visible stigma, which then operates as a sacred sign. The transformation of unseen to discoverable stigmata through tattooing is meant to be indelible testimony of a pact with a deity. At the same time, however, this personal transformation, from a sense of psychological suffering to the voluntary acquisition of a physical stigma, is also a move away from individual suffering and toward the acquisition of a social identity.

Having said this, it is equally important to recognize, as with all stigmata, that the revelation of bodily signs of a pact with La Santa Muerte is not always desirable. Flores Martos's middle-class swimmer was not eager to reveal the sign to his broader social circle. There are others, however, who wear the branded image on their neck or forearm, making the stigma permanently visible, thereby reducing their chances to circulate freely in formal, middle-class jobs and circles while gaining, in exchange, protection from those who fear the tit-for-tat, "jealous" reciprocity that characterizes La Santa Niña. I believe that there is a clue here regarding the nature of the cult: hiding the image in one context as stigma, showing it off in another as protection. How does this dynamic work?

Presumably, an actor who chooses to openly don an allegiance with death prioritizes making that alliance public over the discriminatory effects that carrying a death sign might bring with it. It sets up a hard line between the believer and the dominant society or culture. Such a "hard-line effect" suggests compatibility with modes of precarious living that do not require or entail admission into certain jobs or social circles, for instance white- or pink-collar service jobs that involve serving as a company's face to the public, or domestic employment that involves being accepted within families who might bridle at the idea of having a cult member with regular access to their domestic lives. Indeed, open allegiance to La Santa Muerte suggests forms of existential precarity wherein an announced connection to the saint provides greater protection than the cost of discrimination generated by that same exhibit.

Situations of this sort can be compatible with jobs that don't involve extended relationships with a single patron. For example, a Mexico City taxi driver who exhibits a Santa Muerte figurine on the dashboard of his car probably suffers few consequences if some clients are irked by the figurine—they will be in and out of the cab regardless, with no longer-term consequences. At the same time, the driver might benefit from the protection that his proudly displayed patroness might provide against would-be assailants, who are a key aspect of precariousness for taxi drivers in cities like Mexico City. If the same taxi driver were part of a service such as Uber instead of an independent operator, however, the face of the company, and the feedback mechanisms that exist between Uber users, company management, and drivers, might make public displays of affiliation with La Santa Muerte riskier for the driver.

Indeed, the growth of public identification of the figure since the turn of the twenty-first century may be due at least in part to the relative decline of long-term, face-to-face work relationships, and to the vibrancy of casual work relationships with multiple clients. Taxi drivers, market vendors, and street-walking prostitutes share this characteristic, and there are many devotees among them. Transnational migrants who rely on dangerous border crossings to arrive in the United States may sometimes be in analogous situations of precarity and lack of long-term labor dependencies.

It seems to me that the condition of the cult in prisons also offers a promising avenue of inquiry for understanding the dynamics of open versus discrete modes of identification with La Santa Muerte. There is, after all, a fair indication of the centrality of prison in the development of the Santa Muerte cult. As Wil Pansters recounts in his introduction to this volume, Regnar Kristensen has found a strong correlation between the distribution and density of street altars in Mexico City and the proportion of ex-convicts living in the neighborhood. Moreover, prisoners have for decades improvised altars for La Santa Muerte, and prison studies remarked on the cult long before it became widely known in Mexico City (see Payá, 2006; Yllescas Illescas, 2016). Indeed, it seems possible that the cult that we now know originated in prison.

The relationship between the prison guard and the prisoner around the Santa Muerte stigma may provide clues regarding the connection between open and hidden forms of identification. The prison guard is in a relationship of precarity because of his routine connection to criminals. At the same time, being a prison guard carries social stigma due to their proximity to criminals and crime. Although prison guards engage in both formal and informal rituals that are designed to create a strong solidarity and identity between them, and establish a sharp division between guard and prisoner, these lines often blur. Prisoners have connections to the outside world, and these can be dangerous to the guard. Prisoners and guards develop personal relationships, or at least a level of intimacy that is dangerous and potentially stigmatizing. Such a relationship hinging on the precarity of criminality lends itself to forms of allegiance with La Santa Muerte that can allow guards to hide the death stigma, rather than exhibiting it openly at all times. Presumably, guards who are Santa Muerte devotees will not tattoo their necks, hands, or faces, for instance.

For prisoners, the situation is entirely different. Even when their altars or shrines to La Santa Muerte are personal, they are also necessarily "public," since prison provides no genuine private space for prisoners. For them, not even toilets are "privies." The only private space that prisoners might aspire to is that of their bodies, but even there true privacy is impossible, since prisoners' bodies are easily exposed and violated.[1] Indeed, the prisoner's body is regularly visible in prison and impossible to conceal on a permanent basis. This means that, once a prisoner engages in the Santa Muerte cult, the exhibition of the Santa Muerte image is inevitable.

Because revealing allegiance to La Santa Muerte is inevitable for prisoners who are devotees, there is a tendency among them toward sublimation of the image, which means proudly exhibiting the stigma, rather than hiding it, as a guard will. This sublimation is also encouraged by the nature of the Santa Muerte image itself. Having a dyadic contract with death is believed to provide protection in the highly insecure context that is a Mexican prison. For prison guards, on the other hand, the connection with the same death image is necessarily more ambivalent. This suggests that whereas the cult among prisoners will tend, within the jail, to sublimation and exhibition, the cult among prison guards will tend to be more concealed.

Once prisoners are free, the question of whether maintaining a sublimated relationship with the death image is advantageous or not is less clear. If the stigma of being an ex-convict becomes difficult to hide, former prisoners will tend to occupy a caste-like rung in the broader society, so that what had been an open devotion in prison becomes the sign of something like a fraternity or sodality outside. Much like the signs of Freemasonry in its heyday, shared allegiance to La Santa Muerte can identify two strangers as being part of the same thing. If a policeman and an ex-convict meet as civilians—for instance, in public rosaries to the image—their mutual allegiance to the cult may serve as a bond between them, helping them recognize their shared precarity, and their brotherhood in death.

STRONG AND WEAK FORMS
OF LA SANTA MUERTE DEVOTION

Due to the prominence of stigma in the cult, the tattoo appears in the first instance to be the most significant sign of the compact between the subject and La Santa Muerte. Indeed, in his essay in this volume, Kristensen remarks that the relationship between followers and La Santa Muerte resembles a marriage contract more than a short-lived commercial contract. In this regard, the prominence of tattooing is anything but fortuitous: a lasting vow involves acquiring some visible mark, such as a wedding ring, for instance, or circumcision, in the case of the pact between the children of Abraham and their God. Moreover, until recently in Mexico, tattoos themselves (of any sort) were considered signs of criminality, and police routinely held suspects with tattoos for seventy-two hours in order to investigate whether they were jailbirds (Payá, 2006, p. 278). Thus, with the recent transformation in the meaning of tattoos more broadly, a Santa Muerte tattoo is also a group sign that nods at once to La Santa Muerte and to prison.

The Santa Muerte cult trumpets the signs of its own gravity: believers are bent naturalizing the uneasy admixture of a devouring and jealous death and a caring, nurturing mother figure, for instance, and they stress that asking La Santa Muerte for a favor implies lifelong compulsion of care to the saint, on pain of death. Despite all of this seriousness and consequence, however, it is also clear that the cult has a commercial component that tends to its domestication, equalization to other devotions, and banalization. Ponderously studying Santa Muerte liturgical prayers and religious knickknacks seems sometimes a bit like taking the philosophy of a Chinese fortune cookie deeply into account, or like trying earnestly to parse the significance of the *maneki-neko* "fortune cat" who welcomes patrons at Asian restaurants. The material is meaningful, no doubt, but much Santa Muerte liturgy appears to be a slapdash mixture of elements of Catholic prayers (Our Fathers, Hail Marys, etc.) and the chintzy, made-in-Texas or made-in-China paraphernalia that is routinely sold in magic stores and *botánicas*: black soaps, colored candles, *sábila* cacti wrapped in red ribbons, and the like.

The strength of the Santa Muerte cult is manifest in the body—in the intimate decision to make a binding promise to the death deity, laying down one's own life as the guarantee in the bargain. But the work of making the cult more palatable—via, for instance, the insistence that La Santa Muerte is squarely and firmly "good" (versus frighteningly ambivalent), or the creation of Masses and a mythology harking back to Aztec death deities—allows for shorter-term connections with the deity as opposed to the quasi-familial ties described by several authors in this volume.

Indeed, Santa Muerte commodities are not only popular at botánicas but can also be incorporated in a counterculture market that thrives on the sale of heavy metal and Che Guevara T-shirts, and commodities sold to enthusiasts of the various shades of Mexico's *darketo* subculture. Mexican rock culture has long been an element of urban popular culture, deeply rooted in sectors of the lower classes, and the image of La Santa Muerte is aesthetically assimilable to it. On the other hand, Mexico City's urban counterculture has had long-standing connections to prison and the criminal world as a fount of fashion. This is particularly true in the realm of language; Mexico City *caló* slang is a prime example of this. The assimilation of La Santa Muerte as an image that can be worn on a jacket or T-shirt, or even, these days, in a tattoo, does not require a lifelong dyadic contract. It forms part of a repertoire of images, gestures, and cultural forms of which La Santa Muerte can be a passing element. In other words, the fact that the Santa Muerte cult deals with death and its sovereignty does not necessarily succeed in earning it the gravitas that it no doubt has among many followers.

THE NATURE OF EXCHANGE

In Juan Lope Blanch's (1963) study of idioms and expressions for death in Mexico City, there are several expressions that foreshadow the problems of exchange that are prominent in the Santa Muerte cult. I would like to focus on a few expressions in particular: *la tía Quiteria* (the aunt that takes), *la libera-dora* (the liberator), *la chingada* (the fucked one), *la madre Matiana* (the mother that kills), and *la novia fiel* (the faithful bride). There are several motifs that are relevant to understanding the nature of exchange in the Santa Muerte cult that are already figured in these old Mexico City expressions. Most relevant for comprehending the nature of the dyadic relationship with death is the form of reciprocal exchange that I have elsewhere theorized as "asymmetric negative reciprocity" (2005b). I will summarize the idea briefly, and then return to the lexical forms that Lope Blanche collected in the early sixties.

Classical anthropological treatises on reciprocity recognized a negative form of reciprocity that had feuding, or even haggling in the marketplace, as its models. Negative reciprocity in these modalities involved taking rather than giving, but in order to be conceptualized as a form of reciprocity, the taking needed to be reciprocal. A life for a life, tit for tat.[2] However, classical theories recognized "positive" forms of reciprocity, based on gifting (rather than on taking), that need not be so strictly symmetrical: gifts can be profusely bestowed in one direction with only vague commitments of return and the relationship still be framed as one founded in reciprocity. Similarly, according to my argument, there is a second, asymmetrical, form of negative reciprocity. In it, a relationship begins with a violation—"taking"—that also inaugurates a relationship of subordination. The violent act of taking is then followed by giving as an act of humiliation, because the subordinate must receive, and that forced gift is then meant to launch a relationship of subjugation in a long-term asymmetrical exchange. *Caciquismo* in its classical formulations was often framed in these terms. A cacique approaching a peasant to evict him from his land might ask: "Who shall I buy it from, you or your widow?" Thus, a credible death threat sets off a compulsory exchange, which then launches long-term relations of subordination.

The figure of death as la chingada (the fucked one) is a theme that was analyzed a half century ago by Octavio Paz. Death is a woman who is in eternal and ontological deficit. She has been violated: we live on "borrowed time," so our lives are owed, and death is a form of payment. This idea is reinforced by the not infrequent use of maternal imagery—our collective identity as *hijos de la chingada*, sons of the fucked one (death)—as, for example, in figures for death such as la madre Matiana (the mother who kills) or la tía Quiteria (the aunt who takes). The nurturing mother is all the time owed, hungry, and eager to take back what is her due. This emphasis on death as hungering for the living, on life as a gift that must be repaid, is present and prominent in pre-Columbian imagery, as is well known.

The relationship with death (in the form of La Santa Muerte) is predicated on a form of negotiation in which the time and mode of death is negotiable in exchange for recognition, affection, and advanced payment. This sort of trade-off existed in the baroque era, particularly in exchanges between the living and the souls in Purgatory: making offerings to a soul hastened his or her passage from Purgatory to Glory, but this offering would then be repaid in various ways and could even be used in generating love magic, finding treasure, and the like.

Kristensen's emphasis on La Santa Muerte as providing *paros* is helpful in this regard, because a paro is a temporary form of help, an ad hoc form of aid designed to rescue someone who is in a tight spot, but not to transform his or her normal situation. Death is thus not in a position to effect an ontological life change; it is not a figure of redemption, but of intervention. This is what was implied in a comical expression for death registered by Lope Blanche: la novia fiel, the faithful bride. As opposed to real brides, death will always be there, will never jolt you, will always come through, of course in its macabre and sinister way.

However, the 1960s macabre humor implicit in the formula of death as a faithful bride did at least imply that *life* was what transpires between birth and an expiring individual's final "marriage" to death. One of the puzzles of the Santa Muerte cult is that devotees represent their connection with La Santa Muerte as marriage-like. Thus, there appears to be none of the postponement implicit in the older image of death as the novia fiel. What is it like to be married to death—rather than engaged to death—while one is still alive? This is one of the deeper questions that is implicit in much of the current ethnography but that has not yet been explored directly, although the connection between paro and amparo explored in Kristensen's dissertation (2011) on La Santa Muerte does at least allow some speculation in this regard.

Prayers to La Santa Muerte are modeled on the Catholic rosary, which is a ritual instrument in the cult of the Virgin Mary. And Mary's key role is that of intercession, both for the benefit of the living and, especially, as champion of the souls in Purgatory. Thus, asking for Mary's amparo (protection/intercession) implies not only help in this or that situation but also intercession to gain eternal, transcendental salvation. Thus, as opposed to the Mexican slang term "paro," "amparo" in a religious sense implies salvation. And this La Santa Muerte cannot provide.

The sort of amparo that death may offer is more akin to the Mexican legal injunction—called "amparo"—than to the transcendental amparo provided by the Virgin Mary. This is why I claimed in *Death and the Idea of Mexico* that La Santa Muerte was a symptom of a "second secular revolution," which includes forms of in-worldly religious devotion. Salvation in the Santa Muerte cult is no longer transcendental. It is temporary, transitory, and precarious. Being wedded to La Santa Muerte appears to me to be an act of accepting a life with some possibilities for respite, but no redemption.

NOTES

1. Thus, Victor Payá (2004, p. 296) describes horrifying instances of prisoners who are raped, and then forcibly tattooed with images showing them with tears in their eyes, or with rabbits or mice going into their anuses, so as to mark these individuals as subordinate.

2. Marshall Sahlins provides a classical synthesis of this position (1963).

BIBLIOGRAPHY

Adeath, C., & Kristensen, R. (2007). *La muerte de tu lado*. Mexico City: Fundación del Centro Histórico de la Ciudad de México.

Agar, M. (2006). An ethnography by any other name. *FQS Forum: Qualitative Social Research/Sozialforschung*, 7(4). Retrieved from http://www.qualitative-research. net/index.php/fqs/article/view/177

Aguiar, J. C. G. (2014). Review of the book *Devoted to death: Santa Muerte, the skeleton saint*, by R. A. Chesnut. *European Journal of Latin American and Caribbean Studies*, no. 96, 164–66.

Aguilar, J. (2007, September 23). Santa Muerte, ignorancia, confusión e idolatría. *Desde la Fé: Semanario Católico de Información y Formación*, no. 552. Retrieved from www.churchforum.org

Aguilar Valdés, J. (2007). *Pregúntale al Padre José: Él responde a todas tus dudas*. Mexico City: Diana.

Aisenson Kogan, A. (1981). *Cuerpo y persona: Filosofía y psicología del cuerpo vivido*. Mexico City: Fondo de Cultura Económica.

Alcoceba Hernando, J. A. (2007). El lenguaje del cuerpo a través del tatuaje: De la descripción identitaria a la homogeneizadora democratización de la belleza. *Revista de Estudios de la Juventud*, no. 78, 75–90.

Altares, ofrendas, oraciones y rituales a la Santa Muerte. (2007). Mexico City: Ediciones Viman.

Álvarez, E., Gutiérrez, L., Nuevo, T., Rodríguez, L., Ruiz, A., & Ventura, O. (2007). *Culto a la Santa Muerte: Vida a través de la muerte* (Unpublished master's thesis). Universidad Autónoma Metropolitana Xochimilco, Mexico City.

Amador Marrero, P., & Díaz Cayeros, P. (2014). *Imagen escultórica y retrato*. Paper presented at the thirty-sixth Coloquio Internacional de Historia del Arte: Los estatutos de la imagen, Universidad Nacional Autónoma de México, Instituto de Investigaciones Estéticas, Mexico City. Retrieved from http://www.ebooks. esteticas.unam.mx/items/show/21

Ambrosio, J. (2003). *La Santa Muerte, biografía y culto: Veintiséis rituales personales para conseguir salud, dinero y amor*. Mexico City: Editorial Planeta.

Anónimo. (2015). *La biblia de la Santa Muerte*. Mexico City: Editores Mexicanos Unidos.

Argyriadis, K. (2012). Ritual en el mar a Yemayá: Puerto de Veracruz, primero de noviembre de 2005. In R. de la Torre (Ed.), *El don de la ubicuidad: Rituales étnicos multisituados* (pp. 246–59). Mexico City: Centro de Investigaciones y Estudios Superiores en Antropología Social.

Argyriadis, K. (2014). Católicos, apostólicos y no-satánicos: Representaciones contemporáneas en México y construcciones locales (Veracruz) del culto a la Santa Muerte. *Revista Cultura y Religión*, 8(1), 191–218.

Argyriadis, K., & Juárez, N. (2005). Las redes transnacionales de la santería cubana: Una construcción etnográfica a partir del caso La Habana–Ciudad de México. Unpublished manuscript.

Aridjis, H. (2003). *La Santa Muerte: Sextet del amor, las mujeres, los perros y la muerte*. Mexico City: Alfaguara.

Arvizu, J. (2007, November 3). Fiesta, ante el primer altar de la "santa muerte." *El Universal*. Retrieved from http://archivo.eluniversal.com.mx/ciudad/87487.html

Asad, T. (1993). *Genealogies of religion: Discipline and reasons of power in Christianity and Islam*. Baltimore, MD: Johns Hopkins University Press.

Azaola, E., & Bergman, M. (2008). El sistema penitenciario mexicano. In A. Alvarado (Ed.), *La reforma de la justicia en México* (pp. 745–80). Mexico City: El Colegio de México.

Bandak, A. (2017). Opulence and simplicity: The question of tension in Syrian Catholicism. In K. Norget, V. Napolitano, & M. Mayblin (Eds.), *The anthropology of Catholicism* (pp. 155–69). Berkeley: University of California Press.

Bantjes, A. A. (1998). *As if Jesus walked on earth: Cardenismo, Sonora, and the Mexican Revolution*. Wilmington, DE: Scholarly Resources.

Bantjes, A. A. (2007). Religion and the Mexican Revolution: Toward a new historiography. In M. A. Nesvig (Ed.), *Religious culture in modern Mexico* (pp. 223–55). Albuquerque: University of New Mexico Press.

Barragán Solís, A., & Ramírez de la Roche, O. (2014). Representaciones y experiencias del dolor en un grupo de escolares del Estado de Guerrero, México. *Archivos en Medicina Familiar, 16*(1), 3–11.

Barthes, R. (1985). El cuerpo de nuevo. *Diálogos del Colegio de México*, 21(3), 3–7.

Bartra, R. (1987). *La jaula de la melancolía: Identidad y metamorfosis del mexicano*. Mexico City: Grijalbo.

Bastante, P., & Dickieson, B. (2013). Nuestra Señora de las Sombras: The enigmatic identity of Santa Muerte. *Journal of the Southwest, 55*(4), 435–71.

Baztán Aguirre, Á. (1995). *Etnografía: Metodología cuantitativa en la investigación sociocultural*. Mexico City: Alfaomega/Marcombo.

Beattie, P. (2015). *Punishment in paradise: Race, slavery, human rights, and a nineteenth-century Brazilian penal colony.* Durham, NC: Duke University Press.

Becker, J., Klingan, K., Lanz, S., & Wildner, K. (Eds.). (2014). *Global prayers: Contemporary manifestations of the religious in the city.* Zürich, Switzerland: Lars Müller.

Behar, R. (2003). *Translated woman: Crossing the border with Esperanza's story.* Boston, MA: Beacon Press, 2003.

Benavente, A. (2011). Las "animitas": Testimonio religioso e histórico de piedad popular en Chile. *Estudios Atacameños*, no. 41, pp. 131–38.

Berlanga, M. (2015). Das Spektakel der Gewalt: Von den Frauenmorden zur Verallgemeinerung der Gewalt in Mexiko. In A. Huffschmid, W. Vogel, N. Heidhues, & M. Krämer (Eds.), *TerrorZones: Gewalt und Gegenwehr in Lateinamerika* (pp. 50–59). Berlin, Germany: Assoziation A.

Bigliardi, S. (2016). *La Santa Muerte* and her interventions in human affairs: A theological discussion. *Sophia: International Journal of Philosophy and Traditions, 55*(3), 303–23.

Blair, E. (2005). El exceso codificado en la exclusión social: Muertes anónimas, amenazas y desapariciones. In E. Blair (Ed.), *Muertes violentas: La teatralización del exceso* (pp. 106–20). Medellín, Colombia: Editorial Universidad de Antioquia.

Bolaños Gordillo, L. (2015). El culto a la Santa Muerte en Tuxtla Gutiérrez: De la clandestinidad a la participación colectiva. *Chiapas Paralelo.* Retrieved from https://www.chiapasparalelo.com/opinion/2015/10/el-culto-a-la-santa-muerte-en-tuxtla-gutierrez-de-la-clandestinidad-a-la-participacion-colectiva

Boltanski, L. (1975). *Los usos sociales del cuerpo.* Buenos Aires, Argentina: Ediciones Periferia.

Brandes, S. (2006). *Skulls to the living, bread to the dead: The Day of the Dead in Mexico and beyond.* Oxford, England: Blackwell.

Brandes, S. (2007). Visiones mexicanas de la muerte. In J. A. Flores Martos & L. Abad González (Eds.), *Etnografías de la muerte y las culturas en América Latina* (pp. 31–51). Cuenca, Spain: Universidad de Castilla–La Mancha.

Brandes, S. (2014). Review of the book *Devoted to death: Santa Muerte, the skeleton saint*, by R. A. Chesnut. *Folklore, 125*(1), 132–33.

Bravo Lara, B. (2013). Bajo tu manto nos acogemos: Devotos a la Santa Muerte en la Zona Metropolitana de Guadalajara. *Nueva Antropología, 26*(79), 11–28.

Bricker, V. R. (1981). *The Indian Christ, the Indian king: The historical substrate of Maya myth and ritual.* Austin: University of Texas Press.

Bromley, D. (2016). Santa Muerte as emerging dangerous religion? *Religions, 7*(6), 1–14. https://doi.org/10.3390/rel7060065

Brown, P. (1981) *The cult of saints: Its rise and function in Latin Christianity.* Chicago, IL: University of Chicago Press.

Brunk, S. (2008). *The posthumous career of Emiliano Zapata: Myth, memory, and Mexico's twentieth century.* Austin: University of Texas Press.

Bubandt, N. (2006). Sorcery, corruption, and the dangers of democracy in Indonesia. *Journal of the Royal Anthropological Institute, 12*(2), 413–31.

Bustos, R. (2004). Patrimonialización de valores territoriales: Turismo, sistemas productivos y desarrollo local. *Aportes y Transferencias, 8*(2), 11–24.

Butler, M. (2002). Keeping the faith in revolutionary Mexico: Clerical and lay resistance to religious persecution, east Michoacán, 1926–1929. *The Americas, 59*(1), 9–32.

Butler, M. (2005). God's caciques: Caciquismo and the Cristero Revolt in Coalcomán. In A. Knight & W. Pansters (Eds.), *Caciquismo in twentieth-century Mexico* (pp. 94–112). London, England: Institute for the Study of the Americas.

Butler, M. (2006). Revolution and the ritual year: Religious conflict and innovation in *Cristero* Mexico. *Journal of Latin American Studies, 38*(3), 456–90.

Butler, M. (2007). Introduction: A revolution in spirit, 1910–1940. In M. Butler (Ed.), *Faith and impiety in revolutionary Mexico* (pp. 1–20). London, England: Palgrave.

Cabral Pérez, I. (1995). *Los símbolos cristianos.* Mexico City: Trillas.

Calavia, O. (1996). *Fantasmas falados: Mitos e mortos no campo religioso brasileiro.* Campinas, Brazil: Editora da Unicamp.

Carozzi, M. (2005). Revisando la Difunta Correa: Nuevas perspectivas en el estudio de las canonizaciones populares en el Cono Sur de América. *Revista de Investigaciones Folclóricas, 20,* 13–21.

Carozzi, M. (2006). Antiguos difuntos y difuntos nuevos: Las canonizaciones populares en la década del '90. In D. Miguez & P. Semán (Eds.), *Entre santos, cumbias y piqueteros: Las culturas populares en la Argentina reciente* (pp. 97–110). Buenos Aires, Argentina: Biblos.

Casal Sáenz, H. (2016). *La Santa Muerte: El culto de los que oran y los que matan.* Mexico City: L. D. Books.

Castellanos, L. (2004, May 9). La santa de los desesperados. *La Jornada,* suplemento dominical *Masiosare,* no. 333, pp. 6–9.

Castells Ballarín, P. (2008). La Santa Muerte y la cultura de los derechos humanos. *LiminaR: Estudios Sociales y Humanísticos, 6*(1), 13–25.

Castillo Berthier, H., & Pansters, W. (2007). Mexico City. In K. Koonings & D. Kruijt (Eds.), *Fractured cities: Social exclusion, urban violence and contested spaces in Latin America* (pp. 36–56). London, England: Zed Books.

Ceballos, M. (2013, November 14). Andrew Chesnut: Culto a la Santa Muerte cobra fuerza en toda América. *El País*. Retrieved from http://www.elpais.cr/ frontend/noticia_detalle/7/87929

Chance, J. (1996a). The caciques of Tecali: Class and ethnic identity in late colonial Mexico. *Hispanic American Historical Review*, 76(3), 475–502.

Chance, J. (1996b). The Mixtec nobility under colonial rule. In M. Jansen & L. Reyes García (Eds.), *Codices, caciques y comunidades* (pp. 161–78). Leiden, Netherlands: Asociación de Historiadores Latinoamericanistas Europeos.

Chance, J. (2000). The noble house in colonial Puebla, Mexico: Descent, inheritance, and the Nahua tradition. *American Anthropologist*, 102(3), 485–502.

Chasteen, J. (2006). *Born in blood and fire: A concise history of Latin America*. New York, NY: W. W. Norton.

Chaves Castaño, J. (2010). Cuerpo, poder y territorio en rituales y prácticas funerarias del conflicto armado colombiano: Un análisis antropológico de algunos municipios de Caldas y Risaralda. *Revista Eleuthera*, 4, 230–49.

Chaves Castaño, J. (2011). Entre la violencia sobre el cuerpo y la violencia incorporada. *Revista Hacia la Promoción de la Salud*, 16(2), 162–72.

Chesnut, R. A. (2012a). *Santa muerte: La segadora segura*. Mexico City: Ariel.

Chesnut, R. A. (2012b). *Devoted to death: Santa Muerte, the skeleton saint*. New York, NY: Oxford University Press.

Chesnut, R. A. (2014). Death and roses: Santa Muerte, the love sorceress. *Abraxas: International Journal of Esoteric Studies*, no. 6, 7–16.

Chesnut, R. A. (2015, October 6). Mexico's top two Santa Muerte leaders finally meet. *Huffington Post*. Retrieved from http://www.huffingtonpost.com/r-andrew-chesnut/mexicos-top-two-santa-mue_b_8253318.html

Chouza, P. (2014, January 23). La voz del miedo en Tierra Caliente. *El País*. Retrieved from http://internacional.elpais.com/internacional/2014/01/23/ actualidad/1390514276_718558.html

Christian, W. A., Jr. (1981). *Local religion in sixteenth-century Spain*. Princeton, NJ: Princeton University Press.

Christian, W. A., Jr. (1989). *Person and God in a Spanish Valley*. Princeton, NJ: Princeton University Press. Original work published 1972.

Cipolletti, M., & Langdon, E. (Eds.). (1992). *La muerte y el más allá en las culturas indígenas latinoamericanas*. Quito, Ecuador: Abya-Yala.

Cirlot, J. (1991). *Diccionario de símbolos*. Barcelona, Spain: Editorial Labor.

Ciudad, A., Ruz, M., & Iglesias, M. (Eds.). (2003). *Antropología de la eternidad: La muerte en la cultura maya*. Madrid, Spain: Sociedad Española de Estudios Mayas.

Coleman, S., & Eade, J. (2004). Introduction: Reframing pilgrimage. In S. Coleman & J. Eade (Eds.), *Reframing pilgrimage: Cultures in motion* (pp. 1–26). New York, NY: Routledge.

Comaroff, J., & Comaroff, J. (Eds.). (2001). *Millennial capitalism and the culture of neoliberalism.* Durham, NC: Duke University Press.

Comaroff, J., & Comaroff, J. (2006). *Law and disorder in the postcolony.* Chicago, IL: University of Chicago Press.

Conferencia del Episcopado Mexicano. (2013, October 28). Aclaraciones sobre el culto a la "santa muerte." Retrieved from www.notidiocesis.com

Cornejo Valle, M., Cantón Delgado, M. & Llera Blanes, R. (2008). Introducción: La religión en movimiento. In M. Cornejo Valle, M. Cantón Delgado, & R. Llera Blanes (Eds.), *Teorías y prácticas emergentes en antropología de la religión* (pp. 9–20). San Sebastián, Spain: Ankulegi.

Cornelius, W. A. (1975). *Politics and the migrant poor in Mexico City.* Stanford, CA: Stanford University Press.

Cruz, A. (2006). *La ayuda de la Santa Muerte.* Mexico City: Editorial Planeta.

DaMatta, R. (1987). The quest for citizenship in a relational universe. In J. Wirth, E. De Oliveira Nunes, & T. E. Bogenschild (Eds.), *State and society in Brazil: Continuity and change* (pp. 307–35). Boulder, CO: Westview Press.

DaMatta, R. (1991). *Carnivals, rogues and heroes: An interpretation of the Brazilian dilemma.* Notre Dame, IN: University of Notre Dame Press.

Dansker, L. (2012). I want to believe. In metroZones (Ed.), *Faith is the place: The urban cultures of global prayers.* (pp. 266–77). Berlin, Germany: B_books.

Davis, M. (2006). *Planet of slums.* London, England: Verso.

Davis, N. Z. (1974). Some tasks and themes in the study of popular religion. In C. Trinkaus & H. Oberman (Eds.), *The pursuit of holiness in late medieval and renaissance religion* (pp. 307–36). Leiden, Netherlands: Brill.

Davis, N. Z. (1982). From "popular religion" to religious cultures. In S. Ozment (Ed.), *Reformation Europe: A guide to research* (pp. 56–67). St. Louis, MO: Center for Reformation Research.

Dehouve, D. (2002). Cuando los banqueros eran santos: Historia económica y social de la provincia de Tlapa, Guerrero (B. Chavelas Vázquez, Trans.). Chilpancingo, Mexico: Universidad Autónoma de Guerrero.

De la Fuente Hernández, S. (2013). *La construcción social del culto a La Santa Muerte: Estudio etnográfico en la colonia Ajusco* (Unpublished master's thesis). Universidad Nacional Autónoma de México, Mexico City.

De la Peña, G., & De la Torre, R. (1990). Religión y política en los barrios populares de Guadalajara. *Estudios Sociológicos, 8*(24), 571–602.

Del Bornio, A. (2008). *La Santa Muerte: Altares, oraciones y rituales.* With a prologue by Mons. David Romo Guillén. Mexico City: Skiros.

De León, J. (2015). *The land of open graves: Living and dying on the migrant trail.* Oakland: University of California Press.

Denegri, L. (1978). *Desde la cárcel de mujeres.* Mexico City: Fleischer Editora.

Devoción a La Santa Muerte. (2005, December). La Santa Muerte en la piel. *Colección de oro: Tatuajes de la Santa Muerte.* Mexico City: Mina Editores.

De Vries, P. (2005). The performance and imagination of the cacique: Some ethnographic reflections from Western Mexico. In A. Knight & W. Pansters (Eds.), *Caciquismo in twentieth-century Mexico* (pp. 327–46). London, England: Institute for the Study of the Americas.

Dilthey, W. (1998). *Teoría de las concepciones del mundo.* Mexico City: Consejo Nacional para la Cultura y las Artes.

Dormady, J. (2007). *"Not just a better Mexico": Intentional religious community and the Mexican state, 1940–1964* (Unpublished doctoral dissertation). University of California, Santa Barbara.

Dosal, A. (2014). ¿Cómo pueden funcionar la cultura y el patrimonio como mecanismos de exclusión? *Pasos: Revista de Turismo y Patrimonio Cultural, 12*(1), 137–43.

Ducey, M. T. (2004). *A nation of villages: Riot and rebellion in the Mexican Huasteca, 1750–1850.* Tucson: University of Arizona Press.

Duhau, E., & Giglia, A. (2008). *Las reglas del desorden: Habitar la metrópolis.* Mexico City: Siglo XXI.

Echavarría, J. M. (Director). (2013). *Réquiem NN* [Documentary]. Colombia/Canada: Lulo Films.

Emmel, N., & Clark, A. (2011). Learning to use visual methodologies in our research: A dialogue between two researchers. *FQS Forum: Qualitative Social Research/Sozialforschung, 12*(1).

Escobar Ohmstede, A. (1998). *De la costa a la sierra: Las Huastecas, 1750–1900.* Mexico City: Centro de Investigaciones y Estudios Superiores en Antropología Social.

Escobedo Quijano, E. (2005). *Santa Muerte: El libro total.* Mexico City: Editorial La Luna Negra.

Estrada M., A. (1963). *La grieta en el yugo.* N.p.: n.p.

Fallaw, B. (2013). *Religion and state formation in postrevolutionary Mexico.* Durham, NC: Duke University Press.

Farriss, N. (1984). *Maya society under colonial rule.* Princeton, NJ: Princeton University Press.

Fernández, G. (2013). El "Tío" está sordo: Los mineros bolivianos y el Patrimonio Cultural Inmaterial. *AIBR: Revista de Antropología Iberoamericana, 8*(3), 303–22.

Flanet, V. (1989). *Viviré si Dios quiere: Un estudio de la violencia en la Mixteca de la Costa.* Mexico City: Instituto Nacional Indigenista.

Flores, E., & González, R. E. (2006). Jesús Malverde: plegarias y corridos. *Revista de Literaturas Populares, 6*(1), 32–60.

Flores, R. (1970, June 11). Tijuana: El vicio. *Por Qué?*

Flores Martos, J. A. (2007). La Santísima Muerte en Veracruz, México: Vidas descarnadas y prácticas encarnadas. In J. A. Flores Martos & L. Abad González (Eds.), *Etnografías de la muerte y las culturas en América Latina* (pp. 273–304). Cuenca, Spain: Universidad de Castilla–La Mancha.

Flores Martos, J. A. (2008a). La Santa Muerte y la patrimonialización de la muerte en México. *Humboldt*, no. 150, 28–31.

Flores Martos, J. A. (2008b). Transformismos y transculturación de un culto novomestizo emergente: La Santa Muerte mexicana. In M. Cornejo Valle, M. Cantón Delgado, & R. Llera Blanes (Eds.), *Teorías y prácticas emergentes en antropología de la religión* (pp. 55–76). San Sebastián, Spain: Ankulegi.

Flores Martos, J. A. (2009). Patrimonialización de la cultura indígena y tradicional en Bolivia y México: La UNESCO y los efectos no deseados en la Medicina Kallawaya y el Día de Muertos. In J. López & M. Gutiérrez (Eds.), *América indígena ante el siglo XXI* (pp. 463–98). Mexico City: Siglo XXI.

Flores Martos, J. A. (2014). Iconografías emergentes y muertes patrimonializadas en América Latina: Santa Muerte, muertos milagrosos y muertos adoptados. *AIBR: Revista de Antropología Iberoamericana, 9*(2), 115–40.

Flores Martos, J. A., & Abad González, L. (Eds.). (2007). *Etnografías de la muerte y las culturas en América Latina*. Cuenca, Spain: Universidad de Castilla–La Mancha.

Foster, G. (1979). *Tzintzuntzan: Mexican peasants in a changing world*. New York, NY: Elsevier Press.

Fragoso, P. (2007a). *La muerte santificada: La fe desde la vulnerabilidad; Devoción y culto a la Santa Muerte en la Ciudad de México* (Unpublished master's thesis). Centro de Investigaciones y Estudios Superiores en Antropología Social, Mexico City.

Fragoso, P. (2007b). La muerte santificada: El culto a la Santa Muerte en la ciudad de México. *Revista de El Colegio de San Luis, 9*(26–27), 9–37.

Fragoso, P. (2011). De la "calavera domada" a la subversión santificada: La Santa Muerte, un nuevo imaginario religioso en México. *El Cotidiano*, no. 169, 5–16.

Franco, F. (2009). *Muertos, fantasmas y héroes: El culto a los muertos milagrosos en Venezuela*. Mérida, Venezuela: Universidad de Los Andes.

Fraser, A. (2015). *Santa Muerte*. London, England: Trolley Books.

Freese, K. (n.d.). The death cult of the drug lords: Mexico's patron saint of crime, criminals, and the dispossessed. Retrieved from https://www.globalsecurity.org/military/library/report/2005/santa-muerte.htm

Freitas, E. T. (2007). ¿Cómo nace un santo en el cementerio? Muerte, memoria e historia en el noreste de Brasil. *Ciencias Sociales y Religión, 9*(9), 59–90.

García Olvera, F. (1996). *Reflexiones sobre el diseño*. Mexico City: Universidad Autónoma Metropolitana Azcapotzalco.

Gaytán Alcalá, F. (2008). Santa entre los malditos: Culto a la Santa Muerte en el México del siglo XXI. *LiminaR: Estudios Sociales y Humanísticos*, 6(1), 40–51.

Geschiere, P. (1997). *The modernity of witchcraft: Politics and the occult in postcolonial Africa*. Charlottesville: University Press of Virginia.

Gil Olmos, J. (2010). *La Santa Muerte: La virgen de los olvidados*. Mexico City: Delbolsillo.

Giménez, G. (1997). Materiales para una teoría de las entidades sociales. *Frontera Norte*, 9(18), 9–28.

Giménez, G. (2009). Cultura, identidad y memoria: Materiales para una sociología de los procesos culturales en las franjas fronterizas. *Frontera Norte*, 21(41), 7–32.

Goffman, E. (1991). *Stigma: Notes on the management of spoiled identity*. New York, NY: Simon and Schuster. Original work published 1963.

Goldman, F. (2014). *The interior circuit: A Mexico City chronicle*. New York, NY: Grove Press.

Goldstein, D. (2012). *Outlawed: Between security and rights in a Bolivian city*. Durham, NC: Duke University Press.

González Martínez, J. L. (2002). *Fuerza y sentido: El catolicismo popular al comienzo del siglo XXI*. Mexico City: Ediciones Dabar.

González y González, L. (1985). La Revolución Mexicana desde el punto de vista de los revolucionados. *Historias*, nos. 8–9, 5–13.

Goodman, A. (2006). *Prácticas del culto a la Santa Muerte*. Mexico City: Editores Mexicanos Unidos.

Gosner, K. (1992). *Soldiers of the virgin: The moral economy of a colonial Maya rebellion*. Tucson: University of Arizona Press.

Graeber, D. (2011). *Debt: The first 5,000 years*. New York, NY: Melville House.

Graziano, F. (2007). *Cultures of devotion: Folk saints of Spanish America*. New York, NY: Oxford University Press.

Graziano, F. (2016). *Miraculous images and votive offerings in Mexico*. New York, NY: Oxford University Press.

Gruzinski, S. (1989). *Man-Gods in the Mexican highlands: Indian power and colonial society, 1520–1800*. Stanford, CA: Stanford University Press.

Gruzinski, S. (1990). Indian confraternities, brotherhoods and *mayordomías* in central New Spain: A list of questions for the historian and the anthropologist. In Arij Ouweneel & Simon Miller (Eds.), *The Indian community of colonial Mexico: Fifteen essays on land tenure, corporate organizations, ideology and village politics* (pp. 205–23). Amsterdam, Netherlands: Centro de Estudios y Documentación Latinoamericanos.

Guardino, P. (2006). *The time of liberty: Popular political culture in Oaxaca, 1750–1850*. Durham, NC: Duke University Press.

Guberek, T., Guzmán, D., & Vejarano, B. (2010). Cementerios legales: El uso de información de cementerios en la búsqueda de desaparecidos; Lecciones de un estudio piloto en Rionegro, Antioquía. In Equitas (Ed.), *Propuestas metodológicas para la documentación y búsqueda de personas desaparecidas en Colombia* (pp. 31–43). Bogotá, Colombia: Equitas. Retrieved from https://hrdag.org/wp-content/uploads/2013/02/44.pdf

Gudeman, S. (1988). The manda and the mass. *Journal of Latin American Lore, 14*(1), 17–32.

Guerra Manzo, E. (2005). El fuego sagrado: La segunda Cristiada y el caso de Michoacán (1931–1938). *Historia Mexicana, 55*(2), 513–75.

Guillermoprieto, A. (2010). Troubled Spirits. *National Geographic, 217*(5), 54–73.

Hedenborg-White, M., & Gregorius, F. (2017). The scythe and the pentagram: Santa Muerte from folk Catholicism to occultism. *Religions, 8*(1), 1–14. https://doi.org/10.3390/rel8010001

Hernández i Martí, G.-M. (2008). Un zombi de la modernidad: El patrimonio cultural y sus límites. *La Torre del Virrey: Revista de Estudios Culturales*, no. 5, 27–38.

Hernández R., J. E. (2014). ¿Cómo dejar el culto a la "santa muerte"? *Inquietud Nueva*, no. 179. Retrieved from http://mariaauxiliadoratuxpan.blogspot.co.uk/2015/10/como-dejar-el-culto-la-santa-muerte.html

Hernandez, V. (2013). The country where exorcisms are on the rise. *BBC News Magazine*. Retrieved from http://www.bbc.co.uk/news/magazine-25032305

Hernández Hernández, A. (2011). Devoción a la Santa Muerte y San Judas Tadeo en Tepito y anexas. *El Cotidiano*, no. 169, 39–50.

Hidalgo, C. (Ed.). (2011). *Etnografías de la muerte: Rituales, desapariciones, VIH/SIDA y resignificación de la vida*. Buenos Aires, Argentina: Ediciones CICCUS.

Higuera-Bonfil, A. (2015). Fiestas en honor a la Santa Muerte en el Caribe mexicano. *LiminaR: Estudios Sociales y Humanísticos, 13*(2), 96–109.

Huffschmid, A. (2012a). Another way of knowing: Some notes regarding visual research on ghosts and spirits. In metroZones (Ed.), *Faith is the place: The urban cultures of global prayers* (pp. 164–75). Berlin, Germany: B_books.

Huffschmid, A. (2012b). Devoción satanizada: La Muerte como nuevo culto callejero en la Ciudad de México. *iMex Revista: México Interdisciplinario, 2*(3), 97–107.

Huffschmid, A. (2014). From Padre Múgica to Santa Muerte? Liberation spirits and religious mutations in urban space in Latin America. In J. Becker, K. Klingan, S. Lanz, & K. Wildner (Eds.), *Global Prayers: Contemporary Manifestations of the Religious in the City* (pp. 392–407). Zürich, Switzerland: Lars Müller.

Huffschmid, A. (2015). *Risse im Raum: Erinnerung, Gewalt und städtisches Leben in Lateinamerika*. Wiesbaden, Germany: Springer.

Huffschmid, A., & Spiller, I. (Eds.). (2011). *Mirar y creer/Looking and believing*. Mexico City: Heinrich Böll Stiftung.

Kearney, M. (2004). *Changing fields of anthropology: From local to global*. Lanham, MD: Rowman and Littlefield.

Keenan, T., & Weizman, E. (2012). *Mengele's skull: The advent of a forensic aesthetics*. Berlin, Germany: Sternberg Press.

Kelly, I. (1965). *Folk practices in North Mexico: Birth customs, folk medicine, and spiritualism in the Laguna Zone*. Austin: University of Texas Press.

Kouri, E. (2004). *A pueblo divided: Business, property, and community in Papantla, Mexico*. Stanford, CA: Stanford University Press.

Kraushaar, L. (2013). Crimen y exhibición de prostitutas en el norte de Chile: Producción y uso de las imagenes del cuerpo de mujeres asesinadas. *Aisthesis*, no. 53, 29–51.

Kristensen, R. A. (2011). *Postponing death: Saints and security in Mexico City*. PhD Series, no. 68. Copenhagen, Denmark: Københavns Universitet.

Kristensen, R. A. (2015). La Santa Muerte in Mexico City: The cult and its ambiguities. *Journal of Latin American Studies*, 47(3), 543–66. https://doi.org/10.1017/S0022216X15000024

Kristensen, R. A. (2016a). How did death become a saint in Mexico? *Ethnos: Journal of Anthropology*, 81(3), 402–24.

Kristensen, R. A. (2016b). La Santa Muerte: Inmates' new friend. *Panoramas: Scholarly Platform*. Retrieved from https://www.panoramas.pitt.edu/art-and-culture/la-santa-muerte-inmates%E2%80%99-new-friend

Kselman, T. A. (2016). Ambivalence and assumption in the concept of popular religion. In D. H. Levine (Ed.), *Religion and political conflict in Latin America* (pp. 24–41). Chapel Hill: University of North Carolina Press.

Lafaye, J. (1984). *Quetzalcóatl and Guadalupe: The formation of Mexican national consciousness, 1531–1813*. Chicago, IL: University of Chicago Press.

Lagarriga Attias, I. (1975). *Medicina tradicional y espiritismo: Los Espiritualistas Trinitarios Marianos de Jalapa, Veracruz*. Mexico City: Secretaría de Educación Pública.

Laín Entralgo, P. (1989). *El cuerpo humano: Teoría actual*. Madrid, Spain: Espasa-Calpe.

Lanz, S. (2014). Assembling global prayers in the city: An attempt to repopulate urban theory with religion. In J. Becker, K. Klingan, S. Lanz, & K. Wildner (Eds.), *Global prayers: Contemporary manifestations of the religious in the city* (pp. 17–43). Zürich, Switzerland: Lars Müller.

Lara Cisneros, G. (2007). *El Cristo Viejo de Xichú: Resistencia y rebelión en la Sierra*

Gorda durante el siglo XVIII. Mexico City: Consejo Nacional para la Cultura y las Artes.

Lebner, A. (2012). A Christian politics of friendship on a Brazilian frontier. *Ethnos: Journal of Anthropology, 77*(4), 496–517.

Le Breton, D. (1991). Cuerpo y antropología: De la eficacia simbólica. *Diógenes,* no. 153, 87–98.

Le Breton, D. (1995). *Antropología del cuerpo y modernidad*. Buenos Aires, Argentina: Ediciones Nueva Visión.

Lehmann, D. (2013). Review of the book *Devoted to death: Santa Muerte, the skeleton saint*, by R. A. Chesnut. *Journal of Latin American Studies, 45*(1), 195–97.

Lewis, O. (1963). *The children of Sánchez: Autobiography of a Mexican family*. New York, NY: Vintage Books.

Lewis, O. (1964). *Los hijos de Sánchez*. Mexico City: Fondo de Cultura Económica.

El libro de la Santa Muerte: Rituales, oraciones y ofrendas. (2007). Mexico City: Editorial Época.

Loaeza, S. (1985). *Clases medias y política en México: La querella escolar, 1959–1963*. Mexico City: El Colegio de México.

Lomnitz, C. (2005a). *Death and the idea of Mexico*. New York, NY: Zone Books.

Lomnitz, C. (2005b). Sobre reciprocidad negativa. *Revista de Antropología Social,* no. 14, 311–39.

Lomnitz, C. (2006). *Idea de la muerte en México*. Mexico City: Fondo de Cultura Económica.

Lope Blanch, J. (1963). *Vocabulario mexicano relativo a la muerte*. Mexico City: Universidad Nacional Autónoma de México.

Lorusso, F. (2013). *Santa Muerte: Patronata dell'umanità*. Viterbo, Italy: Stampa Alternativa.

Losonczy, A.-M. (2001). Santificación popular de los muertos en cementerios urbanos colombianos. *Revista Colombiana de Antropología, 37,* 6–23.

Lowry, M. (1947). *Under the volcano*. New York, NY: Reynal and Hitchcock.

Loya, J. (2009, March 24). Militares derrumben altares de Santa Muerte en Nuevo Laredo. *El Universal.*

Lozano, C. (2007). Memoria, violencia e identidad: La canonización popular de María Soledad Morales en la provincia argentina de Catamarca. *Revista Cultura y Religión, 1*(2), 74–89. Retrieved from http://www.revistaculturayreligion.cl/index.php/culturayreligion/article/view/203

Martín, D. (2014). *Borderlands saints: Secular sanctity in Chicano/a and Mexican culture*. New Brunswick, NJ: Rutgers University Press.

Marzal, M. (2002). *Tierra encantada: Tratado de antropología religiosa de América Latina*. Lima, Peru: Pontificia Universidad Católica del Perú.

Mayblin, M. (2010). *Gender, Catholicism, and morality in Brazil: Virtuous husbands, powerful wives*. New York, NY: Palgrave Macmillan.

McNearney, A. (2015, November 1). The death worshipping cult of Santa Muerte. Retrieved from http://www.thedailybeast.com/articles/2015/11/01/the-death-worshipping-cult-of-santa-muerte.html

Mendoza, P. (2009). *Territorios*. Toluca, Mexico: Gobierno del Estado de México.

metroZones (Ed.). (2011). *Urban prayers: Neue religiöse Bewegungen in der globalen Stadt*. Berlin, Germany: Assoziation A.

metroZones (Ed.). (2012). *Faith is the place: The urban cultures of global prayers*. Berlin, Germany: B_books.

México Unido contra la Delincuencia. (2013). *La seguridad pública en México de 2006 a 2012*. Mexico City: México Unido contra la Delincuencia.

Meyer, B. (2012). *Mediation and the genesis of presence: Towards a material approach to religion*. Utrecht, Netherlands: Universiteit Utrecht, Faculteit Geesteswetenschappen.

Meyer, J. (1973–1974). *La Cristiada* (3 vols.). Mexico City: Siglo XXI.

Michalik, P. G. (2011). Death with a bonus pack: New Age spirituality, folk Catholicism, and the cult of Santa Muerte. *Archives de Sciences Sociales des Religions*, no. 153, 159–82.

Michalik, P. G. (2012). The meaning of death: Semiotic approach to analysis of syncretic processes in the cult of Santa Muerte. In *Proceedings of the 10th World Congress of the International Association for Semiotic Studies* (pp. 605–12). Retrieved from http://ruc.udc.es/dspace/bitstream/handle/2183/13361/CC-130_art_61.pdf

Monaghan, J. (1995). *The covenants with earth and rain, exchange, sacrifice, and revelation in Mixtec sociality*. Norman: University of Oklahoma Press.

Moncada, C. (1991). *Del Mexico violento: Periodistas asesinados*. Mexico City: Edamex.

Morín, E. (2009). Agujas en la piel. In E. Morín & A. Nateras (Eds.), *Tinta y carne* (pp. 37–56). Mexico City: Editorial Contracultura.

Müller, M. (2016). *The punitive city: Privatized policing and protection in neoliberal Mexico*. London, England: Zed Books.

Navarrete, C. (1982). *San Pascualito Rey y el culto a la muerte en Chiapas*. Mexico City: Universidad Nacional Autónoma de México.

Navarro, M. (2002). Against *marianismo*. In R. Montoya et al. (Eds.), *Gender's place: Feminist anthropologies of Latin America* (pp. 257–72). New York, NY: Palgrave Macmillan.

Navas Soto, E. (1997). *Ánimas de Guasare*. Coro, Venezuela: Ediciones Do ut Des.

Nieto, P. (2012). *Los escogidos*. Medellín, Colombia: Sílaba Editores.

Oleszkiewicz-Peralba, M. (2015). *Fierce feminine divinities of Eurasia and Latin America*. New York, NY: Palgrave Macmillan.

Orsi, R. (1996). *Thank you, St. Jude: Women's devotion to the Patron Saint of Hopeless Causes*. New Haven, CT: Yale University Press.

Ortega G., C. (1961). *Democracia dirigida con ametralladoras, Baja California, 1958–1960*. El Paso, TX: n.p.

Ortíz, A. (1990). Expresiones religiosas marginales: El caso de Sarita Colonia. In M. Varcálcel (Ed.), *Pobreza urbana: Relaciones económicas y marginalidad religiosa* (pp. 169–201). Lima, Peru: Pontificia Universidad Católica del Perú.

Ortíz Echaniz, S., & Lagarriga Attias, I. (2007). Santería y espiritualismo trinitario mariano: Interrelación e imaginario ideológico en la Ciudad de México. In J. L. Ramírez (Ed.), *Enfermedad y religión: Un juego de miradas sobre el vínculo de la metáfora entre lo mórbido y lo religioso* (pp. 211–26). Mexico City: Universidad Autónoma del Estado de México.

Ortiz Pinchetti, F. (1981). *La Operación Condor*. Mexico City: Proceso.

Osorio Carranza, R. (1994). *La cultura médica materna y la salud infantil: Síntesis de representaciones y prácticas sociales en un grupo de madres de familia* (Unpublished master's thesis). Escuela Nacional de Antropología e Historia, Mexico City.

Ouweneel, A. (1990). Altepeme and Pueblos de Indios: Some comparative theoretical perspectives on the analysis of the colonial Indian communities. In A. Ouweneel & S. Miller (Eds.), *The Indian community of colonial Mexico: Fifteen essays on land tenure, corporate organization, ideology, and village politics* (pp. 1–37). Amsterdam, Netherlands: Centro de Estudios y Documentación Latinoamericanos.

Ouweneel, A. (1995). From *tlahtocayotl* to *gobernadoryotl*: A critical examination of indigenous rule in 18th-century central Mexico. *American Ethnologist, 22*(4), 756–85.

Panfalone, A. (2014). *Formations of death: Instrumentality, cult innovation, and the Templo Santa Muerte in Los Angeles* (Unpublished DPhil thesis). University of Oxford, Oxford, England.

Pansters, W. (2009). *Dubbelspel: Over de betekenis van de informele orde in de Latijns-Amerikaanse moderniteit*. Groningen, Netherlands: Oratiereeks Faculteit der Letteren, Universiteit Groningen.

Pansters, W. (2015). "We had to pay to live!" Competing sovereignties in violent Mexico. *Conflict and Society: Advances in Research, 1*, 144–64.

Pansters, W., Smith, B., & Watt, P. (Eds.). (2018). *Beyond the drug war in Mexico: Human rights, the public sphere and justice*. London, England: Routledge.

Pardo, J. E. (2008). Sin nombres, sin rostros ni rastros. *Revista Número*, no. 58, 10–12.

Pastor, R. (1987). *Campesinos y reformas: La Mixteca, 1700–1856*. Mexico City: El Colegio de México.

Pavez Ojeda, J., & Kraushaar H., L. (2010). Nombre, muerte y santificación de una prostituta: Escritura y culto de Botitas Negras (Calama, Chile, 1969–2008). *AIBR: Revista de Antropología Iberoamericana, 5*(3), 447–92.

Payá, V. (2006). *Vida y muerte en la cárcel: Estudio sobre la situación institucional de los prisioneros*. Mexico City: Universidad Nacional Autónoma de México.

Paz, O. (1998). *El laberinto de la soledad*. Mexico City: Fondo de Cultura Económica. Original work published 1950.

Peebles, G. (2010). The anthropology of credit and debt. *Annual Review of Anthropology, 39*, 225–40.

Perdigón Castañeda, J. K. (2002). La Santísima Muerte. *Boletín Oficial del Instituto Nacional de Antropología e Historia: Antropología*, no. 68, 36–43.

Perdigón Castañeda, J. K. (2008a). *La Santa Muerte: Protectora de los hombres*. Mexico City: Instituto Nacional de Antropología e Historia.

Perdigón Castañeda, J. K. (2008b). Una relación simbiótica entre La Santa Muerte y El Niño de las Suertes. *LiminaR: Estudios Sociales y Humanísticos, 6*(1), 52–67.

Perdigón Castañeda, J. K. (2015a). *Mi Niño Dios: Un acercamiento al concepto, historia, significado y celebración del Niño Jesús para el día de la Candelaria*. Mexico City: Instituto Nacional de Antropología e Historia.

Perdigón Castañeda, J. K. (2015b). La indumentaria para La Santa Muerte. *Cuicuilco, 22*(64), 43–62.

Pérez Sánchez, A. (1992). Trampantojo a lo divino. In Ephialte, Instituto de Estudios Iconográficos (Ed.), *Lecturas de historia del arte III* (pp. 139–55). Vitoria-Gasteiz, Spain: Ephialte.

Perkins, S. M. (2005). Corporate community or corporate houses? Land and society in a colonial Mesoamerican community. *Culture and Agriculture, 27*(1), 16–34.

Pescador, J. J. (2009). *Crossing borders with Santo Niño de Atocha*. Albuquerque: University of New Mexico Press.

Pomeraniec, H. (2014, November 3). ¿Qué cosecha un país cuando siembra cuerpos? *La Nación*. Retrieved from http://www.lanacion.com.ar/1740797-that-cosecha-a-pais-when-siembra-cuerpos

Poniatowska, E. (2002). *Here's to you, Jesusa!* London, England: Penguin Press.

Pope Francis (2016, February 13). Speech to Mexican Bishops. Retrieved from http://www.romereports.com/2016/02/13/full-text-of-the-pope-francis-speech-at-mexican-bishops

Powell, K. (2012). Political practice, everyday political violence, and electoral processes during the neoliberal period in Mexico. In W. Pansters (Ed.), *Violence, coercion, and state-making in twentieth-century Mexico: The other half of the centaur* (pp. 212–32). Stanford, CA: Stanford University Press.

Quiroga, D. (2011). Enriqueta Romero, guardiana de la muerte. *Maguaré*, 25(1), 279–98.

Ramírez Torres, J. L. (2000). *Cuerpo y dolor: Semiótica de la anatomía y la enfermedad en la experiencia humana*. Mexico City: Universidad Autónoma del Estado de México.

Ramos Rodríguez, R. M. (1989). Lo biológico y lo social en el crecimiento físico. *Estudios de Antropología Biológica, 4*, 107–13.

Randel, D. (2009). *Diccionario Harvard de música*. Madrid, Spain: Alianza Editorial.

Reich, P. (2007). Recent research on the legal history of modern Mexico. *Mexican Studies/Estudios Mexicanos, 23*(1), 181–93.

Reyes-Cortez, M. (2012). Material culture, magic and the Santa Muerte in the cemeteries of a megalopolis. *Culture and Religion, 13*(1), 107–31.

Reyes Ruiz, C. (2010). *La Santa Muerte: Historia, realidad y mito de la Niña Blanca; Retratos urbanos de la fe*. Mexico City: Editorial Porrúa.

Riley, C. L., & Hobgood, J. (1959). A recent nativistic movement among the southern Tepehuan Indians. *Southwestern Journal of Anthropology, 15*(4), 355–60.

Rodríguez, A. (Ed.). (2003). *José Guadalupe Posada, 150 años*. Hong Kong: La Mano.

Rodríguez García, L., Villavicencio Rojas, J. M., & Montesinos Maldonado, R. (2004). *Donde se canta y se baila: Evocaciones de Leonor Rodríguez sobre Coicoyán de las Flores*. Oaxaca de Juárez, Mexico: Fondo Editorial.

Rostas, S., & Droogers, A. (1993). The popular use of popular religion in Latin America: Introduction. In S. Rostas & A. Droogers (Eds.), *The popular use of popular religion in Latin America* (pp. 1–16). Amsterdam, Netherlands: Centro de Estudios y Documentación Latinoamericanos.

Rothenstein, J. (Ed.). (1989). *Posada: Messenger of mortality*. Amsterdam, Netherlands: Van Gennep.

Roush, L. (2009). *Notes on the gift exchange at Alfarería Street* (Unpublished doctoral dissertation). New School of Social Research, New York, NY.

Roush, L. (2012). Don't leave me unprotected: The heresy of La Santa Muerte in social context. In metroZones (Ed.), *Faith is the place: The urban cultures of global prayers* (pp. 183–87). Berlin, Germany: B_books.

Roush, L. (2014, July 11). Meet Santa Muerte, the tequila-loving saint comforting both criminals and the marginalized. *Huffington Post*.

Roush, L. (2014). Santa Muerte, protection and *desamparo*: A view from a Mexico City altar [Special issue]. *Latin American Research Review, 49*, 129–48.

Rubin, J., Smilde, D., & Junge, B. (2014). Lived religion and lived citizenship in

Latin America's zones of crisis [Special issue]. *Latin American Research Review*, 49, 7–26.

Rugeley, T. (1996). *Yucatán's Maya peasantry and the origins of the Caste War*. Austin: University of Texas Press.

Rugeley, T. (2009). *Rebellion now and forever: Mayas, Hispanics, and caste war in Yucatán, 1800–1880*. Stanford, CA: Stanford University Press.

Rühling, B. (2013). *La Santa Muerte: Die Konstituierung eines ambulanten Kultes im Straßenhandel von Mexiko-Stadt* (Unpublished master's thesis). Freie Universität Berlin, Berlin, Germany.

Rulfo, J. (1955). *Pedro Páramo*. Mexico City: Fondo de Cultura Económica.

Sahlins, M. (1963). On the sociology of primitive exchange. In M. Gluckman & F. Eggan (Eds.), *The relevance of models for social anthropology* (pp. 139–236). New York, NY: Praeger.

Sahlins, M. (1974). *Stone age economics*. London, England: Tavistock Publications.

Salgado Ponce, J. (2012). *Imágenes de la fé, la creación del mito en el ritual de la Santa Muerte del México contemporáneo: Ensayo fotográfico, Alfarería 12* (Unpublished master's thesis). Universidad Nacional Autónoma de México, Mexico City.

Sánchez, G. (2010, January 28). La memoria comienza a desenterrarse. Retrieved from http://blogs.heraldo.es/gervasiosanchez/?p=741

Sánchez-Carretero, C. (2004). De apodos y diablos transnacionales: Sobrenombres y nuevas identidades documentales como estrategias de supervivencia. In L. Díaz Viana (Ed.), *El nuevo orden del caos: Consecuencias socioculturales de la globalización* (pp. 143–58). Madrid, Spain: Consejo Superior de Investigaciones Científicas.

Sánchez-Carretero, C. (2005). *Santos y misterios* as channels of communication in the diaspora: Afro-Dominican religious practices abroad. *Journal of American Folklore, 118*(469), 308–26.

Sánchez Godoy, J. A. (2009). Procesos de la institucionalización de la narcocultura en Sinaloa. *Frontera Norte, 21*(41), 77–103.

Santa Muerte: Darse a la Muerte, para recibir la vida; Oraciones y rituales para el amor, salud, fortuna y dinero. (2016). Mexico City: Ediciones Enigma Books.

Scheper-Hughes, N. (1997). *La muerte sin llanto: Violencia y vida cotidiana en Brasil*. Barcelona, Spain: Ariel.

Schryer, F. J. (1990). *Ethnicity and class conflict in rural Mexico*. Princeton, NJ: Princeton University Press.

Scott, J. (1976). *Moral economy of the peasant: Rebellion and subsistence in Southeast Asia*. New Haven, CT: Yale University Press.

Scott, J. (1977). Hegemony and the peasantry. *Politics and Society, 7*(3), 267–97.

Segato, R. (2007). Qué es un feminicidio? Notas para un debate emergente. In M. Belausteguigoitia & L. Melgar (Eds.), *Frontera, violencia, justicia: Nuevos discursos* (pp. 35–48). Mexico City: Programa Universitario de Estudios de Género, Universidad Nacional Autónoma de México; UNIFEM.

Semán, P. (2004). *La religiosidad popular: Creencias y vida cotidiana.* Buenos Aires, Argentina: Capital Intelectual.

Smith, B. T. (2010). El Señor del Perdón y los matacristos de Oaxaca: La Revolución desde el punto de vista de los católicos. *Desacatos,* no. 34, 61–76.

Smith, B. T. (2012). *The roots of conservatism in Mexico: Catholicism, society, and politics in the Mixteca Baja, 1750–1962.* Albuquerque: University of New Mexico Press.

Sperber, D. (1989). L'étude anthropologique des représentation: Problèmes et perspectives. In D. Jodelet (Ed.), *Les représentations sociales* (pp. 136–42). Paris: Presses Universitaires de France.

Stephen, L. (2007). *Transborder lives: Indigenous Oaxacans in Mexico, California, and Oregon.* Durham, NC: Duke University Press.

Tackett, T. (1986). *Religion, revolution, and regional culture in eighteenth-century France: The ecclesiastical oath of 1791.* Princeton, NJ: Princeton University Press.

Taylor, S., & Bogdan, S. (1996). *Introducción a los métodos cualitativos de investigación.* Mexico City: Paidós.

Taylor, W. B. (1979). *Drinking, homicide, and rebellion in colonial Mexican villages.* Stanford, CA: Stanford University Press.

Taylor, W. B. (1996). *Magistrates of the sacred: Priests and parishioners in eighteenth-century Mexico.* Stanford, CA: Stanford University Press.

Taylor, W. B. (2010). *Shrines and miraculous images: Religious life in Mexico before the Reforma.* Albuquerque: University of New Mexico Press.

Thompson, E. P. (1971). The moral economy of the English crowd in the eighteenth century. *Past and Present,* no. 50, 76–136.

Thompson, J. (1998). Santísima Muerte: On the origin and development of a Mexican occult image. *Journal of the Southwest,* 40(4), 405–36.

Toor, F. (1947). *A treasury of Mexican folkways.* New York, NY: Crown Publishers.

Torres-Septién, V. & Solís, Y. (2004). El cubilete: De Cerro a Montaña Santa; La construcción del monumento a Cristo Rey (1919–1960). *Historia y Grafía,* no. 22, 113–53.

Tutino, J. (2012). *Making a new world: Founding capitalism in the Bajío and Spanish North America.* Durham, NC: Duke University Press.

Ugalde, A. (1970). *Power and conflict in a Mexican community: A study of political integration.* Albuquerque: University of New Mexico Press.

Uribe Alarcón, M. V. (2011). Against violence and oblivion: The case of Colombia's disappeared. In G. Polit Dueñas & M. H. Rueda (Eds.), *Meanings of violence in contemporary Latin America* (pp. 37–52). New York, NY: Palgrave Macmillan.

Uribe Iniesta, R. (2000). El papel de las representaciones sociales: Su producción en el conflicto e intervención ambiental. In M. Viesca Arrache (Ed.), *Calidad de vida, medio ambiente y educación en el medio rural* (pp. 124–65). Zamora, Mexico: El Colegio de Michoacán.

Vanderwood, P. J. (1998). *The power of God against the guns of government: Religious upheaval in Mexico at the turn of the nineteenth century.* Stanford, CA: Stanford University Press.

Vanderwood, P. J. (2003). The millennium and Mexican independence. In C. I. Archer (Ed.), *The birth of modern Mexico, 1780–1824* (pp. 165–86). Lanham, MD: Rowman and Littlefield.

Vanderwood, P. J. (2004). *Juan Soldado: Rapist, murderer, martyr, saint.* Durham, NC: Duke University Press.

Van Oosterhout, K. A. (2014). *Popular conservatism in Mexico: Religion, land and popular politics in Nayarit and Querétaro, 1750–1873* (Unpublished doctoral dissertation). Michigan State University, East Lansing.

Van Young, E. (1981). *Hacienda and market in eighteenth-century Mexico: The rural economy of the Guadalajara region, 1675–1820.* Berkeley: University of California Press.

Van Young, E. (1986). Millennium in the northern marches: The mad messiah of Durango and popular rebellion in Mexico, 1800–1815. *Comparative Studies in Society and History, 28*(3), 285–413.

Van Young, E. (1989). Quetzalcóatl, King Ferdinand, and Ignacio Allende go to the seashore; or, Messianism and mystical kingship in Mexico, 1800–1821. In J. E. Rodriguez (Ed.), *The independence of Mexico and the creation of the new nation* (pp. 109–27). Los Angeles: UCLA Latin American Center.

Van Young, E. (2001). *The other rebellion: Popular violence, ideology, and the Mexican struggle for independence, 1810–1821.* Stanford, CA: Stanford University Press.

Van Young, E. (2003). In the gloomy caverns of paganism: Popular culture, insurgency, and nation-building in Mexico, 1800–1821. In C. I. Archer (Ed.), *The birth of modern Mexico, 1780–1824* (pp. 41–65). Lanham, MD: Rowman and Littlefield.

Vargas González, A. (2004). ¡Oh Muerte Sagrada, reliquia de Dios! La Santa Muerte: Religiosidad popular en la ribera de Pátzcuaro. *La Palabra y el Hombre,* no. 130, 101–22.

Vatican declares Mexican death saint blasphemous. (2013, May 9). *BBC News.* Retrieved from https://www.bbc.com/news/world-latin-america-22462181

Velásquez López, P. A. (2009). Los cementerios . . . territorios intersticiales. *Revista Hacia la Promoción de la Salud, 14*(2), 24–38.

Velázquez, O. (2013). *El libro de la Santa Muerte*. 7th ed. Mexico City: Editores Mexicanos Unidos.

Vélez-Ibáñez, C. (1983). *Rituals of marginality: Politics, process, and culture change in urban central Mexico, 1969–1974*. Berkeley: University of California Press.

Vergara Figueroa, A. (Ed.). (2001). *Imaginarios: Horizontes plurales*. Mexico City: Instituto Nacional de Antropología e Historia; Escuela Nacional de Antropología e Historia.

Vergara Figueroa, A. (2009). Prólogo: El escorpión y la rosa; Tatuaje: Glocal y urbano, entre transgresión y cosmética. In E. Morín & A. Nateras (Eds.), *Tinta y carne* (pp. 9–32). Mexico City: Editorial Contracultura.

Vicenteño, D. (2012, June 14). Líder de la Santa Muerte recibe 66 años de prisión por secuestro. *Excélsior*. Retrieved from http://www.excelsior.com. mx/2012/06/14/comunidad/841226

Vieira, C. (2008). Nadie podrá pagar ni reparar la orfandad en que hemos quedado. *Humboldt, 50*(150), 56–59.

Villamil Uriarte, R., & Cisneros, J. (2011). De la Niña Blanca y la Flaquita, a la Santa Muerte (Hacia la inversión del mundo religioso). *El Cotidiano*, no. 169, 29–38.

Villaseñor Alonso, I., & Zolla Márquez, E. (2012). Del patrimonio cultural inmaterial o la patrimonialización de la cultura. *Cultura y Representaciones Sociales, 6*(12): 75–101. Retrieved from http://www.revistas.unam.mx/index. php/crs/article/view/30475

Wallace, A. F. C. (1956). Revitalization movements. *American Anthropologist, 58*(2), 264–81.

Westheim, P. (1985). *La calavera*. Mexico City: Fondo de Cultura Económica.

Winslow, D. (2015). *The Cartel*. New York, NY: Alfred A. Knopf.

Wolf, E. (1956). Aspects of group relations in a complex society: Mexico. *American Anthropologist, 58*(5), 1065–78.

Wolf, E. (1957). Closed corporate peasant communities in Mesoamerica and central Java. *Southwestern Journal of Anthropology, 13*(1), 1–18.

Wolf, E. (1959). *Sons of the shaking earth*. Chicago, IL: University of Chicago Press.

Wollen, P. (1989). Introduction. In J. Rothenstein (Ed.), *Posada: Messenger of mortality* (pp. 14–23). Amsterdam, Netherlands: Van Gennep.

Woody, C. (2016, March 17). Saint Death: The secretive and sinister "cult" challenging the power of the Catholic Church. *Business Insider*. Retrieved from https://www.businessinsider.com/what-is-santa-muerte-2016-3?r=UK

Wright, S. (1998). The politicization of culture. *Anthropology Today, 14*(1), 7–15.

Wright-Rios, E. (2009). *Revolutions in Mexican Catholicism: Reform and revelation in Oaxaca, 1887–1934*. Durham, NC: Duke University Press.

Yllescas Illescas, J. (2016). *La Santa Muerte: Historias de vida y fe desde la cárcel* (Unpublished master's thesis). Universidad Nacional Autónoma de México, Mexico City.

Zárate Escamilla, J. (2007). *Huamelula: Pueblo danzante*. Mexico City: Comisión Nacional para el Desarrollo de los Pueblos Indígenas.

Zarazúa Campa, J. L. (2011). *La Santa Muerte, el mal de ojo y otras supersticiones*. Mexico City: Apóstoles de la Palabra.

ABOUT THE AUTHORS

JUAN ANTONIO FLORES MARTOS is an associate professor of social and cultural anthropology at the Universidad de Castilla–La Mancha, Spain. He has done ethnographic fieldwork about the anthropology of the body, emotions, rituals, and new spiritual imaginaries in Mexico, Bolivia, and Spain. In 2012, he was research fellow at the Centro de Investigaciones y Estudios Superiores en Antropología Social (CIESAS) and the Universidad Veracruzana. He has published widely on La Santa Muerte and coedited *Etnografías de la muerte y las culturas en América Latina* (2007).

ANNE HUFFSCHMID holds a PhD in cultural studies and works as a researcher, curator, and author in Berlin. She is affiliated with the Freie Universität Berlin. She specializes in urban studies, social memory and violence, discourse analysis, and visual methods, with a special interest in Latin America. Currently she is involved in a project that explores forensic processes in Mexico. Her books include *Risse im Raum: Erinnerung, Gewalt und städtisches Leben in Lateinamerika* (2015), and the edited volumes *TerrorZones* (2015), *Topografías conflictivas* (2012), and *Metrópolis desbordadas* (2011).

REGNAR KRISTENSEN holds a PhD in social anthropology from Københavns Universitet. Currently an external lecturer in the university's Department of Cross-Cultural and Regional Studies, he specializes in researching the crossroads of law enforcement, crime, and religion in Mexico. He has done fieldwork during many years on the Santa Muerte cult. He has published several articles on the topic as well as *Postponing Death: Saints and Security in Mexico City* (2011).

CLAUDIO LOMNITZ is the Campbell Family Professor of Anthropology at Columbia University, New York. He works on the history, politics, and culture of Latin America, and particularly of Mexico, especially on nation-state formation, public culture, the politics and culture of death, and exile and ideology during the Mexican Revolution. His most important publications include *Exits from the Labyrinth: Culture and Ideology in Mexican National Space* (1992), *Deep Mexico, Silent Mexico: An Anthropology of Nationalism* (2001), *Death and the Idea of Mexico* (2005), *The Return of Comrade Ricardo Flores Magón* (2014), and *La nación desdibujada: México en trece ensayos* (2016). For many years, he has also been a regular contributor to the Mexico City press.

WIL G. PANSTERS is a professor at the Department of Cultural Anthropology and the head of the Department of Social Sciences at University College Utrecht, both at Utrecht University. He has been a research fellow at El Colegio de México, the University of Oxford, and the University of Warwick. He has done ethnographic and historical research in Mexico. Currently he studies drug trafficking, violence, and justice from below. His publications include *Politics and Power in Puebla: The Political History of a Mexican State* (1990); *Caciquismo in Twentieth-Century Mexico* (coedited with Alan Knight, 2005); and *Violence, Coercion, and State-Making in Twentieth-Century Mexico: The Other Half of the Centaur* (editor, 2012).

JUDITH KATIA PERDIGÓN CASTAÑEDA holds a PhD in social anthropology from the Escuela Nacional de Antropología e Historia (ENAH) in Mexico City. Since 1993, she has worked at ENAH's Coordinación Nacional de Conservación del Patrimonio Cultural. She specializes in conservation, restoration, and popular religion. She has done long-term ethnographic research on La Santa Muerte, about which she has published numerous articles as well as the first scholarly book on the cult, *La Santa Muerte: Protectora de los hombres* (2008). She is a member of the Sistema Nacional de Investigadores (I).

BERNARDO ROBLES AGUIRRE holds a PhD in physical anthropology from the Escuela Nacional de Antropología e Historia (ENAH). He does research about the body and disease, especially about living with HIV. He has published and lectured about these topics in Mexico and abroad. He has taught at the Universidad Nacional Autónoma de México and the Universidad Autónoma Metropolitana Xochimilco. Currently he is head of postgraduate studies in anthropology at ENAH in Mexico City.

BENJAMIN T. SMITH is a professor of Latin American history at the University of Warwick, United Kingdom. A historian of nineteenth- and twentieth-century grassroots politics in Mexico, he specializes in postrevolutionary politics, regional bossism, violence, religion, and the press. His most important publications are *Pistoleros and Popular Movements: The Politics of State Formation in Postrevolutionary Oaxaca* (2009), *The Roots of Conservatism in Mexico: Catholicism, Society, and Politics in the Mixteca Baja, 1750–1962* (2012), *The Mexican Press and Civil Society, 1940–1976: Stories from the Newsroom, Stories from the Street* (2018), and two edited volumes, *Dictablanda: Politics, Work, and Culture in Mexico, 1938–1968* (with Paul Gillingham, 2014), and, *Journalism, Satire, and Censorship in Modern Mexico* (with Paul Gillingham and Michael Lettieri, 2018).

INDEX

Page numbers in italic text indicate illustrations.

abandonment, 44, 85, 90, 99; protection
and, 114; as sin, 154
Acción Católica Mexicana, 78
Acta Thomae, 63
addiction, 26–27
adopted dead (NN dead), 85, 102–4,
110n21
adoption, 88, 101; identity given
through, 103; process of, 104
aesthetic interrogation of reality, 116
Agar, Michael, 122
agrarian capitalism, 77
agricultural production, 63, 77, 78
Aguiar, José Carlos, 53n6
alcohol, 28–29
allemande, 85–88, 108n5
All Souls' Day, 15
altars, 10–11, 119, 137, 156n1;
ceremonies at, 146–47; by devotees,
140–41; expansion of public, 25;
growing interest in, 140; guidelines
surrounding, 24; as improvised,
185–86; intermediate, 23; offerings
at, 109n12, 160; tradition of, 94
altruism, 149–51
amarres (love-binding spells), 25–26,
142
Ambrosio, Juan, 4–5, 54n19
amparo. See protection
Andrés, Francisco, 58, 66

anticlericalism, 76
Apóstoles de la Palabra movement,
47–48
Argyriadis, Kali, 6, 38–39, 50, 56n43,
96
Aridjis, Homero, 53n3, 56n46
art, 15, 16–17, 182n9
Asad, Talal, 59
atrezzo (props), 93
authoritarianism, 117
Avilés Pérez, Pedro, 80

Bailón, Pascual, 12
banalization, 114
Bandak, Andreas, 152
Barragán Solís, Anabella, 180, 182n8
Bartra, Roger, 108n9
Bautista Álvarez de Toledo, Juan, 65
Beattie, Peter M., 83n12
beautification, 22, 113
Berger, Peter, 43
betrayal, 34
Biblical Pastoralism, 47
Bigliardi, Stefano, 6, 55n27
Blair, Elsa, 102
bodies, conceptualizing, 164–66
Bolaños, Bartola, 73
Boltanski, Luc, 167
Botitas Negras, Little Black Boots (Iturra
Sáez, Irene del Carmen), 45, 100

Bourbon era, 61, 65–67
bourée, 88, 102–4, 108n5
Brandes, Stanley, 15, 54n14, 92, 135n16
Breton, André, 17
Bricker, Victoria Reifler, 66, 68
bridal representation, 21
Bromley, David, 56n38, 56n47
Bubandt, Nils, 41
Buenos Aires, Argentina, 117
burials, 101, 116, 178
Butler, Matthew, 73

Cabrera, Gerardo, 157n6
caciquismo, 189
calaveras. See skulls
candles, red, 9
candy, 15
cannibalism, 114
Cárcel de Mujeres (women's prison), 9–10
The Cartel (Winslow), 56n46
Casal Sáenz, Heber, 55n33
Castellanos, Laura, 4
Castells Ballarín, Pilar, 43
Castillo Morales, Juan. *See* Juan Soldado
Catholic Church, 29; breaking away from, 11–12; decline of, 74; icons within, 13; as institutional, 58–59; protests by, 37
Catholicism, 2, 59, 106, 158; decline of, 115, 117, 132, 134n5; hierarchical contestation and, 46–50; imageries in, 18–19; as institutionalized, 130; leftist, 118; Mexican folk, 51; opposition to, 113–14; orthodox, 13; political economy, violence, and, 40–42; roots of, 62
Catholicization, of death, 143

Catholic mortuary ritual, 16
Catholic socialization, 137
La Catrina (female skeleton), 15; commercialization of, 17–18; as Día de Muertos icon, 109n11
catrinization, 93–94
cempasúchitl flowers, 15
Charismatic Renovation movement, 56n43
Charlot, Jean, 17
Chaves, Juana, 102
Chesnut, Andrew, 6, 10–11, 55n29, 92, 159; *Devoted to Death*, 55n36; on gender, 34
Chetumal, Mexico, 7, 26, 28
Chiapas, Mexico, 12, 50
Chicahuatzin, Sol, 172–73
The Children of Sánchez (Lewis), 8
Cisneros, José Luis, 56n41
citizenship, 78; disjunctive, 42–43; lived, 41; rights to, 52
Ciudad Juárez, Mexico, 21, 25–26
cleaner (*fontanera*), 92, 108n8
cleansings (*limpias*), 10, 25
cofradías, 61–70, 74–75
collateral damage, 89
Colombia, 45, 85, 101–4
Colonia, Sarita, 98, 109n19
Comaroff, Jean, 41–42
Comaroff, John L., 41–42
commercialization, 15, 97, 114; of La Catrina, 17–18; of death, 49–50
community: coherence within, 78; family as core, 131–32; formation of, 116; histories of, 168; loss of, 42; serenity, companionship, and, 21
Conference of Mexican Bishops, 49
corruption, 16, 41, 79, 137
corruption, religious, 12

cosmovisions, 56n41

courante, 88–92

creativity, 15

crime, 47; glorifying, 56n45; media, violence, and, 5

criminality, 186–87

Cristero War (1926–1929), 12

de la Cruz, Juan, 68

cultural autochthony, 114

cultural defiance, 121

cultural heritage, 86, 87, 107n3, 134n9

cultural resources, 11

curanderismo (healing), 30, 96

curanderos (healers), 26, 50, 158

DaMatta, Roberto, 44

dance, 28–29

Dances of Death, 85

danse macabre, 16, 18, 54n14, 174

darketo subculture, 188

Davis, Mike, 115

Day of the Dead (Día de Muertos), 15–17, 19, 87, 135n16; La Catrina as icon for, 109n11; celebrating, 122; recognition of, 92

death: as blasphemy against religion, 49; Catholicization of, 143; commercialization of, 49–50; cultural preoccupation with, 17; devotion to, 40; figures of, 177–78; history of, in Mexico, 5; as humanized and gendered, 118–19; idioms and expressions for, 188–89; image of, 12, 111; imaginations, 13; intimacy with, 19; manifestations of, 18; meaning of, 33; negotiating, 190; without owners, 101; patrimonialization of, 87; personification of, 29; power of, 13, 18; as protagonist, 85; salvation after, 31; stereotypes of, 92; as triumphant,

32; as widespread, 19. *See also* adopted dead; miraculous dead

democracy, neoliberalism and, 51–52

Denegri, Carlos, 9–10

Denegri, Linda, 9–10

desamparo (lack of protection), 31–32, 42, 80, 91, 132

Devoted to Death (Chesnut), 55n36

devotees: altars by, 140–41; expectations of, 24; growth in number of, 11; imitations by, 156n4; in Puebla, 36; as superstitious, 12; tattoos by, 126; in Tepito neighborhood, 28; in Veracruz, 36; visual representation by, 124

devotion, 4; bodies and, 163–64; complexity of, 6; to death, 40; forms of, 187–88; phenomenology, politics and, 20; within prison system, 41; role of women and, 9; seeking, 180; as socialized, 155; terms of, 35; theology, ritual and, 29–33; transformation from clandestine to public, 7

devotional pictures, 53n12

devotional practices, 20, 158; as acceptable, 78; Catholic traditions associated with, 46; core of, 31; evolution of, 40; financial benefit from, 48; rituals, tattoos and, 84; uniform set of, 181n1; vitality of, 51

Día de Muertos. *See* Day of the Dead

Díaz, Porfirio, 79

Díaz Cuscat, Pedro, 70

Díaz Manfort, Antonio, 71

dislocations, social and economic, 56n38

dispossession, 137

djambe. See witchcraft

domestic abuse, 8, 9–10

domestication, 118

drug consumption, 10, 63
drug traffickers, 3, 80
drug trafficking, 5, 10, 40, 45–48; association with, 56n46; religious conflict and, 81; in Tepito, 120–21

earthquake (1985), 120
ecclesiastical authorities, 59–60, 69, 74–75
Echavarría, Juan Manuel, 102
Echeverría, Bolívar, 14
Echeverría, Luis, 10
education, 78
enchantment, 41
equality, social struggles for, 56n39
erotic performances, 29
Escobedo Quijano, Edgar, 4
esotericism, 48, 51
Espinosa y Dávalos, Pedro, 70
ethos, 161
evangelization, 121, 142–43
excess, 112
exchange, theory of, 148–49
exchange mechanism, 30–31
exclusion, 42–43
exorcism, 56n43
exploitation, 150–51
extortion, 44

factionalism, 38
family, 154, 180; cluster, 150; commitment to, 136, 148–49; as core community, 131–32; gender, intimacy and, 21; kinship, intimacy and, 110n22; micro level of structure of, 104; presence of, 128; relationships within, 33
family relations, 2
Favela, Jorge, 80
fear, 3

female skeleton. See La Catrina
femicide, 133
femininity, stereotypes of, 21
Fernández, Eduardo, "Lalo," 80
figurative exaggeration, 20
figurines, 1, 8, 22; dimensions of, 18, 33; engaging, 13; forms and colors of, 20
Flanet, Veronique, 53n12
folk religion, Mexican, 5
fontanera (cleaner), 92, 108n8
forensic aesthetics, 112
Foster, George, 145–46
fragmentation, 114
Fragoso, Perla, 5, 14, 20, 42, 50; on multireligiosity, 91; observations by, 53n3
Francis, Pope, 49, 132
Franco, Francisco, 97
Frankenstein, 104
Freitas, Eliane Tânia, 99–100
de la Fuente Hernández, Sergio, 54n23

gender, 21, 33–34, 180
Geschiere, Peter, 41
gift exchange, 32
Giger, Hans Ruedi, 175
gigue, 88, 104–7, 108n5
Gil Olmos, José, 119
Giménez Cacho, Daniel, 134n13
global cultural marketplace, 15
Global Prayers: Redemption and Liberation in the City, 114–16, 133n4
Goffman, Erving, 184
Goldman, Francisco, 9
Gómes Checheb, Agustina, 70
Gómez, Sebastian, 66
González Guerrero, Blanca, 164
González Martínez, José Luis, 158
González y González, Luis, 73

Graeber, David, 149–51
Grant, Melvyn, 175
gravestone offerings (*ofrendas*), 15
Graziano, Frank, 30–31, 53n2
Grim Reaper, 23
Gruzinski, Serge, 13, 59, 66–67
Guadalajara, Mexico, 25, 27
Guadalupanization, 94
Guatemala, 12
Guevara, Che, 188
Guillermoprieto, Alma, 53n4

Hartz, Frida, 134n7, 135n19
healers (*curanderos*), 26, 50, 158
healing (*curanderismo*), 30, 96
hell, 2
herbalists, 3
Hernández, Alfonso, 118, 134n12
Hernández, Alfredo, 91
Hernández i Martí, Gil-Manuel, 86
historical continuity, 12
historical roots, 11–14
historiographic gaps, 18–19
Holy Cross of Tonalá, 62–64
humanization, 33–34, 39
human rights, 43–44, 52
human sacrifice, 48
humility, 152
hybridization, 39, 50–51, 94, 108n7
hypervisibility, 125–28
hypocrisy, 16

iconographic continuities, 18–19
iconographic mutations, 94–97
ICP. *See* Intangible Cultural Heritage
identity, 32, 51, 108n9; adoption
    producing, 103; erasing, 102–3; as
    gendered, 34; key elements of, 163
idolatry, 14, 47–48
idolillos, 13

ignorance, 12, 50
illegality, 26, 52, 113
imaginary, 133n3; cultural, 92;
    dominant, 92; of human rights, 43;
    symbolic, 88
impunity, 42–44, 79, 83
independence movement, 59
indigenous peoples, 12
individualism, 90, 118
individualization, 22
Indonesia, 41
insecurity, 133; illegality, vulnerability,
    and, 26, 52; production of, 42;
    violence and, 89
institutionalization, 97
insurrections, 65, 68–71
Intangible Cultural Heritage (ICP),
    86–87
internationalization, 51
International Santa Muerte Shrine, 37
Internet, 3, 10, 51
intimacy, 14, 39; with death, 19; of
    devotional units, 137; gender,
    family, and, 21; kinship, family, and,
    110n22; of social space, 147
Islas Marías, Mexico, 9
Iturra Sáez, Irene del Carmen (Botitas
    Negras, Little Black Boots), 45, 100

Jesus Christ, 24, 31, 47, 71
Juan Soldado, 19, 30, 58, 76, 78–79
Jude Thaddeus, Saint (San Judas
    Tadeo), 3, 30, 50, 106, 155
judgmentalism, 131, 160
Junge, Benjamin, 41

Keenan, Thomas, 112
Kelly, Isabel, 8
kidnapping, 37, 48, 55n33, 137, 170
King, Stephen, 175

kinship, 110n22
Kostner, Evi, 54n13
Kraushaar, Lilith, 100

Lafaye, Jacques, 59
Lagarriga, Isabel, 108
land reforms, 71, 78
leadership, 36, 38
Le Breton, David, 164
legal system, 10
Legaria Vargas, Jonathan, 37–38
Lehmann, David, 53n6, 55n36
Lewis, Oscar, 8, 120
liberation spirits, 122
liberation theology, 117, 121
liminality, 35
limpias (cleansings), 10, 25
Little Black Boots, Botitas Negras (Iturra
    Sáez, Irene del Carmen), 45, 100
Loos, Frederick, 121, 134n13
Lope Blanche, Juan, 188–90
Losonczy, Anne-Marie, 99
love-binding spells (*amarres*), 25–26,
    142
Lovecraft, Howard Phillips, 175
love magic, 8
Lowry, Malcolm, 108n9
loyalty, 33–34; demanding, 76;
    personalistic, 38
Lozada, Manuel, 70

macabre humor, 190
Maldonado Sánchez, Braulio, 79,
    83nn15–16
Malverde, Jesús, 30, 50, 58, 76, 79–80
Malvido, Elsa, 5
mandas (promises), 30, 32, 145–48, 169
marginality, 35
marginalization, 2–3
marianismo complex, 35, 55n30

Marianization, 39, 94–95
marriage, 150, 187
Marschall, Andreas, 175
Martín, Desirée, 36
Martita sanctuary, 25, 39
Marx, Karl, 115
material culture, 21, 115–16
materiality, performativity and, 116
Mauss, Marcel, 149–50
Mayblin, Maya, 152
media, 141, 174, 182n7; crime, violence,
    and, 5; critical focus of, 144; cultural,
    13; digital, 39–40; headlines in,
    48; print, 72; social, 82; suffering
    transmitted by, 98; as superficial, 183
memory, 99
Mendoza, Primo, 134n12
merchandising, 95, 157n7
metroZones, 133n4
Mexicanness, 94–95, 109n13
Mexico United against Delinquency
    (México Unido contra la
    Delincuencia), 89
Michalik, Piotr Grzegorz, 6, 51, 53n8,
    114
micropolitics, 92
Mictlantecuhtli god, 14, 94–95
migration, 10, 51, 76, 185
militarization, 44–45
millennial capitalism, 41
mimetics, 95
Minero, Juan, 8
miracles, 31–32, 92, 160; seeking, 101;
    Virgin of Guadalupe performing, 131
miraculous dead, 97–106, 109n17
modernism, 17
modernity, 86, 90, 104
modernization, 77–78
Monaghan, John, 72
Mondragón, Julio César, 111

money laundering, 37

Monsiváis, Carlos, 118

moral economy, 19, 60; as amenable, 67; as disintegrating, 69; saints, images, and, 61–64

Morales, María Soledad, 98

Morín, Edgar, 170–71

Moscovici, Serge, 181n2

Múgica, Padre, 117

mujer abnegada (self-sacrificing woman), 21, 35, 113

multireligiosity, 91

mutuality, 150

mysteries, 26–27

mythology: Jesus Christ and, 71; localist, 54n24

myths, 28, 35

national identity, 17

nationalism: Hindu, 115; Mexican, 108n9

Navarrete, Carlos, 12, 34

neoliberalism, 45, 51–52, 85, 101

Nevado del Ruiz volcano, 98

Newell, Mike, 182n11

Nieto, Patricia, 102

nihilism, 113

Niño de Atocha, 19, 54n15, 68, 72

Niño de las Suertes, 50

Niño Fidencio, 30, 58

NN dead. *See* adopted dead

Nogales, Mexico, 8

nota roja (sensationalist newspapers), 93

La Novena (prayer collection), 142–43

Oaxaca, Mexico, 53n12, 58; northern, 62; southern, 63; Yanhuitlán, 178

obedience, 62–63

occultism, 51, 57n49

ofrendas (gravestone offerings), 15

Oleszkiewicz-Peralba, Malgorzata, 43, 53n8, 55n31

opulence, 152

organization, 137, 162; lack of, 128; politics and, 35–39; social, 117

Orozco, José Clemente, 17

Ortiz, Jessie, 139, 153–56

Ortíz, Silvia, 108

Padgett, Humberto, 55n33

paganism, 13

Palo Monte, 156

Pancho Villa, 58, 76

Páramo, Jurek, 139, 143–44, 153–56

paraphernalia, 56n45, 70, 188

paro (stoppage), 31–32

Partido Revolucionario Institucional (PRI), 79–80

patrimonialization, 45, 85–86, 107n2; cultural, 93, 99, 104–7; of death, 87; essentialist vision of, 107n3; processes of, 92

Pavez, Jorge, 100

Payá, Victor, 191n1

Paz, Octavio, 108, 189

penny press, 16

Pentecostalism, 105

Pérez, Antonio, 59, 66

performance: power of, 114; of visual excess, 112

performativity, materiality and, 116

Perpetua, Virginia, 75

personalism, 38

personification, 22, 29, 33–34, 39

Pescador, Juan Javier, 54n15

peyote, 13, 58

phenomenology, 20, 21–23

plagues, 13, 15–16, 85, 107

Planet of Slums (Davis), 115

police officers, 3, 187

political economy, violence, Catholicism and, 40–42

politics, 94; organization and, 35–39; phenomenology, devotion and, 20; traditional rules of, 61; vulnerability of patronage, 31. *See also* micropolitics

Posada, José Guadalupe, 16–18, 93

poverty, 99, 120

powers: of dead, 109n17; hierarchy of, 50; resistance against, 41; of spirituality, 182n9; symbolization of, 23; as unlimited, 112

pragmatism, 50, 92

prayer collection (La Novena), 142–43

prayers, for addiction, 26–27

precariousness, 43–45, 52, 88–89, 106, 132, 185–87

PRI. *See* Partido Revolucionario Institucional

prisoners, 186–87, 191n1

prison guards, 186

prison system, 9, 41, 185

promises (*mandas*), 30, 32, 145–48, 169

props (*atrezzo*), 93

prostitution, 79, 83n15, 100–101

protection (*amparo*), 2, 31–32, 52, 55n26, 80, 171–72, 191; abandonment and, 114; as critical, 184; punishment and, 113; seeking, 90–91; vulnerability and, 44

protection, lack of (*desamparo*), 31–32, 42, 80, 91, 132

Protestantism, 2

protests, by Catholic Church, 37

Puebla, Mexico, 22, 36, 62, 77, 138, 156n1, 158; Acatlán town in, 71; ceremonies in, 139; Cholula town in, 74

punishment: condemnation and, 13; protection and, 113

punitive democratization, 53n11

Quijano, Martín George, 154, 163–65

Quintero, Lamberto, 80

radicalization, violence and, 73

Ramírez de la Roche, Omar, 180, 182n8

Ramon Nonato (saint), 30–31, 54n25

Ramos Rodríguez, Rosa María, 162

Ravasi, Gianfranco, 49

rebellion, 59, 68–69

reburials, 109n19

reciprocal dominance, 82n3

reciprocity, 32, 99; exchange and, 106; schemes of, 155; theory of, 149–50; types of, 148–49, 189

redemption, 191

re-Indianization, 39, 94

religion: death as blasphemy against, 49; lived, 41; secular revolution and, 183; as self-made, 116; sociology of, 43

religiosity: clericalizing, 59; displays of, 71; expressions of, 158–59; pragmatism and malleability of, 50; social vulnerability, violence, and, 42–45. *See also* multireligiosity

religious beliefs, 2

religious gatherings, 25

religious revivalism, 58–59

religious uniformity, 136

reputation, 2, 40

Réquiem NN, 102

revitalization movements, 19, 81; Bourbon era, 58–67; of nineteenth century, 67–72; postrevolutionary, 76–80; during Revolution, 73–75

Revolution, 73–75

Reyes-Cortez, Marcel, 57n48
Riggs, Derek, 175
rituals, 88, 99–100, 105; for agricultural
    production, 77; beliefs, symbolism,
    and, 4; Catholic, 16, 26; as complex,
    90; devotion, theology and, 29–33;
    dialogue as, 103–4; fertility, 62–63;
    healing, 50; heretical, 130; magical,
    8; tattoos, devotional practices, and,
    84. See also burials
rivalries, 38, 49; religious, 130–31; in
    Veracruz, 39
Rivera, Diego, 17
Rodríguez Costabella, Alberto, 164,
    169–70
Rojas, Roque, 78
Romero, Enriqueta, "Queta," 7,
    10, 121–22, 143, 151–56; on
    punishment, 149; Santería and,
    129; shrine by, 21, 24, 26, 36, 124,
    137–39
Romo Guillen, David, 36–38, 55n29,
    137–43, 151–56
rosaries, 1, 10, 20, 54n22; monthly, 24;
    shrines and, 23–29; street, 138, 144
rosary services, 26–27
Roush, Laura, 6, 26, 60, 143, 147,
    157n8
Rowling, J. K., 182n11
Royo, Luis, 175
Rubin, Jeffrey, 41
Rühling, Barbara, 129
Rulfo, Juan, 108n9

Safari in Tepito, 134n13
Sahlins, Marshall, 148–51, 191n2
Salomé the Miraculous (Salomé la
    Milagrosa), 97
salvation, 31, 190–91

Sánchez, Gervasio, 102
Sánchez, Omayra, 98, 109n19
Sánchez Chávez, Mónica, 166
Sánchez Marceliano, Miguel, 172
Sandoval, Fernando, 157n6
San Pascualito cult, 11–12
La Santa Muerte. See specific topics
Santa Muerte cult, 2–3
La Santa Muerte: Sextet del amor,
    las mujeres, los perros y la muerte
    (Aridji), 56n46
Santería, 3, 50, 94, 96–97; collars of,
    105; Romero and, 129
Santísima Muerte cult, 7
santo niño peregrino, 141
sarabande, 88, 97–101, 108n5
Satanism, 47, 50, 113
scales of justice, 23
Schryer, Frans, 77
Scott, James, 60
secularization, 76
self-recognition, 27, 50
self-sacrificing woman (mujer abnegada),
    21, 35, 113
semantization, 113
semiotic voracity, 51
sensationalist newspapers (nota roja), 93
senses, human, 163
sexuality, 109n18, 118
sex workers, 44, 100
shrines, 7, 119; destruction of, 48–49;
    for Malverde, 80; by Romero, 21,
    24, 26, 36, 124, 137–39; rosaries
    and, 23–29; security through, 81; to
    Virgin of Guadalupe, 145. See also
    International Santa Muerte Shrine;
    Martita sanctuary
Sigüenza y Góngora, Carlos, 63–64
Simone, Abdou Maliq, 115

skeletons: guises of, 14–18; indigenous worship of, 18–19; materialization of, 114; polysemic image of, 51; presentation of, 112; traditional dress of, 21–22; transformation of, 96; worshiping of, 111

skulls (*calaveras*), 16; familiarization with, 93; materialization of, 114; symbolism of, 17

Smilde, David, 41

social class, 167, 184

social forces, 20, 25, 40

social hierarchies, 66–67

social inequality, 18

socialization, 146–47, 155

social normalization, 88

social processes, 20

The Social Uses of the Body (Los usos sociales del cuerpo) (Boltanski), 167

somatic culture, 167

sorcery, 8, 41

Spanish Inquisition, 12–13, 66

spatial productivity, 132

spectacularization, 93

spiritism, 98

spiritual economy. *See* moral economy

Spiritualist churches, 78, 83n14

statues/statuettes, 8, 20, 27, 114; collecting, 12–13; conversations with, 21; devotion to, 31; dressing up, 22–23; female contours in, 34; images of, in Tepito, 123, 125–27

stereotypes: of death, 92; of femininity, 21

stigmas, 184, 186

stigmatization: confronting, 128; of victims, 99

stoppage (*paro*), 31–32

suite, 88

superstition, 47–48; of devotees, 12; as sin, 49

surrealism, 17

symbolic standardization, 76

symbolism: of powers, 23; rituals, beliefs and, 4; of skulls, 17; in tattoos, 168–71

symbols, 20, 179–80; crow as, 182n10; role of religious, 60; of transgression, 168–69; of wisdom, 54n18

synaesthesia, 163

syncretic overlap, 51

syncretism, 14, 50

talking cross, cult of, 19, 68–69

tattoos, 20, 161–75, 176–77, 178–81; centrality of, 184; choice of, 181n6; criminality and, 187; for devotees, 126; forced, 191n1; as form of gratitude, 160; rituals, devotional practices and, 84; of Virgin of Guadalupe, 119

Tatu Chu, 58, 69

Taylor, William, 64

Teatro Mexicano (de Vetancourt), 64

tenements (*vecindades*), 120

Tepatepec, Mexico, 8

Tepito neighborhood, Mexico City, Mexico, 7–8, 53n10, 90; blessing of images in, 29; devotees in, 28; drug trafficking in, 120–21; images of statue in, 123, 125–27; organization within, 120; shrine by Romero in, 21, 24, 26, 36

Thompson, E. P., 60

Thompson, John, 5–8

Tijuana, Mexico, 19

tolerance, 2

Toor, Frances, 8–9

tourism, 92

traditions, Catholic, 46

transculturation, 14

transformation: analysis of, 21; as apocalyptic, 58–59; from clandestine to public devotion, 7; consequences of, 18; of representations, 33, 55n29; of skeletons, 96; tattoos as, 162

transformation-mutation, 95–96

transformations: vitality through, 39–40

transgression, 112, 168–69

transnationalization, 10, 96, 185

trauma, 90–91, 99, 132

A Treasury of Mexican Folkways (Toor), 8–9

truthfulness, 2

Tuxtla Gutiérrez, Mexico, 7, 11–12

Tzintzuntzan (Foster), 145

United Nations Educational, Scientific and Cultural Organization (UNESCO), 86–87, 92, 107n3

urbanization, 76, 115

urban modernity, 26–27

Uribe Alarcón, María Victoria, 102

Urrea, Teresa, 71

Los usos sociales del cuerpo (*The Social Uses of the Body*) (Boltanski), 167

Valadéz, Luis, 166

Valadéz, Manuel, 164

Vanderwood, Paul, 41, 59

vanity, 18, 34

van Oosterhout, Aaron, 70

van Young, Eric, 59, 81

Vargas, Enriqueta, 37–38

Vargas González, Alfredo, 53n5

Vázquez, Francisco, 12

vecindades (tenements), 120

Vega Aldrete, Alberto, 79

Velásquez, Paula Andrea, 102

de Vetancourt, Agustín, 64

Vieira, Constanza, 102

Villamil Uriarte, Raúl René, 56n41

Villaseñor, Isabel, 107n3

Villoro, Luis, 59

violence, 3; insecurity and, 89, 101; media, crime, and, 5; political economy, Catholicism, and, 40–42; radicalization and, 73; social intervention in scenarios of, 133n2; social vulnerability, religiosity, and, 42–45; spreading, 133; as worsening, 80, 137. *See also* domestic abuse

Virgen del Rosario, 22

Virgin Mary, 190–91

Virgin of Guadalupe, 2, 24, 35, 95, 155; apparition of, 77; miracles performed by, 131; as official icon, 76; as omnipresent, 118; shrine to, 145; tattoos of, 119; worship of, 48

visibility, visuality, 20, 36, 115; digital media and, 39–40; forms of, 46; moment of maximum, 130; as required, 56n41

visual culture of terror, 112

visualization, 112

vitality, 16, 134, 155; of devotional practices, 51; through transformations, 39–40

vulgarization, 114

vulnerability, 14; from crisis, 106; high degrees of, 183–84; insecurity, illegality, and, 26, 52; as normalized, 107; of patronage politics, 31; precarious conditions of, 85; protection and, 44; religiosity, violence, and, 42–45

Wallace, Anthony, 58

Warren, Jim, 175

wealth, 41–42

Weizman, Eyal, 112

Westheim, Paul, 108n9
Winslow, Don, 56n46
witchcraft (*djambe*), 41, 48
Wolf, Eric, 67
women, domestic abuse toward, 9–10
women's prison (Cárcel de Mujeres),
  9–10
Woody, Christopher, 53n4
Wright-Rios, Edward, 73, 75

Yanhuitlán (Oaxaca), 178

Zapata, Emiliano, 76
Zarazúa Campa, Jorge Luis, 47,
  56n43
Zolla, Emiliano, 107n3
zombies, 104–7
zones of crisis, 60–61, 73

CPSIA information can be obtained
at www.ICGtesting.com
Printed in the USA
LVHW111920100920
665606LV00007BA/82

9 780826 360816